The Political Economy of China's Great Transformation

The Political Economy of China's Great Transformation consists of three parts: first, covering the current political transformation, providing a general political background for the economic and fiscal transformation; second, making an in-depth analysis of economic transformation; and third, elaborating from the perspective of fiscal federalism the fiscal transformation in China.

The book analyzes the economic transformation and addresses the shortcomings of existing interpretations of the "Chinese Miracle" and develops a new multi-dimensional framework. In addition, it shows how the private sector has been developing and what a major role it is playing in pushing forward the overall economic development.

The book also focuses on the analysis of China's fiscal transformation. With the set of refined principles of fiscal federalism that the author has developed, it examines the problems of Chinese fiscal federalism in contrast to them. It further elaborates on topics such as the local government debt and explains why further reforms are necessary, making this book a very comprehensive read to understand China's progress.

Xingyuan Feng is Professor and Vice President of the Cathay Institute for Public Affairs in Beijing. He received his PhD in economics from the University of Witten/Herdecke, Germany.

Christer Ljungwall lives in Beijing and works for the Swedish Agency for Growth Policy Analysis, as Science and Innovation Counsellor, Head of Office of Science and Innovation of the Embassy of Sweden. He is also Associate Professor in Economics at the Department of International Economics and Management, Copenhagen Business School. He has published more than 30 academic articles in English, more than 150 reports, and authored and contributed to 5 books. He received his PhD in Economics from Gothenburg University in 2003.

Sujian Guo is Changjiang Scholar, Distinguished Professor at Fudan University, and a tenured professor at San Francisco State University. He is also Editor-in-Chief of the *Journal of Chinese Political Science* (Springer), *Fudan Journal of the Humanities and Social Sciences* (Springer), Executive Editor-in-Chief of *Chinese Political Science Review* (Springer), Co-Editor-in-Chief of the *Journal of Chinese Governance* (Routledge) and Editor of Rowman & Littlefield–Lexington's book series "Challenges Facing Chinese Political Development." He has published more than 20 authored and edited books and more than 40 academic journal articles.

The Political Economy of China's Great Transformation

Xingyuan Feng, Christer Ljungwall and Sujian Guo

With Foreword by Carsten Herrmann-Pillath

Routledge
Taylor & Francis Group
LONDON AND NEW YORK

First published 2017
by Routledge
2 Park Square, Milton Park, Abingdon, Oxon OX14 4RN

and by Routledge
711 Third Avenue, New York, NY 10017

Routledge is an imprint of the Taylor & Francis Group, an informa business

British Library Cataloguing in Publication Data
A catalogue record for this book is available from the British Library

Library of Congress Cataloging-in-Publication Data
Names: Feng, Xingyuan, 1965– author. | Ljungwall, Christer, author. | Guo, Sujian, 1957– author.
Title: The political economy of China's great transformation / by Xingyuan Feng, Christer Ljungwall and Sujian Guo ; with foreword by Carsten Hermann-Pillath.
Description: Abingdon, Oxon; New York, NY : Routledge, 2017. | Series: Routledge studies in the modern world economy ; 160 | Includes bibliographical references and index.
Identifiers: LCCN 2016010185 | ISBN 9781138944008 (hardback) | ISBN 9781315530376 (ebook)
Subjects: LCSH: China—Economic policy—1949– | China—Economic conditions—1949– | China—Politics and government—1949–
Classification: LCC HC427 .F45 2017 | DDC 330.951—dc23
LC record available at https://lccn.loc.gov/2016010185

ISBN: 978-1-138-94400-8 (hbk)
ISBN: 978-1-315-53037-6 (ebk)

Typeset in Galliard
by Apex CoVantage, LLC

Contents

Figures

Tables

Foreword

State-building and market transition: the two faces of China's great transformation

In the past 30 years, China has undergone fundamental and rapid institutional changes which duly deserve the label of "great transformation." These changes have been documented in ten thousands of books and articles, making China one of the best-researched regions of the world. So, what can another book on China add to this vast pool of knowledge? I wish to offer my personal interpretation of the contributions collected in the book, which goes beyond their specific contents. I argue that the contributions and their scope actually reflect something about the deeper structure of the Chinese transformation, and that it is these more fundamental aspects that warrant the term "great" in describing them.

The book has a focus on fiscal and financial aspects of reforms and embeds this research into the broader picture of theorizing about institutional change, including the normative perspective. The latter comes into play when considering the functional requirements of a market economy and, for that purpose, also market society. So, we may ask why fiscal and financial topics deserve to be at the core of a book that aims at understanding China's "great transformation." Indeed, this is a perspective that is different from what most economists would emphasize about the Chinese experience, namely, the simultaneous process of market transition and development in the sense of structural change: fiscal structures would just be seen as elements of the institutional framework of these larger patterns, with mostly practical consequences, for example, for funding the necessary public infrastructure. However, as I have argued in my own research three decades ago, this economic perspective tends to neglect the third core process in China's modernization, which is state-building. I argue that market transition is deeply intertwined with the process of state-building, and that to a large degree specific results of reforms are partly unintended side effects of this more fundamental process. If we recognize this, we also clearly realize that the fiscal system and public finance stay at the center of state-building. This also closely relates with development as structural change, since one of the remarkable characteristics of recent Chinese reforms is the gradual transformation of the fiscal system in the rural areas.

Routledge Studies in the Modern World Economy

For a full list of titles in this series, please visit https://www.routledge.com/series/SE0432

151 Cultural Differences and Economic Globalization
Effects on trade, foreign direct investment and migration
Roger White

152 Human Development and Capacity Building
Asia Pacific trends, challenges and prospects for the future
Edited by Maria Fay Rola-Rubzen and John Burgess

153 The Economics of Terrorism
Peter J. Phillips

154 Culture, Institution, and Development in China
The economics of national character
C. Simon Fan

155 The Economics of Waste Management in East Asia
Edited by Masashi Yamamoto and Eiji Hosoda

156 Global Economic Crisis and Local Economic Development
International cases and policy responses
Edited by Jason Begley, Dan Coffey, Tom Donnelly and Carole Thornley

157 Liberalism and Chinese Economic Development
Perspectives from Europe and Asia
Edited by Gilles Campagnolo

158 The Financialization of Housing
A political economy approach
Manuel B. Aalbers

159 Fiscal Policy in Dynamic Economies
Kim Heng Tan

160 The Political Economy of China's Great Transformation
Xingyuan Feng, Christer Ljungwall and Sujian Guo

The perspective on state-building puts the Chinese reforms in the context of the *longue durée* of Chinese modernization since the 19th century. This also opens up fresh perspectives in understanding China in comparative terms. In the ongoing debates about China's failure to achieve the transition to "capitalism," fiscal and financial structures have obtained a central place: one aspect is the comparative weakness of the Imperial fiscal state as compared to emerging capitalist-led economies in the 18th and 19th century, the other is the lack of modern financial instruments of government debt which triggered the emergence of capital markets and modern banking in the West.

The most remarkable characteristics of the Imperial fiscal system were a systematic organizational dualism: formal fiscal administration of central government on the one hand, whereas county-level administration was based on informal structures on the other hand. The two economic and social domains were fiscally connected via the mandatory contributions of the local level to the central power. In Qing Dynasty China, the system was ideologically supported by the Confucian doctrine of keeping the tax burden low for the people, which stood in tension with the reality of informal taxation which put much pressure on local communities. This dual structure was also reflected in the dualism between a vigorous market system, today often dubbed a "Smithian economy," and the tributary public economy of the Empire.

This traditional fiscal system proved to be too weak to raise the resources necessary to create a strong state that could withstand the aggression by the Western and the newly emerging powers, in particular Japan. In Republican China, there was clear awareness that reforming the fiscal system was a key to building strong government in China, while also creating legitimacy of rule. The main challenge was to expand the formal fiscal administration to the local level, together with a comprehensive effort of state-building, which means the extension of government encompassing all levels and groups in society. However, the Republican government ended up in what Prasenjit Duara has called "state involution": this means, even though the scale of administrative structures grew, the net result for funding government was declining, and the contribution of government to local society was even negative; in particular, the dual structure of government could not be overhauled, with local society plunging into disorder and facing the growing strain of informal taxes, fees and outright plundering by local strongmen. Hence, Republican China ended up as a "failed state" in the chaos of Japanese aggression and civil war. This was the most important reason why the many successful initiatives at development and industrialization eventually did not achieve the "great transformation," and at the eve of the founding of the People's Republic, China remained an agricultural economy and a predominantly rural society.

Now, considering what happened after 1949, probably the unique feature of China as compared to other developing economies was the establishment of a rigid dualist institutional structure that separated rural and urban economic and social systems, such as the different organization of land ownership and the household registration system. Seen in the light of the *longue durée*, this was tantamount to freezing the status of state involution, and to stabilizing the dual structure of the Imperial fiscal state. That means, rural society was connected with the central state only via mandatory contributions to the project of industrialization and remained "self-reliant" in all other respects. Government administration did not advance beyond the county level, with the People's Communes governed by the Communist Party and the newly emerging cadre stratum. This system resulted in what Vivienne Shue has dubbed a "cellularized" rural society, since in the planned economy the vital role of markets in connecting villages with the larger regional economic and social fabric was suppressed. In the end, this cellularization therefore also contributed to maintaining the pattern of "economic involution" in Imperial China, thus only achieving low rates of growth (Gross Domestic Product, GDP), GDP per capita and of living standards in spite of a substantial increase of the share of industry in GDP.

So, we think that Philip Kuhn was right when he argued recently that the economic system established after 1949 was mainly aiming at solving the fiscal problem in creating a strong state in as short a time as possible. In other words, the planned economy can be interpreted as a special formation of comprehensive taxation that came at the price of subduing the dynamic and productive roles of markets. However, the system produced mixed results in terms of the crucial challenge of state-building, because it maintained the dual structure of the Empire in the shape of People's Communes. This became immediately evident when market forces were released again. In the context of the dual institutional structure, market forces initially speeded up state involution.

This fact is visible in what we believe was probably the most important single event in Chinese reforms, namely, the tax reform of 1994. It became necessary because the immensely successful first stage of market transition had triggered the rapid decline of the fiscal power of the central state, reflecting the rise of what has been called the "local state" in China studies. So, market transition turned out to be a fundamental challenge to state-building in China, which was reflected in many popular and scholarly visions of China possibly falling apart like the Soviet Union or the former Yugoslavia, as the Chinese scholars Wang Shaoguan and Hu Angang wrote at that time. This was highly misguided, because it underestimated the strength of the central state, and it erroneously misinterpreted the fragmentation of the local states as the growing autonomy of higher-level administrative entities, in particular the provinces.

In Chinese studies, the phenomenon of the "local state" is mainly related to the county level and hence reflects the historical continuity with the pivotal role of the county in separating formal and informal governance in Imperial times. In modern China, on the county level the schism between rural and urban society crystallizes, hence reflecting the failure of state-building in rural society during the Maoist era. So, the tax reform of 1994 easily succeeded in recentralizing revenue on higher levels, but left the local state in a quandary, with a large and growing gap between revenues and factual expenditure requirements of county governments. China developed a fiscal system that is unique in international comparison, with a high degree of revenue centralization and a high degree of expenditure decentralization. That could resolve the fiscal crisis of the central state, but created the fiscal crisis of the local state.

Interestingly, the tax reform of 1994 came hand in hand with the first design of the "socialist market economy" in conceptual terms. It was the trigger for many further and crucial reform processes, such as the silent privatization of Township and Village Enterprises and many smaller state-owned enterprises since local governments wanted to get rid of the burden of subsidizing them, or the speeding up of urbanization via the mobilization of land use rights by local governments for funding their budgets. So, fiscal reforms were actually driving marketization and privatization without a centrally determined master plan, setting the incentives for the much appraised Chinese experimentalism on the local level. This is why we can say that the dynamics of state-building has been shaping the transition to the market economy.

On the other hand, the fiscal crisis of the local state can be seen as a resurgence of the forces of state involution in contemporary China. The expressions of state involution were similar to the conditions of Republican times, without the disorder resulting from political instability and internal strife, and were mainly visible in rural society. That means, the burden of informal taxation grew incessantly in the 1990s and early 2000s, because the local state desperately had to fund its needs, and at the same time the quality and scale of public services declined, manifest, for example, in worsening conditions of health care and education in many rural areas. Rising income inequality between rural and urban society therefore can be seen as an expression of failures of state-building. In many parts of China, state involution even went hand in hand with economic involution, when the developmental efforts of local governments failed to achieve momentum, because of ill-judged local policies and lack of market opportunities and because of locational and other environmental factors. Often, these vicious circles also involved the local financial sector, thus also worsening the environment for private business.

Consequently, the turn of the millennium also saw renewed efforts of reforming the local state, with tax reforms staying at the center. Initiatives such as "Building a New Socialist Countryside" are not simply measures of economic development, but part and parcel of a state-building effort. Again, if we look at this in the *longue durée*, it is straightforward to see that only these efforts finally overcome the dual structure of public finance which was the hallmark of the Empire. This is what I call the "Great Transformation." This is why the study of fiscal institutions duly stays at the center of any attempt to understand the political economy of reforms in China.

To summarize, the "Great Transformation" is the phenomenon that during China's economic and political development in the 20th century, a mismatch and de-synchronization of institutional change in the economic domain and of the structures of the state, manifest in institutions of government, in particular fiscal, materialized. This mismatch resulted in the cellularization of the Maoist times, the coupled rise of the local state and the market in the early reform era, and is only gradually resolved with the most recent reforms of the fiscal and the financial system. In other words, institutional deep structures of Empire survived into the twenty-first century, and the completion of China's transition to the market economy requires the completion of Chinese state-building. This is what we see as the core challenge of the Xi Jinping leadership, hence to fulfilling the "China Dream."

State-building in the twenty-first century is of course a different challenge than in the nineteenth and the twentieth century, since for any state-building effort the global context matters crucially. In somewhat simplistic terms, these are different contexts of what "modernity" and "modernization" might mean, in the larger patterns of relating economy, society and politics in a track of sustainable development and constant change. One of the core challenges is to balance state power and market freedom. We believe this is where reference to the German tradition of "Ordo-liberalism" looms large, which is also central concern in this book.

If we relate this to the problem of state-building, the fundamental dilemma in relating market freedom and state power is the question of knowledge. The problem of knowledge has been highlighted by another representative of the Freiburg school, Friedrich August Hayek. In China, state-building under the auspices of modernization was always interpreted as giving the state the role of the avant-garde, thus also claiming superior knowledge about the societal needs of future developments. Economists rarely discuss Ordo-liberalism in the context of state-building, so it is illuminating to consider Foucault's seminal and deep discussion of German Ordo-liberalism in the context of his treatment of "bio-politics." China certainly is an exemplary case of "bio-politics" in the Foucaultian sense, with the state aiming at penetrating the economy and society with the goal to achieve stabilization of institutional structures and developmental trajectories: Chinese population policy is a case in point. However, there is the fundamental epistemological issue where the knowledge originates that the state mobilizes in its bio-politics, and how it can be effectively deployed. This creates the fundamental challenge at designing an "economic order" in which state and market assume their autonomous positions, mutually limiting their scope, and thus creating the realms of freedom in which new knowledge is created.

The Ordo-liberal school of thinking argues that there are fundamental limits to the powers of the state in discovering and exploiting the knowledge which is also necessary for fulfilling its role. In an increasingly complex modernizing society, this knowledge is dispersed across myriads of epistemic subjects, in the context of markets, entrepreneurs, consumers or managers. The state is only one actor among many others who produce this knowledge. That implies that the state can no longer claim the role of the avant-garde of change and development. This is the fundamental paradox of state-building in China today: a strong state needs to bind its visible hand precisely in order to enable itself to make it operational in maintaining and further developing the structures of the state in the context of global society.

In fact, this paradox already is well recognized in China and there are even creative solutions: this relates to the pivotal role of territorial competition in

Chinese reforms. The dysfunctional aspects of the tensions between local state and central state also had the positive side in fostering the generation of knowledge about reform strategies and institutional alternatives by the local states which compete against each other. This "regional decentralized authoritarianism" and the resulting pervasive pattern of experimentalism meant that realms of autonomy of the local level are being implicitly recognized by the central authorities. Territorial competition can be seen in the Hayekian light of being a process that generates new knowledge about ways of providing public services and establishing alternative governance schemes. I think that building on these experiences, it is obvious that further institutionalization of these autonomies is a key to successfully continuing the "great transformation" in the future. A core challenge to state-building in China is establishing a stable institutional framework for the interaction between the local and the central state. I think that points toward another family resemblance to Imperial China, namely, the dynamic role of provinces and municipalities in the late nineteenth-century reform movements.

To conclude, we believe that the key to understanding the political economy of China's Great Transformation is the interaction between state-building and market transition, which is evolving in the context of economic development. Reading the contributions in this volume helps to analytically and empirically decipher the institutional mechanisms driving these changes.

Professor Carsten Herrmann-Pillath
Witten/Herdecke University
Germany
Beijing, February 15, 2016

Preface

The term "transformation" is different from "transition." Although both refer to a given starting point of the change of a system such as a planning system, "transformation" doesn't imply a preset goal such as a market economy while "transition" does. This differentiation is especially important as regards the case of China. China didn't clearly define her goal of transformation from the outset. This kind of reform strategy was once summarized by Deng Xiaoping as "crossing the river by touching stones in the river bed." Therefore, the Chinese transformation has been characterized as gradualist, phased-in, partial and experimental.

This book focuses on the elaboration of features and problems of China's great transformation since China opened her door to the world in 1978, and necessary conditions and reform policies for her further transformation. It deals with a triple transformation, i.e. the political, economic and fiscal transformation in China. Accordingly, the book consists of three parts discussing these three dimensions, respectively.

Part I includes two chapters. Chapter 1 focuses on the examination and analysis of the political development in post-Mao China from Deng, through Jiang and Hu, to Xi. According to the authors, the Communist Party of China followed the Marxist and Leninist principles to create a "vanguard party," modeled on the Leninist party in the former Soviet Union during the Chinese Communist revolution. After the Communist takeover of power, the making of the Chinese Communist state was modeled on the former Soviet Union, which is called the "Party–state." In the Chinese Party–state, the Party stands at the top of the pyramid of the power structure, and assumes the total representation of the nation and total guidance of national goals. The Party commands, controls, integrates and completely intertwines with all sectors of the state: the government (the executive), congress (the legislative), courts (the judiciary), political consultative conference, the military, mass organizations and all other political organizations and institutions, from top to bottom.

With the Leninist Party–state as the analytical framework, the chapter examines the political change in post-Mao China from Deng, through Jiang and Hu, to Xi, along the most critical empirical dimensions and demonstrates that the post-Mao regime has remained in the fundamental sense the Communist Party–state, which retains the defining characteristics of all Communist regimes in the making. The post-Mao regime maintains a Leninist party that is the locus or – to use the regime's official terminology – "the core of leadership" or "the political nucleus" for all state institutions and social organizations. China has not made any fundamental political change from the Communist Party–state regime in any of those fields despite the considerable economic change and some administrative and institutional changes made in the last three decades.

Chapter 2 analyzes the characteristics and problems of the values and institutions of the "Chinese Dream" proclaimed by the Chinese president Xi Jinping and considerations of some values and institutions necessary for China to realize the "Chinese Dream." This chapter serves to provide a general political background for the socio-economic and fiscal transformation, and urban and rural transformation in China. The new Chinese leadership promised to deliver a "Chinese Dream" with the rejuvenation and the prosperity of the Chinese nation and the happiness of the people as China's development goal. While articulating the necessity of the further reform and opening-up, they also put an emphasis on the adherence to a so-called peculiar socialist way of Chinese characteristics in that the one-party rule is regarded as its imperative. For the "Chinese Dream" to be realized, a set of values was proclaimed, among others the "core socialist values," including prosperity, democracy, civility, harmony, freedom, equality, justice, rule of law, patriotism, dedication, integrity and friendship. Beside the existing institutions such as the system of democratic centralism, the CCP-led multi-party cooperation and system of people's congresses, a set of institutions was proclaimed as well, including a brand-new "socialist" system of rule of law.

This part shows that these newly proclaimed values and institutions are an important new foundation for China to gain high economic efficiency and escape from a "middle-income trap," and thus to realize the "Chinese Dream." However, its realization depends still on whether the new leadership can successfully enforce the property right protection, a system of rule of law and political constitutionalism.

Part II includes three chapters, Chapters 3–5. Chapter 3 analyzes characteristics of the economic transformation in China and tries to re-interpret the "Chinese Miracle." As is well known across the world, the rapid economic development and transformation of Chinese society over the past three decades has, by a large mass of analysts, been called the "Chinese Miracle." This chapter not only addresses the shortcomings of existing interpretations but also develops a new multi-dimensional framework based on North's theory of institutional change and Hayek's theory of institutional evolution to explain China's miraculous growth. Its analysis shows that both Hayekian spontaneous order and Popper's "piecemeal social engineering" played a major role in attaining China's miraculous growth. In concrete, such a "Miracle" is to be traced back to a large degree to the unintended and selective approximation to a competition order advocated by Walter Eucken, which includes a set of constitutive principles, including a functioning price system, stability of monetary value (primacy of monetary policy), private property, open market, freedom of contract, liability and constancy of economic policies (which means consistently enforcing all these principles).

Chapter 4 shows how the private sector has been developing and what a major role it is playing in pushing forward the overall economic development in China. Private enterprises are an important and integral part of China's economy today. Whether in terms of sheer numbers or contribution to GDP, employment or technological innovation (measured by number of registered patents), they far outpace state-owned enterprises. Although the private sector in China is playing a major role in Chinese development, the outlook for many private enterprises remains less than positive and has continued to deteriorate in recent years. There is a variety of reasons for the deterioration of the environment for the survival and development of private enterprises in China, including system and policy problems, market issues and internal management problems. One system and policy problem is that the Decision of the 3rd Plenary Session of the 18th Central Committee of CCP supports the development of a mixed ownership economy in the sense that state-owned enterprises and private enterprises are encouraged to hold equity in each other. But this is a double-edged sword for the development of the private sector and jeopardizes the principle of subsidiarity. The authors suggest that China should switch to a full-scale protection of property rights and market openness, and a low-tax regime to facilitate the private sector development in China.

Chapter 5 introduces a corporate capital freedom index for Chinese provinces. It analyzes the different scores and rankings of capital freedom in various provinces and their relationship with economic performance. The combined degree of capital freedom improved in 2011 as compared to all years since 2006 and, hence China has ended the decline observed in 2008. The scores and rankings of various provinces show the strength and weakness of the respective province. It helps them to identify their strengths and weaknesses.

Part III focuses on the analysis of the fiscal transformation in China. It includes four chapters, Chapters 6–9. Chapter 6 shows that the Chinese fiscal federalism features a combination of a close link between local fiscal revenue and expenditure with fierce territorial competition, which generates immense incentives for local governments to run own businesses or promote local economic development in order to generate profits, taxes or other revenues. Furthermore, the Chinese fiscal federalism is characterized by a high centralization of the tax revenue and the formal power to tax. However, local governments have de facto autonomy to a large extent in terms of deviations from the formal laws and regulations. This chapter shows that the Chinese fiscal federalism is still far from being perfect, compared with traditional normative principles of fiscal federalism. However, these traditional principles are themselves not fully free of pitfalls. Centralization tendencies are inherent. Therefore, some principles are to be refined, or even added up (such as the principle of protecting basic rights or that of subsidiarity) for the normative analysis of future Chinese fiscal federalism. The author develops a set of refined principles of fiscal federalism and analyzes the problems of Chinese fiscal federalism in contrast to them. This chapter concludes that it is necessary for China to take further steps toward fiscal constitutionalism.

Chapter 7 elaborates the size, structure and problems of local government debt and municipal bonds. Local governments in China are facing heavy debt burdens, a low level of fiscal transparency and a lack of constraints by local democracy. Since 2008, local government debts have skyrocketed. This chapter analyzes the current state and features of local government debts and the two kinds of "quasi municipal bonds" in China – urban investment bonds and local government bonds – along with their problems and risks. It examines the risks connected with local government debts and these bonds from the perspectives of public finance and political economy. It concludes with a discussion of a framework of rules for local government debt financing, especially for the issuance of municipal bonds in China.

Chapter 8 introduces the analytical framework of "government competition," which encompasses current models of Chinese local government like the "developmental state" or "entrepreneurial state" as special cases. The argument is based on a detailed empirical case study of Gujiao Municipality (Shanxi Province) which is put into perspective with reference to two other cases (Tongxiang, Zhejiang Province, and Zhangjiagang, Jiangsu Province). It is argued that the specific interaction between fiscal reforms and local approaches to infrastructure finance is the outcome of vertical and horizontal competition among governments. This competition is conceived as a complex system of formal and informal institutions undergoing endogenous change. Rooted in historically determined institutions like the regional property rights system in local resources, the system evolves through political entrepreneurship crafting competitive strategies and institutional innovations. The peculiar features of Chinese local government like budgetary dualism, local resource ownership or fiscal bargaining should not be conceived as "policy failures" in terms of deviations from centrally imposed formal institutions. They are defining features of the institutional framework of government competition in China, in which the central government is only one player.

Chapter 9 addresses the features, problems and reform of the county and township fiscal administration system in China. That China's counties and townships are in a fiscal predicament is an acknowledged fact. This problem is largely attributed to the current multi-tier fiscal system, the county and township fiscal administration system in particular. So far, we still lack overall analytic research on the county and township fiscal administration system and the relationship between functions and powers and fiscal powers at county and township levels in the context of the multi-tier fiscal system and its structure; a sound normative framework for a county and township fiscal system depends on such research. By analyzing the multi-tier fiscal system and its structure, this chapter discusses the status, features, problems and causes of the county and township fiscal administration system, sorts out distribution and operation of functions and powers, expenditure responsibilities and fiscal powers across levels of government, and, from the angle of the theory of fiscal federalism, puts forward some thoughts for resolving these problems. The research finds that the fiscal administration system of "supervising the lower level" and the functions and powers "mandated by higher levels" not only conflict with the internationally accepted principle of fiscal federalism, but are free from the restriction of local democratic fiscal rules and procedures, both unfavorable to the efficient operation of the county and township fiscal administration system. This is why further reforms are necessary.

The authors of this book welcome any comments and critiques. We would like to thank Yongling Lam of Routledge for her patience and able assistance in our manuscript preparation and Professor Carsten Herrmann-Pillath for writing the foreword for this book.

Xingyuan Feng
Christer Ljungwall
Sujian Guo
Beijing, February 15, 2016

Bibliography

Eucken, W. *Grundsätze der Wirtschaftspolitik,* 6th ed. (Tübingen: J.C.B. Mohr, Paul Siebeck), 1952.

Hayek, F.A. *Law, Legislation, and Liberty.* (Chicago: University of Chicago Press), 1973.

Hayek, F.A. *The Fatal Conceit: The Errors of Socialism.* (London: Routledge), 1988.

North, D. C. 'Sources of Productivity Change in Ocean Shipping, 1600–1850'. Journal of Political Economy. Vol. 76, 1968, p. 953.

North, D. C. *Institutions, institutional change, and economic performance.* (Cambridge University Press), 1990.

North, D. C., and Davis, L. E. *The Theory on Institutional Change: the Concept and Cause.* See Coase, Ronald H., Armen A. Alchian and Douglass C. North: Property Rights and Institutional Change. (Shanghai Sanlian Joint Publishing House and Shanghai People's Publishing House), 1994, pp. 266–294.

Popper, K.R. *Objective Knowledge as an Evolutionary Approach.* (London: Oxford University Press), 1972.

Popper, K.R. *Die Offene Gesellschaft und ihre Feinde.* Band 1: Der Zauber Platons. (Tübingen: Mohr Siebeck), 1945/1992.

Part I

Political transformation in China

1 Political development in contemporary China[1]

During the Chinese Communist revolution, the Communist Party of China (CPC) followed Marxist and Leninist principles to create a "vanguard party," modeled on the Leninist party in the former Soviet Union. After the Communist takeover, the Chinese Communist state was modeled on the former Soviet Union, which had a system known as a "Party–state." The Party has been the center of power in Chinese politics, both in Mao's China and in post-Mao China. The Party–state has been maintained and developed according to the so-called Four Cardinal Principles (四项基本原则) in post-Mao China: the adherence to Marxism-Leninism and Mao Zedong Thought, the leadership of the Communist Party of China, the socialist system, and the dictatorship of the proletariat.[2]

In the Chinese Party–state, the Party stands at the top of the power structure, where it assumes total representation of the nation and total guidance of national goals. The Party is recently defined as not only the vanguard of the working class but also the vanguard of the Chinese people, and the entire nation (Jiang, 2001). "In this way, the Party's claims to political representation became, in a sense, more totalizing, and one may well ask whether or not this effort of inclusion was more or less totalitarian. Nevertheless, it was, arguably, more 'Leninist'" (Mahoney, 2011). The Party commands, controls, integrates and completely intertwines all sectors of the state: the government (the executive branch), congress (the legislative branch), courts (the judiciary), the political consultative conference, the military, mass organizations and all other political organizations and institutions, from top to bottom. The Party–state therefore accurately captures the nature and function of China's political reality.

The CPC is the Leninist vanguard party

The CPC has since its very birth been a Leninist party, proclaiming itself as the "vanguard of the proletariat and all working classes" and following the principle of "democratic centralism" according to Leninist principles. As a result the CPC leadership not only requires the whole party to be subject unconditionally to its leadership, but also requires the state, the military, society and individuals to be subject to the Party's leadership and policy.

The post-Mao regime has continued to follow Bolshevik lines, or Maoist style, in its organization, though it has taken some measures to rationalize the organizational system and decision making. New policy rhetoric such as "cadre four modernization" (*ganbu sihua*干部四化)[3] or the "Three Represents" (*sange daibiao*三个代表)[4] in post-Mao China has, however, not really changed the organization of the political system. The current organization can be traced to the same origin as the Leninist or Maoist system in the following two respects:

1 The CPC under the post-Mao regime continues to claim that it is a "revolutionary vanguard" of the proletariat; an elitist party acting as the enlightened trustee of the working class, and acting on behalf of society. As Jiang Zemin declared, "our party is the Marxist-Leninist party standing in the forefront of the times and leading in the direction of the future. Our party will lead the people towards the full prosperity of the nation in the twenty-first century" (Dangjian, 1998). In a speech in 2001, "Uphold the Four Cardinal Principles," Jiang describes the principle of Party leadership as follows: "Maintaining the leadership of the CPC means maintaining the political leadership of the CPC over major state policy and overall work. It means maintaining absolute leadership of the CPC over state apparatuses, including the army and other facets of the people's democratic dictatorship."[5] The "vanguard" status of the CPC is the keystone of Party power and its ideological power, which little resembles political parties in Western democracies, or the elite single party in authoritarian regimes. The Three Represents is the most recent formulation of the Party's vanguard status, which was announced at the 16th Party Congress in 2002. This concept stipulates that the Communist Party of China is representative of advanced social productive forces, advanced culture and the fundamental interests of the Chinese people of all ethnic groups. The total representation of the nation and total guidance of national goals are codified into the Constitution: "under the guidance of Marxism-Leninism, Mao Zedong Thought, Deng Xiaoping Theory and the important thought of 'Three Represents'" (PRC Constitution 2004, Preamble).
2 The Party exercises the principle of "democratic centralism" (*minzhu jizhongzhi*民主集中制), which in fact has everything to do with centralized control and nothing to do with democracy. Party organizations, from the national level to the workplace, neighborhood or village level, are rigidly hierarchical. The whole Party must obey the Party Central Committee (PCC) and look to the PCC as the correct interpreter of ideology and the core leadership of political action. According to the principle of "democratic centralism," the whole Party is ultimately subject to a paramount leader and a small group of the Politburo standing members. Discussion may be allowed, but Party leadership decisions are final and non-debatable. Dissent or even objective thinking is *prima facie* evidence of "bourgeois liberalism" that must be purged with "criticism and self-criticism," if not expelled from the Party.

To maintain "vanguard" status, carry out the principle of "democratic centralism," and accomplish its historical mission, the Party has to be kept in a constant rectification movement. The rectification movement has been the main vehicle for the post-Mao regime to re-establish ideological purity and organizational rule. The earliest rectification movement after the death of Mao was the purge of the followers of the "Gang of Four," lasting for a number of years. This was followed by the 1984–1987 rectification movement which was carefully planned to be systematic, thorough and inclusive.

The main purpose of the rectification movement in early post-Mao China was to purge the "three kinds of people" who had benefited from the Cultural Revolution (that is, those who rose to prominent positions by following the Jiang Qing and Lin Biao "cliques," those imbued with factionalism and those who engaged in "beating, smashing and looting"[6]), strengthen Party discipline, restore the Party tradition of the period before the Cultural Revolution, and attack "new unhealthy tendencies" and intra-Party factionalism (Young, 1990). In the earlier stages of the movement, the "liaison groups" were sent out by the Commission to supervise and coordinate rectification activities at lower levels. "Inspection groups" were often used later on to check on lower levels.[7]

Purges have been periodically conducted among Party cadres and Party members in "party construction" and "rectification" movements to ensure that "the party organization is pure" and to guarantee that "various leadership positions and functions are taken up by true Marxists."[8] The most extensive housecleaning after the Cultural Revolution was the purges that were carried out after 1989. "Work teams" were stationed in almost all key central government organs and their subordinate mass organizations. All government functionaries, particularly Party members and cadres, were required to give a detailed account of their "involvement" in the event. An unprecedented Party membership "re-registration" campaign was launched in the first half of 1990. All Party members automatically lost their membership unless they were allowed to re-register after satisfying the authorities of their total devotion to the "Four Cardinal Principles." The result of the purges was announced by the *People's Daily* on May 30, 1991. The total number of CPC members had declined to 50.3 million. In 1990, 127,000 Party members were either expelled, or asked to leave the CPC. In addition, 166,000 Party members were subjected to internal Party discipline (Lam, 1995).

During these purges the emphasis had been on restoring the Party's past values and practices and on using "tradition" to address current problems. Jiang Zemin urged the Party–state cadres to uphold the ultimate ideal and firm faith in communism, strengthen the "party nature," resist various temptations, and try to be exemplary models in upholding and developing the Party's fine tradition and style.[9] "Party style" (*Dangfeng*) refers to a combination of all the prescribed political norms and relationships crucial to the Party's operations and the maintenance of organizational coherence and obedience. The various elements of Party style were first fully articulated in the early 1940s, and it is this articulation that is regarded as establishing Party "tradition." If a tradition is to have any current political relevance, then it implies continuity of application. Emphasis on "Party style" suggests a continued insistence on the Party's vanguard character and on the qualitative difference between the CPC and other types of political organizations. The notion of "Party style" demands commitment to Party goals as the basis for members' political actions and relationships (Young, 1990). However, this emphasis on Party "traditions" is not considered to conflict with the "shift in focus" on economic modernization. Instead, it is considered crucial for the Party's survival during economic marketization and liberalization to offset the threat posed to organizational discipline and ideological purity.

The Party controls every sector of the state and central-local governments

The CPC Party–state continues its commitment to the same ideology – Marxism-Leninism-Maoist Thought, with the same ultimate goal and the same fundamental principles of the Leninist Party–state, despite some changes and modifications in post-Mao China.

As in the Leninist "Party–state," the Communist Party is the center of the power in China, or "a state within a state." All the key policy decisions since 1949 have been made outside the government, but have been entirely monopolized by the Party. The Party defines its function as that of making all the crucial decisions, which the government must carry out. The existence of Party leading groups in units of the state organ ensures the structural dominance of the Party. Members of Party standing committees at various levels are in charge of one or several governmental functions and operations. As in Western states China has political institutions, for example, three branches of the government, but they are organized differently. If we simply look at the three branches of government (executive, legislative and judiciary) and their relationships, we will lose sight of the most important features of the Leninist Party–state. In the politics of the People's Republic of China, we must look at the power relationships among the three big tightly interlocked *xitongs* or systems (系统), called "party – state – military" (党政军), under the direct leadership of the Party Politburo standing committee members, and many sub-*xitongs* headed by high-ranking Party officials.

In both horizontal and vertical power relationships, the Party is the center of the power structure, and controls every level of government through an array of Party organizations from top to bottom. As China is a highly centralized unitary system, a provincial or local government is subject to the "dual leadership" (双重领导) of both higher-level Party organizations and the local Party organization. The Leninist Party–state emphasizes centralism as its organizational principle, and applies it to the organization of state institutions. Each administrative level in the power hierarchy is responsible for overseeing the work carried out by lower levels of the administrative strata. Although provincial and local governments are given more autonomy in economic policy making, they are subservient to their superiors at higher levels of administration, and ultimately to the central government. At each level of administration below the central-level government, there are two important political figures, out of which both are Party members and ranking Party officials. One is the Party Secretary of the Party committee who is "first-hand figure" (第一把手) and acts like a policy maker, while the other is "second-hand figure" (第二把手) in the Party committee, and serves as the head of the government to carry out the Party's policy and administrative work. The Party Secretary is always ranked above the head of the government. Both figures are actually appointed by the higher-level Party committees, but are in theory elected by the people or by the people's congresses.

In summary, the Party is the center of power while the function of government is to implement the Party's political guidelines and policies. The Party's guidelines and policies set national goals, justify the means to achieve them, and provide the basis for government policies. It is the Party's congress that sets guidelines, not the NPC and people's congresses. As a Chinese American scholar put it, "if the latter are the bones and flesh of Chinese body politics, the Party is undoubtedly its brain, its nerve center and its sinews. The Party commands, controls and integrates all other political organizations and institutions in China. The Party-state, or 'partocracy,' accurately captures China's political reality" (Ming, 2002). The Party–state structure and the relationships of various political institutions demonstrate the following key features:

1 Party/state/military are combined and intertwined, with four parallel and highly interlocked structural arrangements: parallel positions of Party leaders and state officials, parallel structures of Party organization and state institutions, Party ideology being the governing ideology, and Party principles being the guiding principles of government.
2 No checks and balances between different branches of the government, with the Party being the center of the power and the supreme authority of all politics and public life.
3 The CPC controls every sector of the state and penetrates every corner of society with a political consultation conference to incorporate non-CPC social elite into the political system and justify its rule.
4 The CPC declares that it works within the constitutional and legal system, but in actual reality it is the lawmaker, and therefore above the law. Laws are defined and made according to the Party's ideology, norms and political needs. There is no independent judicial system.

The Leninist Party–state is the pillar that sustains the CPC rule and maintains the political order in contemporary China. The Party–state governing principles and its ruling model are not only codified in the Chinese Constitution but also grounded in Marxist-Leninist principles under which the state is organized and through which it is governed.

Post-Mao political development

Since 1978, China's economic reforms and open-door policy have brought about considerable change in many aspects of politics. However, our theoretical picture of post-Mao China's political development and our interpretation of the nature of the changes have been complicated and confused by contrasting situations that coexist in China:[10] these changes have complicated our understanding of the Chinese state and beg this question: is post-Mao China still a Leninist party-state? Many scholars have used "fragmented authoritarian state" (Lieberthal, 1992), "local state corporatism" (Oi, 1998), or "political decay" (Gilley, 2001, 2003) to describe the changing nature of the Chinese state.

- Ideological campaigns are still employed, while more emphasis is placed on economic development.
- The Party still maintains its monopoly of power and its organizational control. It is still pervasive, while the Party–state control over people's daily lives and economic activities is relaxed.
- The Party control over information and media is still tight, while some civil publications are allowed within non-political areas.
- Political persecutions continue, while greater individual freedom is evident.
- The Party still adheres to its ideological commitment, while its influence on the general population is weakening. Party control over private morality is less effective than under Mao, while official Communist morality is still a whip over the Chinese society.

To many people, both scholars and non-academic analysts, post-Mao China represents a contradiction, which suggests the need to assess the changes over the last three decades and evaluate the nature of the politics. As Joseph Fewsmith, a leading scholar on Chinese politics, pointed out, "Any observer of contemporary China will note two seemingly contradictory facts: first, there is considerable political innovation in China, and, second, to date, none of these political reforms have gathered momentum"(Fewsmith, 2013).

The Chinese political system is the area of least change in post-Mao China, compared with the economic, social and legal areas, though the post-Mao regime has attempted some within-the-system "political reforms." This includes decentralization, establishment of a legal system, inclusion of the eight "democratic parties" into the political process, broadening the powers of the legislature, streamlining administration, redefining the role of Party organizations and their relationships with state institutions and economic organizations, and experimenting with local grassroots elections under the Party leadership, and so forth. More recently, under Xi Jingping, the Party has started to embrace the ideas of democracy, freedom and rule of law into the core value of socialism, and implement the idea of rule by constitution (依宪治国), rule by law (依法治国), and government by law (依法行政), independent jurisprudence (独立司法审判),

modernization of state governance (国家治理现代化), and so forth. To many China analysts, these reforms and changes have led to a fundamental regime change in post-Mao China – transitioning away from the Leninist Party–state Communism, and thus, they conclude that the Party–state conceptualization of the current Chinese political system is no longer relevant or outdated.

The contradiction begs the question whether post-Mao China has experienced such a "fundamental" change in the political system, and, whether a new political system has come into being due to these reforms. The answer to the question depends on how we define the hard core of the political regime and the key indicators of fundamental change at the regime level. For example, Communist China has always repeated the cycles of streamlining–bloating and decentralizing–recentralizing. Such institutional changes and rationalizations are not indicators of fundamental change in the hard core of the Leninist Party–state. Therefore, the answer to the question requires a coherent theory of regime identity or a clear conceptual framework by which we are able to distinguish between systemic and developmental changes, and between a change *of* a political regime and a change *within* a political regime.

This chapter has constructed a conceptual model of real-world Leninist Party–state Communism to distinguish the "hard core" of the Party–state from other operative features, and establish the criteria for assessing the nature of political change in post-Mao China (Guo, 2012). According to the model, the above changes only suggest the regime's attempt at institutionalization of the Leninist Party–state and rationalization of its administrative, legislative and legal systems. It does not point to liquidation of the Party's power, ideology and organization, or political liberalization from the Party–state power.

In post-Mao China, political development is institutional and administrative in nature, and political reforms are based on rationalization. Rationalization is a central concept used by Max Weber to refer both to institutional changes involving differentiation, specialization, standardization, and bureaucratization of political and social organizations (Gerth et al., 1998). This has been more associated with the adjustment of action means and the functioning of the regime at the operative level. The post-Mao regime from Deng to Xi has retained the Leninist Party–state hard core, the Party's vanguard status as a total representation of the working class, and goal culture (Three Represents, Chinese Dream, etc.), the pervasiveness of Party organizations and control in every sector of the state. Only changes associated with the hard-core components of the regime are the key indicators of a fundamental change at the regime level. Distinguishing between the two levels or the two different types of changes is the key to our understanding the nature of political change in post-Mao China.

The Post-Mao "political reform"

Has political reform made any fundamental or systemic change of the Leninist Party–state? By "political reform" the post-Mao leadership has never meant a transition from the Party-led Party–state Communism, but primarily the modernization and professionalization of the Party–state institution. The "political reform" is not aimed at systemic change but at so-called self-improvement and moral self-restraint of the Party and the government. This goal is no different from a utopia, in which government is expected to be self-disciplined, self-restrained and self-improved without a real external check – a system of checks and balances, constitutional democracy and rule of law (Meisner, 1998). The aim of political reform, as Deng Xiaoping has clearly prescribed for China, is to "raise working efficiency and overcome bureaucratism" and to make Party–state cadres at various levels "better educated, professionally more competent, and younger." Its content has included "separation of the functioning of the party and the government," "decentralization of power" and "streamlining the administrative structure," although "westernization and liberalization," "separation of powers" and "Western parliamentary system" are not allowed.[11] The CPC under reiterated "Five Nos" (*wudebugao*五个不搞): "We have made a solemn declaration that we will not employ a system of multiple parties holding office in rotation; diversify our guiding thought; separate executive, legislative and judicial powers; use a bicameral or federal system; or carry out privatisation."[12] This is crucial for determining the nature of the reform and its limitations. Particularly, the post-Mao leadership emphasized that the "Four Cardinal Principles" are a fundamental prerequisite to the socialist reforms and the Four Modernizations. This means that changes brought about by the reform have not made the core features of the Leninist Party–state insignificant.[13]

The "Four Cardinal Principles" are by no means considered by the post-Mao regime merely as rituals, but as defining core elements of the system, and any attempt to weaken these principles has never been tolerated. During the 1980s the top reformist leaders attempted to open more political space or create a "more relaxed political environment," such as allowing more debate on political reforms, more press freedom and lifting political taboos within the Party. Their limited liberal reform efforts had the unintended effect of ideological decay and increasing student and dissident activities. These reformist leaders and their political allies were removed from office by Deng Xiaoping and Party elders. Steps toward a more "relaxed" political environment were quickly reversed in the late 1980s. Instead, legitimization of the regime and the individual leaders was sought through traditional political forms, such as the leadership cult and the resurrection of Maoism. We have observed more conservative backlashes in every aspect of political life.

Political reform determines the nature and degree of political change. However, there has been no evidence to prove any essential change in the political system and the power structure since reform in 1978. The post-Mao reform, either under Deng, Jiang, or Hu, and Xi has pursued a pattern of economic modernization with no attempt to fundamentally transform the Chinese Communist Party–state. Political reforms were officially regarded as a means of facilitating economic reforms, and served the purpose of strengthening and improving the Party leadership and governing capacity. Party leadership claimed that successful and further economic reform required "social stability and unity," and should be carried out only under Party leadership. Thus any tendency toward political liberalization and democratization was seen as a threat. Democratic reform had little place on the political agenda (Zaijun, 2011).

From the very beginning of Deng's reform in 1978, the Chinese Party leadership never intended to have a true and thorough reform of the political system. Instead they attempted to ease domestic conflict and serious political tension through a readjustment of economic policy, or later economic liberalization and administrative rationalization, and continued to maintain the Party's power while relaxing control on citizens' daily life and economic activities. Therefore, the focus of the reform policy was the economic realm, which served to facilitate economic development and attract foreign investment. The focus was on economic liberalization and not on privatization of ownership in the economic system and democratization of the political system, which would enhance and guarantee individual freedoms and rights. The post-Mao Communist regime has attempted to graft a "market economy" on a Party–state political structure originally designed for a socialist planned economy. Such a reform strategy has led to the incompatibility between the requirement of a market economy and the political structure, between the market economy and state ownership, as China's former Premier Wen Jiabao recognized in an interview with CNN in October 2010.[14]

Political reforms have been based on rationality and pragmatism, and have been administrative in nature. It was not a systemic reform and involved no significant and fundamental transformation of the political system, power structure and ideology. Therefore, as Tatsumi Okabe points out, "it was not a regime transition, but a within-system change (*tizhi gaige*体制改革)" (Okabe, 1992). Even these rationalization programs in administrative, legislative and legal systems are slow and remain weakly institutionalized, and the actual achievements are meager.

A major reform step taken at the 9th National People's Congress (NPC) following the 15th Party Congress was the government restructuring program intended to streamline the size of the central government to 29 departments. The reduction of the size at this time is comparable to the one in the Cultural Revolution under Mao, during which the standing bodies of the State Council were reduced to 33 (Qingkui, 1998). Does this suggest that Mao's regime is less communist, or less capable than the post-Mao regime? This is another perfect example that suggests that the change in governmental size does not prove a systemic or fundamental change of the regime. The plan at the 9th NPC involved greater changes. However, the purpose of the government restructuring program was to "transform functions, put relations in order, streamline administration, and improve efficiency."[15] Within four years, from 1993 to 1997, the departments and standing bodies of the State Council increased from 68 to 86, and the non-standing bodies increased from 49 to 85; on average, 14 standing and non-standing bodies increased per year (Qingkui, 1998). In fact, the sixth governmental restructuring did not break the "vicious circle" of history, but just repeated it.

The 11th National People's Congress in 2008 was the most recent major government restructuring and streamlining, which received wide attention internationally. However, today the state council has 27 ministries, 1 state assets administration commission, 16 agencies under its direct supervision, 14 public institutions under its direct supervision, 22 bureaus under ministerial direct supervision, totaling 80 organizations under its supervision. Besides, there are 28 consultative and coordinating organs. We can simply count over 100 central government organs that rely on the state budgetary expending. Not to mention the huge duplicated and overlapped organizations at all levels.[16] In short, the Chinese Communist regime has undertaken major institutional restructuring at least seven times since the Communist takeover in 1949, but it has always repeated the circle of "streamlining–bloating – streamlining again–bloating again." The purpose of the restructuring program is not to reduce the strength of the state, or to weaken the Party leadership, or to promote the separation of Party and government. The principle or slogan is clearly stated as "streamlining, unification and efficiency."

In fact, instead of the separation of Party and state, a major setback since the 14th Party Congress was to reinforce the "cross leadership" of the Party and the state. This refers to the fact that Politburo members and other top leaders can concurrently take up positions in the Party, government, legislature and the CPPCC. Jiang Zemin or Hu Jintao is head of the state, the Party, and the army-President of the state, General Secretary of the CPC Central Committee, and Chairman of the Central Military Commission (CMC), in addition to many other substantial and ceremonial titles. Other Politburo members double as heads of the executive or the legislature.

All the key Party leaders also occupy senior positions in the government. While the Party's constitution provides that the Party congress is responsible for setting political policy, that authority in fact rests with a half dozen or so top Party leaders who are members of the Politburo Standing Committee of the Party Central Committee. Under Deng's regime, this small group had to refer all major decisions to Deng Xiaoping (Starr, 1997). The Party has two means for ensuring that its policies are implemented by the government officials. The first is the power of appointment, since at each government level appointments are the responsibility of the Party organization at the level just above – the central Party organization appoints provincial officials, while provincial Party organizations, in turn, appoint officials at the city and county level. Second, the performance of officials appointed by the Party is then supervised by Party organizations. At each government level and in public enterprises, a leading Party group or a Party committee supervises political correctness and ensures that Party policies are carried out.

In fact, since the 15th Party Congress, in an effort to strengthen and improve work in the Party-state organs and bring the Party grassroots organizations into full play, the Politburo of the Party Central Committee issued "Guidelines for the Party Grassroots Organizations Build-up in the Party and State Organs" and asked the Party committees and the Party leading groups in all political and military organs and all major military regions to carry out the guidelines without delay.[17]

The "black box" operation of the Party's National Congress suggests a big retrenchment in "intra-Party democracy," of which the CPC is model for the whole nation. The election of the members of the Central Committee is separately held in the hotels where various delegations or deputy groups stay during the Party's congress. No information exchange is allowed between delegations or deputy groups during this period of time. In principle, deputies are not allowed to meet visitors or go home in the course of the congress. The specially designed envelopes containing the official slates and the form of election are picked up by specially appointed congress work personnel from Zhong Nan Hai (headquarters of the Party Central Committee of the CPC) and then sent to the hotels to distribute among the deputies. Deputies have no idea of the content of the envelopes until they open them up.[18] Such a "black box" operation of the election suggests no fundamental change of the Communist Party–state system. This Party congress operation mechanism applies to all Party congresses and the people's congresses at all levels.

The Party continues to exercise the principle of "democratic centralism" (*minzhu jizhongzhi* 民主集中制) in all sectors of the state and central-local governments. In both horizontal and vertical power relationships, the Party is the center of the power structure, and controls every level of government through an array of Party organizations from top to bottom. The People's Liberation Army (PLA) and other armed forces have always been considered as a "strong pillar of the people's democratic dictatorship," and subject to the absolute command of the CPC and the Central Military Commission (CMC). The PLA has extensive political, social and economic duties to serve as "the defender and the builder of the socialist system and modernization."

The relationship between the CPC and the People's Congress remains fundamentally unchanged. The CPC proposes directly to the NPC or its Standing Committee and other special legislative committees legislative bills in important state affairs, and such a practice is duplicated at all levels of the Party committees and people's congresses. The CPC exercises the leadership of the routine work of the NPC Standing Committee and those at lower levels through specific directives or decisions. The CPC exercises the leadership of the election work of people's congresses and the leadership of people's congress sessions. All major leaders of the Party and governmental organizations must be in charge of some work during people's congress sessions. The important personnel decisions are all made by Party committees. In practice, all the leading positions of people's congresses are held by Party secretaries, deputy secretaries, or Party committee members. Therefore, the Chinese legislature, as a political institution of the Leninist Party–state system, continues to serve the Party's goals, acts as a rubber stamp on the Party's policy change, and provides legitimation for the Party rule, though it is declared as the "supreme power body" of the Chinese political structure.

The relationship between the CPC and other "Democratic Parties" at the CPPCC also remains fundamentally unchanged. The post-Mao regime has re-instituted "multi-party cooperation" into its political operation, and emphasized the enhanced role of the Chinese People's Political Consultative Conference (CPPCC). However, the CPPCC serves as a political instrument of the Party–state to "incorporate" the eight so-called democratic parties, which are actually subordinate satellites of the CPC. These so-called parties have no independence and must accept the leadership of the CPC. The political foundation of cooperation between the CPC and the democratic parties is based on the CPC leadership and the Four Cardinal Principles. The purpose of the CPC's efforts to develop the "united front" was to help strengthen the unity of people from various sectors, maintain political stability and support the CPC rule. Therefore, the CPPCC is after all a window dressing for democracy and only serves as a "think-tank" or "talent bank" for the CPC.

Major core elements of and many of the political practices of the Leninist Party–state still remain essentially unchanged. Although some institutional factors might be functional in determining short-term policy and personnel issues, they operate within the political and structural constraints that stem from the basic nature or essence of the Leninist Party–state system.

Political development under Hu Jintao

The 16th Party Congress in 2002 officially marked the beginning of Hu Jintao's era. Some changes have taken place under his generation of leadership, in response to new challenges facing the ruling party. As a result of three decades of economic reform, economic freedom expanded and private business boomed. However, the economic success also created new problems due to the lack of political reform. The market-driven reform under the Party–state rule led to serious government corruption; social injustice; a widening of income gaps and regional disparities; collapses of the old social system, health and income safety networks; public unrest; and a deteriorating environment. All these problems have posed serious challenges to the ruling party, jeopardized the political stability and cast a shadow on the moral foundation of market-oriented economic reform (Guo and Guo, 2008).

The World Bank has developed a Political Stability Indicator (PSI) as part of its World Governance Indicators (WGI). The PSI measures the perception of the likelihood that a government in power will be destabilized or overthrown by unconstitutional and/or violent means. A negative value indicates a high level of instability. In 2000, China's PSI was –0.01. By 2006, that figure has dropped to –0.37, which indicated declining trust in China's political stability (Kaufmann et al., 2007). In 2003, there were 58,000 "mass incidents" reported by the government, and in 2005 over 74,000 incidents of public unrest were reported.[19] In 2008, there were an estimated 124,000 instances of "mass unrest" in China (Less, 2010). However, despite the increase in the number of reported incidents, China has remained relatively stable (Minxin, 2008). Nevertheless, these numbers should send an alarming signal to the Party leaders.

The 16th CPC Party Congress, held in November 2002, and the 10th National People's Congress, held in March 2003, completed the power transfer from the "third generation" to the "fourth generation." Since many key leaders are protégés of Jiang Zemin, there is continuity in the Party's policies. Therefore, the new leaders did not "rock the boat."[20] However, they seem to have reached a consensus that reform had reached a critical point where some policy adjustments were needed. There were growing interests in an alternative development model which emphasizes sustainable development, more equitable distribution of wealth and the creation of a "harmonious society." It seemed that some changes were going to happen, though not in a radical form (Guo and Guo, 2008). We have observed some face changes in official declaration but not much in effect.

The new generation leadership under Hu Jintao began to search for solutions and directions. "Building a Harmonious Society" based on "Scientific Outlook of Development" became a new catchphrase and slogan in political and academic discourse in China (Guo and Guo, 2008). The new concept was viewed by many as a significant departure from the previous efficiency-oriented developmental strategy, and a "model for the world" (Qin, 2006). However, the focal point of this departure was mainly economic, social and environmental, aiming to solve these problems without changing the Leninist Party–state rule. In practice, however, the implementation of new policies and programs has achieved very limited success and the problems have remained unresolved.

It is in this context the 17th Party Congress was held in October 2007. The 17th Party Congress declared to set the historical course and path of the "socialist democratic building," featuring gradual, phased-in, grassroots self-governance and intra-Party democratization. The guidelines and slogans were set as follows:

- Developing the "four democracies": "democratic elections, democratic decision making, democratic management, and democratic oversight"
- Developing grassroots democracy: "self-management, self-service, self-education and self-oversight"
- Furthering administrative reform and building a service-orientated government (the "four separations"): separating the functions of the government from those of enterprises, state assets management authorities, public institutions and market-based intermediaries
- Establishing a system of checks and balances, stressing that "power must be exercised in the sunshine to ensure that it is exercised correctly."
- The Party should become democratic first. The Party will reform the intra-Party electoral system and improve the system for nominating candidates and electoral methods at the grassroots level.

These Party guidelines and slogans have generated high expectations and exciting discussions for almost eight years both within and outside China. However, these reforms are set within the limit of maintaining the Leninist Party–state instead of undermining it, with a goal for its "self-improvement." Hu Jintao, in a speech at the ceremony in December 2008 marking the 30th anniversary of China's adopting the economic policy of reform and opening-up, elaborated on what kind of political reform the Party has pursued, which deserves a long quote:

> China's political reform is characterized by the self-improvement and development of the socialist political system. We must adhere to the path of political development under socialism with Chinese characteristics, integrate the leadership of the Party, the position of the people as masters of the country and the rule of law, maintain the features and advantages of the socialist political system, and proceed from national conditions . . .[21]

Hu's political report actually reiterates and defines the nature, direction and principle of political reform and claims that "socialism with Chinese characteristics" depends on "the leadership of the Party." In fact, Hu Jintao, Jiang Zemin and Deng Xiaoping have talked about remarkably similar things regarding "political reform." Therefore, the three keystones of the Leninist Party–state remain fundamentally unchanged. A comparison of the CPC under Mao's regime and under the post-Mao regime is further illustrated in Table 1.1.

Table 1.1 The CPC under Mao's regime and under the post-Mao regime

	Under Mao's Regime	*Under Deng's Regime*
Power	Monopolistic and personalistic (based on the principle of "Democratic Centralism")	Monopolistic and oligarchic (based on the principle of "Democratic Centralism")
Ideology	Strong commitment, exclusive, compulsory and coherent	Strong commitment, exclusive, compulsory and less coherent
Goal	Twin-goal: industrialization and Communism	Twin-goal: modernization and Communism
Means	Mass mobilization and universal participation of all social members in the political system via constant and direct mass political campaigns for carrying out political objectives	Bureaucratic rationalization, combined with limited mass mobilization and participation in the political system via Party-controlled mass organizations, political institutions and state-licensed or controlled social organizations
Leadership	Infallible charisma (Mao)	Infallible charisma (Deng)
Membership	Elitist vanguard	Elitist vanguard
Legitimacy sources	Communist revolution and Marxist-Leninist-Maoist ideology	Communist revolution and Marxist-Leninist-Maoist-Deng-Jiang-Hu ideology

Table 1.2 Party–state relationship under Mao's regime and under the post-Mao regime

	Mao's Regime	*Post-Mao Regime*
Government/ regime/state	The distinction between the three is blurred and fused through the CPC. The CPC constructs and molds government, regime and state in its own ideology, principles, norms, rules, image and need.	Unaltered
Party–state apparatus	Party apparatus is hierarchically organized, superior to and intertwined with the state apparatus.	Unaltered
State institutions	Fusion of powers of various state institutions under the CPC leadership.	Unaltered
Party dictatorship	CPC dictates politics, and party organizations lead, dominate and penetrate every sector of the state.	Unaltered

A comparison of the Party–state relationship under Mao's regime and under the post-Mao regime is illustrated in Table 1.2.

According to Pan Wei, a Peking University professor, China's supreme power rests on the Politburo Standing Committee of the Communist Party of China, and China's political structure is led and controlled by the Chinese Communist Party in six major ways:

1 Communist Party and its core decision-making departments, such as Central Committee of the Communist Party of China, Politburo of the Communist Party of China, Propaganda Department of the Communist Party of China, Central Commission for Discipline Inspection of the Communist Party of China, Political and Legislative Affairs Committee of the Communist Party of China, Organization Department of the Communist Party of China Central Committee.
2 The all-powerful National People's Congress has always been under the control of the CPC.
3 All the PRC governmental departments are under the control of the CPC.
4 People's Liberation Army is under control of the CPC.
5 Chinese People's Political Consultative Conference is under control of the CPC.
6 All the semi-governmental departments, such as trade unions, women's associations, Communist youth groups, are all under control of the CPC.[22]

Under Hu Jintao, the PLA has continued to be under the control of the CPC without any change. As early as 1938, Mao Zedong stated: "our principle is that the Party commands the gun, and the gun must never be allowed to command the Party."[23] Deng, Jiang and Hu have made remarkably similar remarks: the army must be under the Party's absolute command. On April 1, 2009, General Li Jinai, the PLA's top political commissar who sits on the 11-member Chinese Communist Party Central Committee, reiterated that People's Liberation Army must continue taking orders exclusively from the Communist Party in an essay published in the Party's official theoretical journal, *Qiushi*. He stated:

- "Unshakingly uphold the basic principle and system of the party's absolute leadership over the army";
- "Resolutely oppose the wrong thinking of 'army-party separation, depoliticization, and army nationalization' ";
- "At all times, make the party flag the army's flag and . . . in all things listen to the commands of the party, Central Military Commission and President Hu."[24]

Political development under Xi Jingping

The 18th Party Congress held on November 15, 2012 formally made Xi Jinping the paramount leader of the CCP. He became General Secretary of the Communist Party and Chairman of the CPC Central Military Commission, and President of the State in 2013. After Xi become the leader of the new generation, he made a number of public announcements of his new doctrines, such as "Three Confidences" (三个自信), "Chinese Dream" (中国梦) and "Four Comprehensives" (四个全面), which have become central themes in CCP's political slogans, being often recited by state media, official meetings, political discourse and conferences.

The "Three Confidences" refers to "confidence in our chosen socialist path, confidence in our political system, and confidence in our guiding theories." Xi Jinping has a deeply held belief that the Communist Party created the best political system and institutions to govern China and its political development and has more advantages than the Western-style democracy. These political institutions include the People's Congress, People's Political Consultative Conference under the CCP leadership, and Regional Ethnic Autonomy.

Xi also promoted the idea of the "Chinese Dream" in his visit to the National Museum of China in November 2012. Since then, the phrase has become widespread in official announcements and has become Party lexicon as the embodiment of the political ideology of the leadership under Xi Jinping. Xi has described the dream as "national rejuvenation, improvement of people's livelihoods, prosperity, construction of a better society and a strengthened military" (Osnos, 2013). Xi's Chinese Dream aims to achieve the "Two 100s": China will become a "moderately well-off society" by 2021, the 100th anniversary of the Communist Party of China, and a fully developed nation by about 2049, the 100th anniversary of the founding of the People's Republic.[25]

To achieve the Chinese Dream, Xi began to promote four most important strategic measures, which are called "Four Comprehensives": comprehensively building a moderately prosperous society; comprehensively deepening reform; comprehensively governing the nation according to law; and comprehensively strictly governing the Communist Party. Within the CPC's system, new leaders must always explicate their vision and policies for the country as an extension of the canon of Marxism-Leninism and Mao Zedong thought, as Deng Xiaoping, Jiang Zemin and Hu Jintao did in post-Mao China. This provides a leader's mandate to rule, and defends their policies against those who may criticize their policies as going against the ideological tenets of the CPC.[26]

Along with Xi's ideological campaign to consolidate his power, he laid down the boundaries of deepening reform in his era, promoting modernization of state governance and governing capacity, governing state by law and constitution, all of which must be carried out by the CPC leadership. However, in the meantime, Xi acknowledges the challenges to the legitimacy of Communist rule, particularly corruption by Party–state officials and its serious consequences. His solution is two-fold: strengthening the Party from within, by initiating a large-scale anti-corruption campaign to remove unsavory elements from within the Party, and instituting Mao-style "mass line" campaigns externally to make Party–state officials better serve the needs of ordinary people.

However, Xi believes that just as the Party must be at the apex of political leadership of the state, the Party's central authorities (i.e., the Politburo and himself as general secretary) must exercise full and direct political control of all Party–state affairs, including political, economic, cultural, legal and social governance (Veg, 2014). Therefore, despite some new features, Xi's thought has demonstrated continuity of Mao Zedong and Deng Xiaoping ideology, i.e., CPC leadership, socialist core values and Party–state institutions. In fact, the "administrative state" and "administrative society" of the Leninist Party–state have remained fundamentally unchanged, and the state power has continued to perform comprehensive or all-embracing functions of administration. In an effort to curb Western influence, China's leadership under Xi has reportedly ordered universities in China to steer clear of seven subjects in the classroom, including universal values, press freedom and civil rights and the historical mistakes of the Chinese Communist Party.[27]

Concluding discussion

We have examined the political change in post-Mao China along the most critical empirical dimensions and demonstrated that the post-Mao regime has remained in the fundamental sense a Communist Party–state. The post-Mao regime has attempted to resurrect the political tradition and political theory of the mid-1950s and base the political doctrine of the post-Mao regime on the "Four Cardinal Principles." The post-Mao regime has continued to consolidate and institutionalize the totalistic Party–state apparatus that has come down from Mao's era. There has been no genuine separation of party and state and political liberalization, as reform has consisted of "rationalization" of the government functions.

The state institutions and social organizations are established and institutionalized as an appendage of the Party, which is consistent with the Leninist Party–state. State agencies are generally facades for corresponding Party organizations wherein the real power lies. State institutions and social organizations act as Party instruments in carrying out the wishes of the Party leadership, while the Party acts to ensure its predominance in all aspects of the society – political, legal, economic, social, cultural, ideological and military arenas. All state institutions, including the NPC, the CPPCC, and the PLA are the instrument of the Party, which the Party either disregarded entirely (under Mao's regime) or manipulates for its own ends (under the post-Mao regime). Moreover, in the post-Mao era, the security forces, synthesized with the military, are greatly strengthened and heavily politicized so that they can defend the Party and its ruling order against real and imagined threats and opposition. The military and the security forces serve as sword and shield of the Party.

Therefore, the post-Mao regime retains the defining characteristics of all Communist regimes and maintains a Leninist party that is the locus or – to use the regime's official terminology – "the core of leadership" or "the political nucleus" for all state institutions and social organizations. China has not made any significant political change from the Communist Party–state regime in any of those fields despite considerable economic change and some administrative and institutional changes made in the last three decades.

Notes

1 The authors thank Routledge for permission to adapt and reproduce pp. 131–139 in Chapter 9, and Chapter 10 of *Chinese Politics and Government: Power, Ideology, and Organization* (Routledge, 2013).

2 Deng Xiaoping, "Uphold the Four Cardinal Principles," *Selected Works*, Vol. II (Beijing: Foreign Language Press, 1995), p. 168.

3 This new policy adopted in the post-Mao era refers to the four criteria for choosing and promoting Party–state cadres: younger, better educated, revolutionary and modernized.

4 Jiang Zemin's political report at the 16th CPC Congress, November, 2002.

5 Jiang Zemin, "Uphold the Four Cardinal Principles," *Selected Works*, Vol. III (Beijing: Foreign Language Press, 2010), pp. 224–225.

6 *Beijing Review*, no. 42, 1993, p. v.

7 *People's Daily*, March 13, 1985, p. 4.

8 Ibid., June 25, 1991.

9 *People's Daily*, April 2, 1998, p. 4.

10 The discussion in this section incorporates some material from Sujian Guo, *Post-Mao China: From Totalitarianism to Authoritarianism* (Westport, CT: Praeger Publishers, 2000), pp. 70–92.

11 Deng Xiaoping, *Selected Works of Deng Xiaoping*, Vol. III (Beijing: People's Publishing House, 1993), pp. 177–178.

12 http://www.theaustralian.com.au/news/world/china-rules-out-political-reform/story-e6frg6so-1226020720813

13 For a detailed discussion on the actual practices and political/ideological campaigns to enforce these principles, see Guo (2012).

14 CNN's interview with Wen Jiabao, http://transcripts.cnn.com/TRANSCRIPTS/1010/03/fzgps.01.html; http://www.telegraph.co.uk/news/worldnews/asia/china/8040534/Wen-Jiabao-promises-political-reform-for-China.html
15 *People's Daily*, October 17, 1995, p. 1.
16 http://www.gov.cn/gjjg/2005–08/01/content_18608.htm; http://www.gov.cn/gjjg/2005–08/28/content_27083.htm
17 *People's Daily*, May 7, 1998, p. 1.
18 *Press Freedom Guardian*, November 21, 1997, p. 4.
19 "National Poverty Does Not Affect Political Stability in China," *Pravda*, August 15, 2005. Available at: http://english.pravda.ru/ world/20/91/366/15985_China.html
20 "The Survivors Take Over," *Economist* 366 (March 22, 2003): pp. 37–38.
21 Hu Jintao's Speech at the Meeting Marking the 30th Anniversary of Reform and Opening Up. Available at: http://www.china.org.cn/archive/2009–05/11/content_17753659_9.htm
22 P. Wei, "China's Party-Government System – The Origins of the Current Political Regime" (in Chinese). Available at: http://www.chinaelections.org/NewsInfo.asp?NewsID=111152
23 Mao Zedong, "War and Problems of Strategy," *Selected Works*, Vol. II (Beijing: People's Publishing House, 1991). Available at: http://baike.baidu.com/view/139621.htm
24 "China Military Still under Communist Party Control," Victoria Advocate Publishing Co. Available at: http://www.victoriaadvocate.com/news/2009/apr/01/bc-as-china-communist-party-military
25 http://www.nytimes.com/2013/06/05/opinion/global/xi-jinpings-chinese-dream.html?pagewanted=all&_r=0
26 "Xi Jinping's Four Comprehensives," *Economy Watch*, April 22, 2015. Available at: http://www.economywatch.com/features/Xi-Jinpings-Four-Comprehensives.04–22–15.html
27 http://www.scmp.com/news/china/article/1234453/seven-subjects-limits-teaching-chinese-universities-told

Bibliography

Beijing Review, no. 42, 1993, p. v.

Dangjian, Y. [*Party construction studies*], no. 4, 1998.

Deng, X. *Selected Works of Deng Xiaoping*. (Beijing: People's Publishing House), 1993, vol. III, pp. 177–178.

Deng, X. "Uphold the Four Cardinal Principles," in *Selected Works*, Vol. 2. (Beijing, China: Foreign Language Press), 1995, p. 168.

Fewsmith, J. *The Logic and Limits of Political Reform in China*. (New York: Cambridge University Press), 2013, p. 232.

Gerth, H.H. and Wright Mills, C. "Introduction: The Man and His Work," in H.H. Gerth and C. Wright Mills, eds., *From Max Weber: Essays in Sociology*. (New York: Oxford University Press), 1958, pp. 3–74.

Gilley, B. The Limits of Authoritarian Resilience. *Journal of Democracy*, 14(1), 2003.

Gilley, B. From Decay to Democracy. *Foreign Policy*, May/June, 2006.

Guo, B. and Sujian Guo, S. "Challenges Facing Chinese Political Development," in Sujian Guo and Baogang Guo, eds., *Challenges Facing Chinese Political Development*. (Lanham, MD: Rowman & Littlefield-Lexington), 2008, p. 3.

Guo, S. *Post-Mao China: From Totalitarianism to Authoritarianism*. (Westport, CT: Praeger Publishers), 2000, pp. 70–92.

Guo, S. *Chinese Politics and Government: Power, Ideology, and Organization.* (London: Routledge), 2012, pp. 1–32.

Jiang, Z. "Uphold the Four Cardinal Principles," in *Selected Works*, Vol. III. (Beijing: Foreign Language Press), 2010, pp. 224–225.

Kaufmann, D., Aart, K. and Mastruzzu, M. *Governance Matter IV: Aggregate and Individual Governance Indicators (1996–2006)*, World Bank Policy Research Paper 4280, July 2007 (Washington, DC: World Bank).

Lam, W.W-L. *China after Deng Xiaoping.* (New York: John Wiley & Sons), 1995, pp. 155–156.

Less, J. China Won't Revalue the Yuan. *Foreign Policy*, September 24, 2010. http://www.foreignpolicy.com/articles/2010/09/24/china_won_t_revalue_the_yuan?page=0,1

Lieberthal, G.K. "Introduction: The 'Fragmented Authoritarianism' Model and Its Limitations," in G.K. Lieberthal and David M. Lampton, eds., *Bureaucracy, Politics, and Decision Making in Post-Mao China.* (Berkeley, CA: University of California Press), 1992.

Mahoney, J.G. "Legitimizing Leninism," in Deng Zhenglai and Sujian Guo, eds., *Reviving Legitimacy: Lessons for and from China.* (Lanham, MD: Rowman & Littlefield-Lexington), 2011.

Mao, Z. "War and Problems of Strategy," in *Selected Works*, Vol. 2. (Beijing: People's Publishing House, 1991). Available at: http://baike.baidu.com/view/139621.htm

Meisner, J.M. *The Deng Xiaoping Era: An Inquiry into the Fate of Chinese Socialism, 1978–1994.* (New York: Hill and Wang), 1996, p. 481.

Ming, X. *The Communist Party of China and the 'Party-State'*, 2002. Available at: http://www.nytimes.com/ref/college/coll-china-politics-002.html

Minxin, P. Is China Unstable? *American Diplomacy*, on-line, accessed on January 21, 2008. Available at: http://www.unc.edu/depts/diplomat/AD_Issues/amdipl_13/china_pei.html

Nathan, A. *China's Crisis: Dilemmas of Reform and Prospects for Democracy.* (New York: Columbia University Press), 1990, pp. 178–179.

Oi, J. "The Evolution of Local State Corporatism," in Andrew Walder, ed., *Zouping in Transition: The Process of Reform in Rural North China.* (Cambridge, MA: Harvard University Press), 1998, pp. 35–61.

Okabe, T. "China: The Process of Reform," in Gilbert Rozman, Seizaburo Sato and Gerald Segal, eds., *Dismantling Communism: Common Causes and Regional Variations.* (Washington, DC: The Woodrow Wilson Center Press), 1992, p. 190.

Osnos, E. Can China Deliver the China Dream(s)? *New Yorker*, March 26, 2013.

Pan, W. *China's Party-Government System – The Origins of the Current Political Regime* (in Chinese). Available at: http://www.chinaelections.org/NewsInfo.asp?NewsID=111152

People's Daily, March 13, 1985, p. 4.

People's Daily, October 17, 1995, p. 1.

People's Daily, April 2, 1998, p. 4.

People's Daily, May 7, 1998, p. 1.

Press Freedom Guardian, November 21, 1997, p. 4.

Qin, X. Harmonious Society to Be a Model for the World. *China Daily*, October 13, 2006.

Sondrol, P.C. *Castro's Cuba and Stroessner's Paraguay: A Comparison of the Totalitarian/authoritarian taxonomy*, Doctoral Dissertation in Political Science, The University of Arizona, 1990, p. 14.

Starr, J.B. *Understanding China: A Guide to China's Economy, History, and Political Structure.* (New York: Hill and Wang), 1997, pp. 64–65.

The Survivors Take Over. *Economist*, 366, March 22, 2003, pp. 37–38.

Veg, S. China's Political Spectrum under Xi Jinping. *The Diplomat*, August 11, 2014.

Xi Jinping's Four Comprehensives. *Economy Watch*, April 22, 2015, http://www.economywatch.com/features/Xi-Jinpings-Four-Comprehensives.04-22-15.html

Xie, Q. Retrospect and Prospect of Restructuring China's Administrative Institutions. [*Zhongguo xingzheng gaige de huigu yu zhanwan*], *XinHua Wenzhai* [New China Digest], no. 3, 1998, p. 4.

Young, G. "Party Reforms," in Joseph Y.S. Cheng, ed., *China: Modernization in the 1980s.* (New York: St. Martin's Press), 1990, pp. 75–86.

Zaijun, Y. *The Failure of China's "Democratic" Reforms.* (Lanham, MD: Rowman & Littlefield-Lexington), 2011.

Zhang, X. From Totalitarianism to Hegemony: The Reconfiguration of the Party-State and the Transformation of Chinese Communication. *Journal of Contemporary China*, 20(68), January, 2011, pp. 103–115.

2 The "Chinese Dream" deconstructed

Values and institutions

China became the world's second-largest economy in terms of Gross Domestic Product (GDP) in 2010 and joined the club of middle-income economies with a per capita GDP of USD 5,432 and 6,100 in 2011 and 2012 according to Chinese statistics. This long-term speedy economic growth contributed enormously to the strengthening of the political legitimacy of the authoritarian rule of the Communist Party of China (Heberer et al., 2006; Herrmann-Pillath, 2009). However, the slow-down of economic growth since 2012 has become a long-term tendency, which is quite understandable after over 30 years of high-speed growth. Not to mention that the GDP base for further growth is simply much larger than in 1978, the beginning year of China's reform and opening-up, there are a number of political, economic and social problems that have created bottlenecks for maintaining sustainable economic growth, such as the expansion of state power, growth of interest groups, renationalization of the economy, lack of democracy, low level of protection of individual rights, farmers' group resistances, outdated industrial structures, and low level of social, labor and environmental protection. As has been seen in many other middle-income economies, this can result in a "middle-income trap" (The World Bank et al., 2012).

It is the phenomenon of hitherto rapidly growing economies stagnating at middle-income levels and failing to graduate into the ranks of high-income countries (Aiyar et al., 2013). To avoid or escape this "trap," and also to foster the political legitimacy of the Party's rule, China must work to improve the efficiency of the allocation of production factors to maintain a relatively high economic growth rate over an extended period of time. Such a move is also a necessary step for any country that ultimately wishes to move into the high-income bracket. Some analyses (Sachs et al., 2000; North et al., 2009) even conclude that for China to attain this goal, there is the necessity of a constitutional transition.

China's new president Xi Jinping (2013) started his presidency promising to deliver a "Chinese Dream" (*zhongguo meng*, in the following "CD") of national rejuvenation and prosperity in his speech at the closing ceremony of the 1st Plenary of the 12th National People's Congress on March 17, 2013. This should be the guiding vision of the new leadership over the next five to 10 years. It emphasizes the "Chinese way" (*zhongguo daolu*) of development with "Chinese characteristics" (*zhongguo tese*) such as the CCP leadership, traditional Chinese culture and "socialism." This chapter scrutinizes values and institutions proclaimed by Xi to support the realization of the "CD" and their potential effects upon it. It studies some general rules for economic development, especially for a country's escape from a so-called middle-income trap, and discusses how those values and institutions can be conducive to the realization of the development goals anchored in the "CD" concept.

Major ingredients of the "Chinese Dream"

In Xi's concept (Xi, 2013), the goal of the "CD" is the economic prosperity and strength of the country (*guojia fuqiang*), the rejuvenation of the nation (*minzu zhenxing*) and the happiness of the people (*renmin xingfu*). Accordingly, Xi reemphasizes sticking to Deng Xiaoping's guiding strategic thinking that "development is the last word" (*fazhan caishi ying daoli*). However, while Deng stressed economic growth, Xi and his predecessor Hu Jintao already switched their focus on relatively high-speed economic growth and, in connection to it, a more balanced development. To fortify the foundation of the realization of the "material civilization" (*wuzhi wenming*), which is nothing else but economic prosperity and strength of the country, Xi (2013) commits to "further reform and opening-up" and a reemphasis on "scientific development" that was put forward by Hu Jintao (2003) on July 28, 2003, and stresses "adhering to the people-centered, comprehensive, coordinated and sustainable development concept, to promote comprehensive economic, social and human development." The above "development" notion is found again in the expression "economic construction" (Xi, 2013), which means proactively pushing forward economic growth and development and is at the center of the work of the new Party leadership.

The above development goals are expressed in the CCP's mid-term target of China's becoming a "moderately well-off society" (*xiaokang shehui*) in full scale by the end of 2020, which is anchored both in the resolution of the 18th Party Congress held in November 2012 and Xi's above-mentioned speech. Furthermore, as a long-term goal, "a prosperous, democratic, civilized, harmonious and modernized socialist country" is to be constructed (Xi, 2013).

According to the blueprint of realizing such a "moderately well-off society" announced by the 18th Party Congress, both the total GDP size and per capita income of urban and rural residents are to be doubled by the end of 2020 in comparison to those in 2010. Figure 2.1 shows that China has to keep a pace of annual GDP or per capita GDP growth of 7.18 percent from 2010 to double its size of GDP and per capita GDP by the end of 2020. In contrast, the US economy will still keep its No. 1 position in the world, far ahead of China in terms of both the size of its GDP and per capita GDP in the same period, if we take a moderate growth scenario by extrapolating its annual GDP and per capita GDP growth from 2010, i.e., taking its moderate annual GDP growth

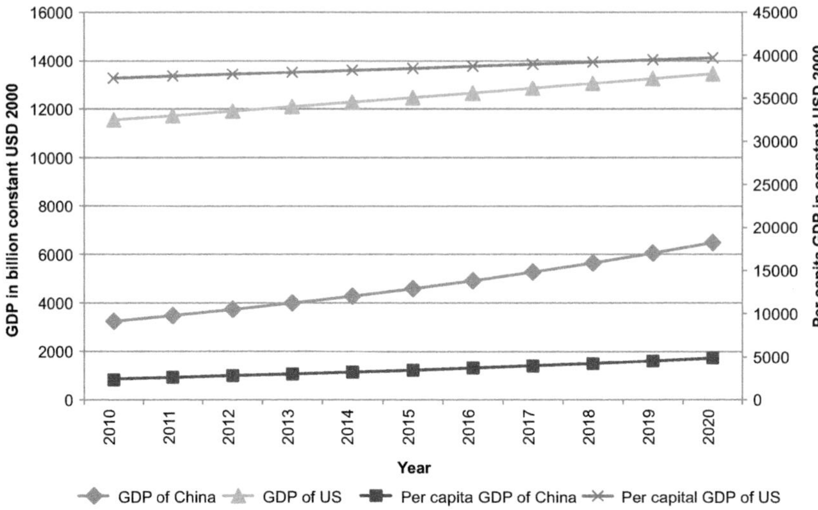

Figure 2.1 GDP and per capita GDP development: China and the US (2010–2020)

Source: World Development Indicators and the authors' own calculations.

Note: China has to keep a pace of annual GDP or per capita GDP growth of 7.18% from 2010 to double its size of GDP and per capita GDP by the end of 2020. The US data reflect a moderate growth scenario and are extrapolated from the base year 2010, by taking its annual GDP growth rate of 1.55% and annual per capita GDP growth rate of 0.62% in the period of 2000–2010 as the respective annual reference growth rates for the period of 2010–2020.

rate of 1.55 percent and annual per capita GDP growth rate of 0.62 percent in the period of 2000–2010 as the reference rates for the period of 2010–2020. Even a progress as such should be a major one. Moreover, if measured in terms of purchasing power parity, China's GDP will climb to $17.6 trillion, while the US grows to $17.4 trillion in 2014, as the IMF projections show on October 8, 2014 (Chandra, 2014).

Xi's "CD" concept emphasizes the "Chinese Way" (*zhongguo daolu*), which is accounted as a "road of socialism of Chinese characteristics" (*zhongguo tese shehui zhuyi daolu*) and is regarded as "a development path suited to China's national conditions" (Xi, 2013). The "CD" concept stresses also bringing into play the "Chinese spirit" (*zhongguo jingshen*), i.e., the "national spirit" with patriotism as its core, in pushing forward reform and innovation that are to be regarded as the core of the Zeitgeist inspiring the Chinese people to attain the goal (Xi, 2013). Furthermore, the "CD" is regarded by Xi (2013) as a dream of the entire nation and that of every Chinese as well. This individualized conceptualization of the "CD" renders an immense space for imagination, including that of building up a harmonious commonwealth based on protection of every individual's basic rights.

Proclaimed values and institutions in support for the "Chinese Dream"

To support the realization of the "CD," the new Party leaders proclaimed among others a set of "core socialist values" and a set of new institutions, especially a system of "socialist rule of law," both of which can be seen as path-breaking and epoch-marking in the CCP history.

Proclaimed values

There is a series of so-called core socialist values first announced in the Report of the 18th Party Congress delivered by the former Party Secretary-General Hu Jintao and endorsed by Xi in his "CD" concept. They include prosperity, democracy, civility, harmony, freedom, equality, and justice, rule of law, patriotism, dedication, integrity and friendship. Some additional values are also embedded in Xi's concept, including socialism, scientific development and traditional Chinese culture.

The Chinese reform and opening-up mark a certain degree of disenchantment of the orthodox ideology and the loosening of control of society in China. New Party leaders often choose to add some reform-oriented fresh value or policy formulations to the existing ones proclaimed by their predecessors, or rephrased the latter ones. However, the validity of such additional or rephrased catchphrases has been often compromised or neutralized by the resistance from the left wing and conservatives within the Party. On the occasion of celebrating the 30th anniversary of the implementation of the Chinese constitution of December 4, 2012, i.e., shortly after Xi's taking his position as the Secretary-General of the CCP at the 18th Party Congress, he stated that "the full implementation of the Chinese constitution is the primary task and the foundational work for building up a socialist country under rule of law" and "any organization or individual, is not allowed to hold privileges out of the constitutional and legal boundaries. All activities that violate the Constitution and laws, must be investigated and punished" (Xi, 2012). However, ironically, "constitutionalism" was viewed by the left wing and the conservatives within the Party as a threat to the CCP-led regime. From May 2013 on, the party propaganda apparatus arranged the release of a series of news articles criticizing reformers' efforts to realize constitutionalism in China. Only in the 3rd Plenary Session of the 18th Central Committee between November 9 and 12, 2013, did Xi manage to include his idea of the implementation of the Constitution in the Decision of the CPC Central Committee on Several Important Issues Pertaining to Comprehensively Deepening the Reform (in the following "Decision") of November 12, 2013. According to the Decision, the Party is to "preserve the legal authority of the Constitution." The epoch-marking Decision of the 4th Plenary Session of the 18th Central Committee on October 20–23, 2014, set a general target of forming a system of "socialist rule of law with Chinese characteristics" and building a country under "the socialist rule of law." In such a system, the

Constitution is taken as the core, the implementation of the Constitution is to be strengthened, and all state affairs are to be managed in line with the Constitution (*yi xian zhi guo*).

However, the enforcement of the proclaimed values is incredibly important and difficult, and may face many challenges. First, different individuals in the society understand and perceive differently the meanings and importance of these values. Second, some proclaimed values, for instance democracy or rule of law on one side, and socialism on other side, if referring to its traditional orthodox ideas, are contradictory and incompatible with each other (Hayek, 1944). Third, a value can be interpreted differently by Party leaders in different periods, or even its meaning can be kept vague in the same period. Fourth, in different periods of time, different values have been emphasized by Party leaders. Which values are taken more seriously at a given period of time depends on their ad hoc political need. Therefore, one has to be alert to the undertones of the Party rhetoric. Last but not least, for most Chinese, including most members and leaders of the CCP, some proclaimed values such as "rule of law" might not be the values they believe in, but taken as instruments for governing China. However, some of above values are relevant to the realization of the "CD" and deserve more attention.

Socialism

The "CD" concept puts a particular emphasis on the value of "socialism." The CCP has been facing criticism from its left wing each time it moves further away from its orthodox socialism (Lawrence et al., 2013). To reconcile and balance between the left-wing ideology and the reform policy, the CCP has reformulated socialism for more than 20 years so that China will remain in the "primary stage of socialism" (*shehui zhuyi chuji jieduan*) for a long period of time. This statement found its entry into the 1993 amendments to the Chinese Constitution. The essence of this statement lies in its relativizing the orthodox ideology of socialism to allow the profit seeking by investors and entrepreneurs for quite a long period of time in the future. With this re-interpretation of socialism, the CCP has quite successfully played down the contradiction between the orthodox socialism and values such as development, democracy and rule of law. Because China is in such a primary stage of socialism, the CCP can allow various market values and institutions of capitalism to develop in China to help China achieve the goals of economic development.

Democracy

Accordingly, the CCP defines the concept in its own way and practices democracy as "socialist democracy," "people's democracy" or "democratic centralism" through the Party leadership. In the Chinese context, the Chinese term of "democracy" (*minzhu*) has multiple meanings, ranging from multi-party elections to consultative leadership to "benign autocracy" (Taylor et al., 2010).

Accordingly, strictly speaking, the notion of "socialist democracy" can mean a range of polities from "proletariat dictatorship" to "enlightened authoritarianism" (Cabestan, 2004) or "benign autocracy" here allowing "deliberative democracy," but normally excludes Western democracy in the American sense. However, in an extreme case, Western democracy can also be re-interpreted as a type of "socialist democracy" if the CCP finds it necessary and helpful. The reason is that the Party can explain and adopt everything good as "socialism," just as Deng had already done to some extent.

Freedom

The value of freedom has been mentioned rarely in Party documents or speeches until recently. In China, the term "liberalism" got a bad reputation among the people since it was criticized by Mao Tzetung (1969) in his famous 1937 article "Against Liberalism" in the sense that he related "non-obedience" of CCP members to the CCP leadership to the term "liberalism." The Report of the 18th Party Congress, delivered by the former Party Secretary-General on November 8, 2012, unprecedentedly stresses that the CCP should "uphold freedom, equality, justice and the rule of law and advocate patriotism, dedication, integrity, and friendship," and "ensure that the people enjoy extensive rights and freedoms as prescribed by law." This new inclusion of the term "freedom" in the Party Document was formally and explicitly coined and propagated as one of the twelve "core socialist values" across China in early 2014. The Decision of the 4th Plenary Session of the Central Committee of the CCP further provides that China is to "ensure that the people enjoy a wide range of rights and freedom." In combination with the Party's repeated emphasis on the establishment of a system of rule of law, the inclusion of the term "freedom" cannot be understood as mere rhetoric, but seen as a remarkable turn to embrace a new value, which is indeed a "Great Leap Forward" in the CCP's history of ideological development.

Rule of law

"Rule of law" is expressed as "socialist rule of law" (*shehui zhuyi fazhi*), or "rule of the country by the law" (*yifa zhiguo*), implying that "rule of law" is to be run under the CCP leadership. This proclaimed value was first anchored in the 1995 Constitution and re-emphasized as a goal of the legal reform in the Report of the 15th Party Congress of September 12, 1997. It is an upgrade from the former formulation of the construction of a "socialist legal system" (*shehui zhuyi fazhi*) in Deng's era. Again, one can't undervalue this renewed phrasing since the real move can take place under this name. More and more government officials are quite sensitive to what is provided by the law, which is a desirable phenomenon across China. The report of the 4th Plenary Session of the 18th Central Committee of the CCP provides a blueprint and a huge bundle of reform measures for realizing the "socialist rule of law," which is to take place under the leadership of the CCP given its special status rooted in Chinese history.

Equality

Equality is regarded as a major source of legitimacy of any government, including the Chinese government. Equality as a value and goal has been stressed by Party leaders since the very beginning after the founding of the Party. Mao Tzetung put strong emphasis on income equality. However, his enforcement of a planning economy led to severe destruction of productive capability and a situation of equal poverty. Deng Xiaoping (1986) stressed the long-term goal of "common prosperity" (*gongtong fuyu*) while encouraging a part of the population to get rich first. The result was the rapid rise of the per capita income of urban and rural residents. However, the income disparity between urban and rural residents became larger later on and the ratio of the per capita income of urban residents to the per capita net cash income of rural residents reached a record high of 3.111 in 2002 (Figure 2.2), i.e., at the end of the period of Party Secretary-General Jiang Zemin. The period of Party Secretary-General Hu Jintao and Premier Wen Jiabao (end of 2002–2012) marked a policy re-orientation toward a focus on income redistribution, featured by building up a social safety network for all, and interregional equalization of basic public services. However, the above ratio kept rising in the early period then reached a record high and a turning point as well in 2009. The Gini coefficient shows a similar trend. According to the statistics, it fell from 0.491 in 2008 to 0.474 in 2012 (Xu, 2013).

In the era of Xi, the new leadership is to continue expanding the social safety net. According to the Report of the 18th Party Congress, equality will be measured by two target indicators of the people's life to be attained by the end of 2020: first, the equalization of basic public services is in general realized; second, the gap of income distribution is narrowed.

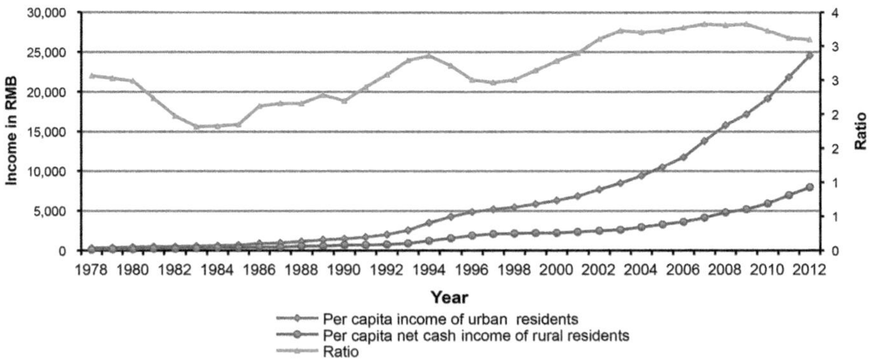

Figure 2.2 Income disparities between urban and rural residents in China (1978–2012)

Source: National Bureau of Statistics of China (2013). *China Statistical Abstract 2013*, Beijing: China Statistical Press.

Justice

In China, the protection of basic individual rights has often been given away in many cases to the protection of the so-called development right (*fazhan quan*) of the Chinese people. The most obvious cases are land takeovers that have occurred so pervasively, given the rapid urbanization and unlimited power of local governments. Land takeover has been perpetrated by local governments in the name of "public interest." In these cases, local governments pay in general compensation for only the land use for a certain period of time, not the land ownership collectively held by farm households. In this regard, most farm households who lost their land were given only low compensation. This has given rise to much resistance from the peasants and made the land takeover the premier source of rural social instability. Therefore, the new leadership under Xi Jinping realizes that the value of justice is of utmost importance if the CCP is to hold a society together and achieve Chinese dreams.

Scientific development

The Chinese Dream has re-emphasized the concept of "scientific development" already proclaimed by former President Hu Jintao. The promise of a clean environment and air is to be seriously kept by the government since environmental pollution has already become unbearable in major cities. The new leadership under Xi has advocated a green development and eco-civilization strategy as a part of their efforts to achieve a balanced and sustainable development in China. The Chinese government has the fiscal strength to support their endeavors and deal with pollution.

Traditional cultural values

There is also a place for traditional Chinese values in the "CD" concept. Confucianism is an inevitable part of this since it provided the prevailing ethical guide in ancient China. Some Confucian values, such as "harmony" (*he*, or *hexie*), were already introduced during the era of Hu Jintao, with his concept of developing a "harmonious society" (*hexie shehui*), and is also adopted in Xi's "CD" concept. China is far behind building up such a society. The socio-political instability problem became severe during Hu's period. For instance, it is estimated that the number of incidents of group resistance doubled from 2006 to 2009, and rose to ca 180,000 across China (Du, 2011). The amount of budgetary spending on stability maintenance has been larger than that of national defense spending for three years since 2011 (Ministry of Finance, 2011, 2012, 2013). According to the budget plan of the Ministry of Finance (2013), the amount of budgeted spending on stability maintenance is RMB 769 billion, larger than that of national defense spending which amounts to RMB 720.2 billion in 2013.

When considering Confucian ethic values, these are in fact not unique features of Confucianism, but exist everywhere in other civilized societies – values such as benevolence (*ren*), righteousness (*yi*), etiquette (*li*), wisdom (*zhi*) and honesty (*xin*), or behavioral norms for good conduct such as moderate (*wen*), beneficent (*liang*), respectful (*gong*), sparing (*jian*) and tolerant (*rang*). These values can be traced back to at least four often interrelated sources: (1) revelations from religions such as Christianity or Buddhism (Walvoord, 1966); (2) natural laws (Spooner, 1882); (3) human interactions, including games of interest and learning (North et al., 2009); and (4) pure logical inferences as considered by Kant (1785). For instance, the Kantian ethic concept of "categorical imperative" is a product of pure logical inferences. The First Formulation is "Act only according to that maxim by which you can at the same time will that it should become a universal law" (Kant, 1785, 2002), which is almost the same as what Confucius said in *The Analects* (Confucius, 540–400 BC): "Do not do to others what you do not want them to do to you," or what is meant by Adam Smith (1759) under the term "sympathy." These are basic ethics that are of the utmost importance to human life, which exist in every human society, and are not specific to Chinese. Therefore, these Chinese values are corresponding to those of other civilizations in the world.

However, some ingredients of Confucianism are not fully compatible with a market economy. For instance, Confucianism looked down on profit-seeking merchants in moral terms and regarded them as "ordinary people" or "little ones" (*xiaoren*) , while regarding non-profit-seeking persons as "gentlemen" (*junzi*) (Liew et al., 2004). Among the Confucianists, Mencius (ca 372–ca 289 BC) is the second most important figure after Confucius and the most famous pro-market figure in the Confucian school. Even he advocated only for the possession of property of moderate value and the realization of a richness of moderate scale, far away from allowing the emergence of business tycoons such as Bill Gates or Steven Jobs. Also, the mainstream thought of Confucianism demands that the pursuance of self-interest (*li*) is to be coordinated by "justice" (*yi*) (see "The Book of Changes" of the Zhou Dynasty). However, "justice" can be defined by a ruler or as a part of the tradition in very suppressive terms, affecting business development in a society.

Patriotism

Patriotism, or nationalism, is strongly advocated by the new Chinese leader Xi (2013). And two out of the three goals of his "CD" concept, the prosperity and rejuvenation of the Chinese nation, are related to the "Chinese nation." Such an emphasis is a response to nationalist sentiments existing in Chinese society and should help foster his leadership position and reputation, and maintain China's territorial integrity. Patriotism is somewhat supported by traditional Chinese culture. In ancient times, China found unity through the strength of its own culture, rather than through politics. For millennia, the power of Chinese culture served, sometimes more and sometimes less, to assimilate external threats (Liang, 1997; Liew et al., 2004). National pride was undermined by the Western powers beginning from the Opium War to the Japanese invasions, during which

Chinese people suffered from tremendous loss, humiliation, psychological trauma and disillusionment in traditional culture, which failed to resist the Japanese invasions and challenges from the West. It seems to Chinese people that Chinese culture was not strong enough to assimilate as previously when facing the powerful military technology and power of other nations (Liew et al., 2004; Hu, 2009). This development provoked in turn the development of nationalism in China (Liew et al., 2004; Wang, 2008). The May Fourth Movement, Sun Yet-sen's uprising and Mao's founding of the PRC were all efforts to build up a strong modern nation-state of China (Liew et al., 2004). And the only force that could represent such a modernization vision and endeavor would be a strong state with a strong leadership (Herrmann-Pillath, 2005). With the advancement of reform and opening-up, China has become economically stronger and stronger. Accordingly, a strong national pride came back to the government and people, so did an interest in traditional Chinese culture, including Confucianism.

Proclaimed institutions

Xi's "CD" concept relies on a system of so-called democratic centralism based on a set of existing principles which are re-proclaimed and will be enforced at the present time: the CCP's leadership, the "people's sovereignty," "rule of law," the maintaining of the people's "principal position" (*zhuti diwei*) and "people's democracy." Among them the CCP's leadership is the leading principle. However, recently, as a new step, the principle of "rule of law" is unprecedentedly emphasized by the current Party leadership, as is clearly shown in the Decision of the 4th Plenary Session of the 18th Central Committee of the CCP.

Some fundamental political institutions or systems are re-proclaimed by Xi. They include the people's congresses, "multi-party cooperation" and the political consultation system, regional ethnic autonomy and the grassroots mass self-government and other institutions, with all being run under the Party leadership. Obviously, the above-mentioned existing institutions re-proclaimed by Xi in his "CD" vision need to be reformed to realize this dream. To improve the current institutions, further new institutional reforms are anchored in the Decision of the 3rd Session of the 18th Central Committee. The CCP takes the perfecting and development of a "socialist system of Chinese characteristics" based on the above-mentioned core values as one major goal of comprehensively deepening the reform, and for the first time the modernization of the governance system and governing capacity of the country as further major goals. The development of governance and governability under the rule of law is part of the political reform advocated by Xi. Other political reforms include judicial exercise of power independently, and more checks and balances are to be introduced in executive, legislative and judicial branches of government, and within the Party. The Party and government are to preserve the legal authority of the Chinese Constitution. Each level of administration is to report to the same level of people's congress before the former launches any major decision. The system of re-education through labor (*laojiao*) is to be abolished. The Decision of the 4th Session of the 18th Central Committee further delivers a blueprint for establishing and implementing a system of rule of law in China. For instance, it provides unprecedentedly that China is to enforce "rule by constitution of the country" (*yi xian zhi guo*) and "judicial supervision" (*si fa jian du*, similar to the term "judicial review" in the US) of illegal administrative acts, and strengthen the judicial protection of human rights. Although the "CD" concept doesn't refer to the "socialist market economy" as its institution, this system is implicitly included and was included in the Report of the 18th Party Congress and also reconfirmed in the Decision.

One breakthrough is that the Decision provides that China is to make "the market play a decisive role in allocating resources." However, this is a mixed message. Just as already announced in the Report of the 18th Party Congress, the Decision re-emphasizes that "one must unswervingly consolidate and develop the public-owned economy, adhere to the mainstay of public ownership and the leading role of the state-owned economy, and strengthen the viability, and controlling and influencing power of the state-owned economy," while it provides that "one must unswervingly encourage, support and lead the development of the non-public economy," where the private sector is to play a subordinate role, led by the government.

Moreover, the Decision advocates for the equal treatment of various ownership systems and a mixed ownership economy in which enterprises of various ownership systems are allowed to hold shares in each other. Here the scope of the "market" also seems to encompass state-owned enterprises (SOEs) and mixed economies, and thus is mixed up with the state. Again here the instrumentalized orthodox ideology is still a hindrance to any further transformation to a market economy. The obvious "phenotype" of such an ideology is the "dinosaur" role of SOEs in the Chinese economy.

However, a mixed ownership economy with the SOEs in dominant position could lead to a low efficiency of the economy since the SOEs are generally inefficient in the allocation of the resources, and SOEs tend to monopolize the most important resources, which undermines the competitive market order and thus the competitiveness of the economy. According to a report (Sheng et al., 2012), the SOEs in industrial sectors remained profitable according to the book record between 2001 and 2009, but they actually ran losses during that period of time. The reason is that these SOEs paid very little or even nothing for land and raw materials, paid less in interest on loans, less in taxes, and received massive government subsidies. When all of these are put together, this total non-included input is greater than the profit on the book. In general, SOEs are facing up to many problems which lead to their loss; one problem is that of "insider control." Most SOEs are de facto owned by insiders: According to the statistics of the Ministry of Finance, only 6.45 percent of the profits of central government-owned enterprises were transferred to the central government in 2012 or 0.27 percent after deducting the central transfer to them.

Universal rules for development to be followed

It is clear that the new Chinese leaders plan at least nominally to go a peculiar "Chinese Way," that is, a "way of socialism of Chinese characteristics" (Xi, 2013). But China has already fallen away from traditional socialism, with the abolition of the planning economy that is one of its core ingredients, and transformation toward a market economy. Also the public ownership, another of its core ingredients, is quite shaky and vulnerable, as shown above.

Before we go further determining which values and institutions are necessary to keep the dynamic of Chinese economy and enter into the high-income club of the world, it is necessary to discuss some general rules for economic development that are universal and thus to be followed. This is because the above emphasis on the "peculiarity" of the Chinese way of development could easily invoke misunderstanding that there would be no universal rule which is applicable to the Chinese case. Denying the existing universal rules is obviously inadequate. To take an example, no one can deny the demand and supply law of economics if one is to deal with market exchanges. Such a law is a universal rule from which no country can escape. There are actually many general or universal rules in economic development.

The first general rule is that high economic performance is in general the outcome of efficient allocation of resources to where sufficiently high rates of return can be generated. This rule is widely accepted.

The second general rule is that two factors are important for an economy to realize a relatively high long-term economic growth: first, a certain degree of economic freedom in the market is ensured, and second, a stable environment for economic activities is safeguarded. This rule is explained further by differentiating three levels of economic development: low, middle and high in terms of per capita GDP or GNP. Which ranges of per capita income belong exactly to low, middle or high level of economic development is an empirical matter. The above definition of economic development in terms of per capita income of an economy is still one-sided. One has to consider economic development in terms of technical progress in a Schumpeterian sense as a more essential dimension of the definition. With regard to the levels of economic development, we can explain the second rule as follows.

First, at a low level of economic development, it is easy for either a system of constitutional democracy or a pro-development authoritarian system to ensure a certain level of economic freedom and provide a relatively stable environment for economic activity and can be both conducive to economic development to a certain extent, with the per capita income continuing to rise, but in a descending speed from a certain point of time. In such a stage, the GDP base is small while the per capita GDP is low. A high growth rate on such a base is easily achievable under both systems.

Second, at a middle level of economic development, one economy faces a bundle of bottlenecks hampering further economic development, including problems with the rise of production cost, squeezing of wage and profit margin, pollution, social security, labor protection, income discrepancy, formation of strong vested interests, etc., and it is easy to fall into the so-called middle-income trap (Agénor et al., 2012; The World Bank et al., 2012; Aiyar et al., 2013).

Although the term "middle-income trap" is a provocative metaphor, the phenomena are pervasive and non-neglectable. Between 1960 and 2009, only about one third of low-income countries of the world reached at least middle-income status, and many of the middle-income countries have been stuck in the "middle-income trap" (Lin, 2012). Out of 101 middle-income economies in 1960, only 13 became high income by 2008 (Flaaen et al., 2013). Of the countries that were independent and had middle-income status in 1960, almost three fourths remained middle income or had regressed to low income by 2009 (Flaaen et al., 2013). The countries that made it to high-income status are those in Western Europe, Japan, the Asian Dragons, and two island economies in Latin America – Barbados, and Trinidad and Tobago.

At this middle-income level of development, the difference in the nature of government matters if an economy is to escape from the "middle-income trap" to enter the high level of economic development. With the exception of some small economies or even "point economies" such as Singapore, and energy-rich countries such as Russia or Kuwait, for countries to switch to the stage of a high level of economic development, only a system of constitutional democracy or a system that is close to such has the best opportunity of keeping the momentum to finally attain such a goal (Sachs et al., 2000; North et al., 2009).

The Fraser Institute's report on economic freedom of the world (Gwartney et al., 2013) shows that countries with more economic freedom have substantially higher per capita incomes (Figure 2.3).

To enter the stage of a high level of economic development, a high degree of economic freedom and a stable environment for economic activities are

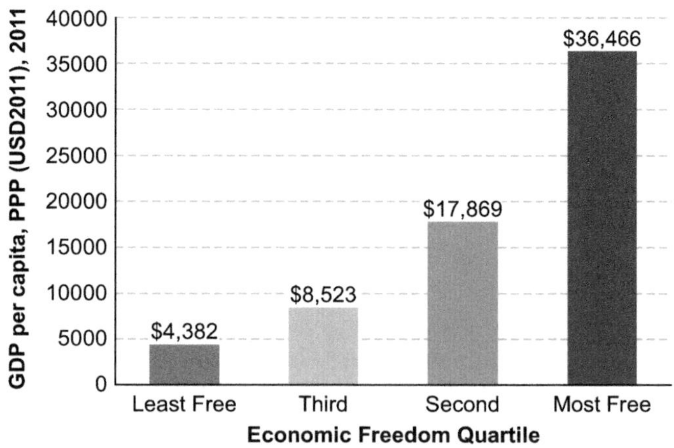

Figure 2.3 Per capita income and economic freedom quartile in the world
Source: Gwartney et al. (2013), Economic Freedom of the World: 2013 Annual Report.

required to further liberate the productive force of an economy. This can be ensured in large probability by a constitutional democracy. In contrast, there is a small probability among authoritarian governments that happen to choose a series of policies to ensure such a degree of freedom and stability. The advantage of a system of constitutional democracy over an authoritarian system can be traced back to such a fact: on many occasions, it is very likely that it might be the better way not to further liberate the productive forces and the market for an authoritarian leader to capture the best for her/his own interest. Without limiting the power of government, an authoritarian system has more alternatives for government officials' pursuing their own interest than a system of constitutional democracy that protects individual rights and limits government power. Also under an authoritarian system, even if one authoritarian government behaves benevolently in one field, it doesn't exclude the possibility of malevolent behavior in another field.

Even if one authoritarian government behaves benevolently, its successor might abandon such a behavior. It is also a small probability that an authoritarian government chooses to establish and maintain a fair competition order. In most cases, an authoritarian government prefers interventionism to attain a high growth in a small number of branches while neglecting and limiting the growth in other branches, so that the overall growth is easily relativized. A "benevolent despot" (Fukuyama et al., 2012), "benevolent autocrat," "enlightened despot" (Kow, 2005), or "enlightened authoritarian" (Wissenbach, 2008) should exercise political power for the benefit of the "whole population" rather than exclusively for the benefit of himself or herself or only a small portion of the population, and substitutes his own preferences for those of all individuals and it is impossible for him to be benevolent to each individual of the society, especially her/his rivals or opponents. At least a part of the "body politic" will be sacrificed.

According to the authors' own calculation, among 214 countries or regions, there are 68 which exceeded per capita GDP of USD 20,000 (current USD, PPP) in 2011, out of which there are only 20 countries or regions with a population of more than 10 million people, or only 8 countries or regions with an area of more than 500,000 square meters. Among these 20 population-rich countries or regions, there are 18 constitutional democracies such as the US, Japan and Taiwan, and 2 energy-rich countries including Saudi Arabia and Russia. These 8 wide-area countries or regions include again the same two energy-rich countries, with another 6 being constitutional democracies. Small economies or even "point economies" can be easily "managed" by any government-like enterprises, which implies that a part of them can be successful in attaining economic performance if their government "manages" well. Energy-rich economies easily can become members of rich clubs. However, they depend too much on returns from energy. Their economic structure is often featured by a monostructure and suffers from a so-called resource curse (Wright et al., 2004). In such cases, although their per capita income can reach a high level, there is little development in the Schumpeterian sense behind it.

Values and institutions necessary for rule compliance

To follow the above rules, it might be necessary for China to adjust and update its value systems and relevant institutions and adopt some further necessary values and institutions.

Necessary values

Among the "core socialist values," almost all are necessary values that have to be accepted in their very authentic term. Even the value "patriotism" is to some degree conducive if it doesn't go too far to back the economic protectionism in foreign trade and investment relations. Three points are of utmost important for China to really get started with the adoption of these proclaimed core values.

First, the traditional value of honesty, also one of the core values, is to be fully revived in the society, which can be seen as the key to the recognition of government's wrong-doings, the building up of people's trust in government and the initiation of an open process of trial and error in further policy making and reform (Spooner, 1882; Popper, 2004).

Second, values such as democracy and rule of law are regarded widely as universal values in modern market economies, and they were embraced and formally recognized by the Party at the 18th Party Congress as the core values of socialism in China, as mentioned above. China has to implement these values in their original sense to enhance individual autonomy, self-responsibility, economic efficiency, restriction on the exercise of power, and thus increase the probability of China's upgrade to the rich club of the world.

Third, although freedom is included as one core value, it has to be fully adopted as a basic value in its original sense. Accordingly, the protection of the basic rights of individuals is a must. This is because it is the foundation of realization of the "CD" that is to be every Chinese person's dream according to Xi (2013).

Necessary institutions

In order to keep a relatively high economic growth rate in a long period of time, the Chinese government needs to further enhance economic freedom and to provide a more stable economic environment. In this regard, future success depends on the implementation of the core part of economic reform that is completely different from reforms up to now. Over the past 30 years, the government has made use of neo-authoritarianism to maintain and increase economic freedom to a certain extent and by this to maintain a high economic growth. In the future, the hard core economic reform can only be done in parallel with political and legal system reform, partly because some part of hard-core economic reform itself, such as reform of SOEs, is already a part of political reform. In order to push forward relatively high economic growth, just as Sachs and colleagues have figured out, what China in the past has done is a technical imitation of the Western experiences, and the next step is to implement economic reform with political reform to change the functions of government and implement a set of institutional arrangements of "rule by constitution," "rule of law," "state governance" and "social governance." These institutional reforms and arrangements should include both economic and political areas, one for the market, i.e., a competitive market order, and the other for the government, i.e. "rule by constitution" and "rule of law."

A competitive market order

A competitive order or competitive market economy is a key to the achievement of sustainable economic development and prosperity. China started with its market transformation 35 years ago. Since 1992, the establishment of a market economy has been regarded as the goal of the Party. According to the Report of the 14th Party Congress of 1992, in such a system, market has to play a "basic role" in resource allocation in combination with "macro-controls" by government and under the "basic socialist system." The 2013 Decision provides that the market is to play a "decisive role." What China should do is to implement economic reforms to make the real market play a genuine decisive role.

The new CCP leaders, just like the old ones, put emphasis on maintaining the socio-political stability of China. Since they see the maintenance of one-party rule as the prerequisite of their reform, they regard any challenge to the one-party rule as the breaking of the socio-political stability. A satisfactory overall economic performance is regarded as a key source of the legitimacy of the one-party rule. So for the new leadership, the key is to keep the economy growing at a relatively high speed.

The current high growth of the economy can be partly traced back to the "overdraft" of the Chinese future: less social, labor and environmental protection, and less human rights protection. The inefficiency of SOEs is compensated for by this overall "efficiency" of the economy. To remove the inefficiency of the economy, SOEs are to leave the competitive and profitable sectors. A competitive market institution is to be introduced.

In this regard, a competition order can serve as such a required market institution. According to Eucken (1952), it is essential that the state should establish and maintain a competition order that consists of two sets of principles, the constitutional principles that establish this order, and the regulatory principles that help maintain it. The constitutional principles include a functioning price system (with a sufficiently large number of suppliers and demanders), primacy of monetary policy (maintenance of currency value), private properties, open market, freedom of contract, liability (each person is to be liable for her/his own behavior) and continuity and consistency of economic policy. The regulatory principles include mainly anti-monopoly policy and social policies. The American "economic miracle" and the German *Wirtschaftswunder* (economic miracle) can be traced back to such a competition order. China is no exception: the so-called Chinese miracle was partly traced back to sometimes intended, sometimes unintended approximations of such a competition order (Feng et al.,

2011). Only such a competition order would tend to maximize the efficiency of an economy. Up to now, China has approached such a competition order in a selective manner. To escape from the "middle-income trap," China should switch to establishing and maintaining such a competition order in a systemic manner to maximize the probability of attaining the highest efficiency.

Premier Li Keqiang's economic policies mark in general a positive turn and a correct direction in the history of Chinese reform, which are quite different from those of his predecessor, the former Premier Wen Jiabao. In 2008, Wen's government launched a stimulus package of RMB 4 trillion to spur economic growth by mainly expanding public spending. Although a high growth was secured in the following three years, private sector development and the adjustment of industrial structure have been neglected. Since the "re-nationalization" has been taking place and the external demand has remained sluggish at the same time, the survival environment of private enterprises has deteriorated (Feng et al., 2013). At the same time, local government debt amounted to a nearly unsustainable level, which is reflected by local governments' busy raising of new debts for the repayment of old debts.

With Li Keqiang's taking the position of the new premier, it has been almost impossible for him to continue the old approach of the reliance on expansion of government spending on public investment to boost the sluggish economic growth, which is regarded by the new leadership as "the new normal" (Gu et al., 2014). The only feasible way is now to rely on building up and boosting the dynamics of the private enterprises, while restrained spending on public infrastructure is still needed. Many private enterprises are suffering from the crisis of the manufacturing sector in the coastal area, which is regarded as one of the manufacturing centers of the world. Therefore, the "Likonomics" (named after Li Keqiang) is the proper and only feasible choice, which is characterized by no stimulus, deleveraging and structural reform according to *The Economist* (2013), and also generally by continuing Deng Xiaoping's policy of "reform, opening-up and revitalization." This marks a good step forward in the direction of establishing and maintaining an above-mentioned competition order and the attainment of a high efficiency of the economy. Of course, the real-world development is a little bit different from the theoretical abstraction in term of "Likonomics": because of the slow-down of the economic development, the Chinese government turned to so-called micro-stimulus (International Finance News, 2014). However, the features of the government's practice of the supply-side economics are still visible. If the SOEs can be reformed so that the state can leave the competitive and profitable sector, it would mark another major step toward such a competition order.

Rule by "Constitution" and "rule of law"

Rule by Constitution and rule of law are needed political conditions to realize a high degree of economic freedom, a competitive market order and a stable environment for economic activities, to maximize thus the probability of capturing the highest economic efficiency, and to escape from an eventual "middle-income trap."

Xi stressed "safeguarding the authority of the constitution," "defending the dignity of the constitution," and "ensuring implementation of the constitution" at the meeting celebrating the 30th anniversary of the current Chinese Constitution on December 4, 2012. He also figured out that "governing the country by rule of law is reflected by rule of constitution in the first place." Xi also advocated for the enforcement of the Constitution under the CCP leadership that is provided by the Constitution itself. The Decision of the 3rd Plenary Session of the 18th Central Committee of the Party of November 15, 2013, provides that the Party is to preserve the legal authority of the Constitution and realize the modernization of the governance in China, thus paving a way toward the establishment of more checks and balances. Rule by Constitution and rule of law mean that both ruling party and government must follow the Constitution in the exercise of power, and both are subject to the constitutional restrictions, and respect the Constitution as the supreme authority. All society members and organizations, including Party leaders and Party members, must respect the Constitution and follow the norms of rule of law, and everyone is equal before the law. The judicial branch must exercise its power independent from political intervention or any political influence from the Party and government officials. Individual rights and freedom based on the rule of law must be respected and protected. Political reforms along the new line proposed by Xi's new Party leadership should help China realize a "CD" for all, especially for every Chinese. Otherwise it would not be every Chinese person's dream. In this regard, Prof. Yu Keping argues that the high degree of democracy and rule of law is an integrated part of the "CD" and one should push forward an "ordered democracy."

Concluding discussion

The "Chinese Dream" concept is definitely a switch to a new vision of China's future that is more open-minded than before. It is not only a new symbol or rhetoric since the new Party leadership has to do something in setting the new direction toward a greater economic freedom and rule of law for state governance. However, the outcome of the interplay of newly proclaimed values and institutions depends partly upon the leadership's determination, perseverance and competence though the new leadership may face many daunting challenges.

However, there are uncertainties about keeping a high economic growth in China. Currently, China is facing up to a series of bottleneck problems, indicating that China might be stuck in a so-called middle-income trap, which doesn't mean that the Chinese economy will not grow. In fact, given the still quite low level of per capita income and immense degree of entrepreneurial enthusiasm of a huge number of entrepreneurs in China, the economy can maintain a relatively high growth rate. In general, however, a slow-down of economic growth is already a general trend. Also the degree of economic freedom has been reduced during last years if looking at re-nationalization, strengthened government monopolies and the increasingly unruly expansion of government power.

China needs to push forward the hard-core part of its economic reform. The new government has introduced lending rate liberalization and promised to allow the establishment of private banks shortly before the launch of the Decision. The Decision reconfirmed such a policy and direction by promising to launch many open market measures for private enterprises. However, it is still uncertain whether economic freedom can be increased significantly even after the Decision provides that the "market" is to play a "decisive role" in resource allocation if the government continues to maintain a tight grip on the economy and SOEs continue to monopolize key economic sectors without deepening reforms both in political and economic arenas.

Bibliography

The original source of this chapter is: Feng, Xingyuan. The "Chinese Dream" Deconstructed: Values and Institutions, in *Journal of Chinese Political Science*, Volume 20, No. 2, 2015:163–183.

Agénor, P.-R., Canuto, O. and Jelenic, M. *Avoiding Middle-Income Growth Traps.* The World Bank Economic Premise, 2012.

Aiyar, S., Duval, R., Puy, D., Wu, Y., and Zhang, L. *Growth Slowdowns and the Middle-Income Trap.* IMF Working Paper, International Monetary Fund, 2013.

Cabestan, J.-P. Is China Moving Towards 'Enlightened' But Plutocratic Authoritarianism? *China Perspectives*, 55, 2004, pp. 2–10.

Chandra, S. Hold on China, U.S. Still World's Top Economy by Main Benchmark. *Bloomberg News*, October 9, 2014.

Chen, R. Chinese Government's Debt Might Reach RMB 50 Trillion and It Can Collapse Because of Pension Payments. *China Securities Daily*, February 21, 2013.

Confucius (540–400 BC). *The Analects*, pp. 1–13. Available at: www.classics.mit.edu

Deng, X. *Opinions Expressed During the Listening to the Reports of Local Government Officials and Inspection in Tianjin from August 19 to 21*, 1986.

Du, J. The Chinese Origins of Group Resistances. *Consensus Net (gongshi wang)*, October 15, 2011.

Eucken, W. *Grundsätze der Wirtschaftspolitik.* (Tübingen: J.C.B. Mohr, Paul Siebeck), 1952.

Feng, X. and He, G. *The Survival Environment of Private Enterprises in China.* (Beijing: China Economic Publishing House), 2013.

Feng, X., Ljungwall, C. and Guo, S. Re-Interpreting the 'Chinese Miracle'. *International Journal on World Peace*, XXVIII(1), 2011, pp. 7–40.

Flaaen, A., Ghani, E. and Mishra, S. *How to Avoid Middle Income Traps?* Economic Policy and Debt Unit, Poverty Reduction and Economic Management Network, The World Bank, 2013, pp. 1–53.

Fukuyama, F. The Patterns of History. *Journal of Democracy*, 23(1), January, 2012, pp. 15–26.

Gao, H. *How Did the Red Sun Rise?* (Hong Kong: Chinese University Press), 2000.

The Government Admitted that 'Micro-stimulus' Exists and Is Reasonable. *International Finance News*, June 2, 2014.

Gu, Q., Zhang, Z. and Wang, X. Xi Jinping Interprets 'The New Normal' for the First Time. *Xinhua Net*, November 10, 2014.

Gwartney, J., Lawson, R. and Hall, J. *Economic Freedom of the World: 2013 Annual Report*. With Alice M. Crisp, Bodo Knoll, Hans Pitlik, & Martin Rode. (Vancouver: Fraser Institute), 2013.

Hayek, F.A. *The Road to Serfdom*. (London: Routledge & Sons), 1944.

He, Y. and Man, Y. *Local Debt Scale in China and an Analysis of Its Risk*. Working Paper of Peking University–Lincoln Institute Urban Development and Land Policy Research Center, No. W093, October 2011.

Heberer, T. and Schubert, G. Political Reform and Regime Legitimacy in Contemporary China. *Asien*, 99, April, 2006, pp. 9–28.

Herrmann-Pillath, C. *Culture, Economic Style and the Nature of the Chinese Economic System*. Proceeding Submitted to the China Roundtable of the International Economic Association, January 15, 2005, Hong Kong.

Herrmann-Pillath, C. *Kulturelle Hybridisierung und Wirtschaftstransformation in China*. Frankfurt School of Finance and Management Working Paper Series, No. 115, March 2009.

Hu, D. *Nationalism and the Change of Chinese Politics of Modern Times*. (Beijing: Property Right Press), 2009.

Hu, J. *Speech Delivered at the National Meeting on 'SARS' Prevention and Treatment*, July 28, 2003.

Kant, I. *Grundlegung zur Metaphysik der Sitten*. (Riga: bey Johann Friedrich Harknoch), 1785.

Kant, I. *Groundwork of the Metaphysics of Morals*. (New Haven and London: Yale University Press), 2002.

Kow, S. *The Idea of China in Modern Political Thought: Leibniz and Montesquieu, 2005*. Available at: http://www.cpsa-acsp.ca/papers-2005/kow.pdf

Lawrence, S.V. and Martin, M.F. *Understanding China's Political System, CRS Report for Congress*. Prepared for Members and Committees of Congress. Congressional Research Service, 2013.

Liang, S. *The Essentials of Chinese Culture*. (Shanghai: Xuelin Press), 1987.

Liew, L.H. and Smith, D. "The Nexus between Nationalism, Democracy and National Integration," in L.H. Liew and S. Wang, eds., *Nationalism, Democracy and National Integration in China*. (London and New York: RoutledgeCurzon), 2004, pp. 1–20.

Likonomics: What's not to like. *The Economist*, July 1, 2013.

Lin, J.Y. *New Structural Economics: A Framework for Rethinking Development and Policy*. (Washington, DC: The World Bank), 2012.

Mao, T. "Against Liberalism," in Committee for Publishing Selected Works of Mao Tzetung, ed., *Selected Works of Mao Tzetung*, Vol. 2. (Beijing: People's Press), 1969, pp. 359–361.

Ministry of Finance. *Report on the Situation of Implementation of the Central and Local Budget in 2010 and the Draft Plan of the Central and Local Budget in 2011*, March 17, 2011.

Ministry of Finance. *Report on the Situation of Implementation of the Central and Local Budget in 2011 and the Draft Plan of the Central and Local Budget in 2012*, March 16, 2012.

Ministry of Finance. *Report on the Situation of Implementation of the Central and Local Budget in 2012 and the Draft Plan of the Central and Local Budget in 2013*, March 5, 2013.

Mises, L.V. *Socialism*. (Indianapolis: Liberty Classics), 1981.

National Audit Office. *Audit Results on the Debt of Local Governments of 36 Local Jurisdictions*, Audit Report No. 24, 2013.

North, D., Wallis, J.J. and Weingast, B.R. *Violence and Social Orders: A Conceptual Framework for Interpreting Recorded Human History.* (Cambridge and New York: Cambridge University Press), 2009.

Orwell, G. *1984.* (San Diego: Harcourt Brace Jovanovich), 1984.

Popper, K.R. What Is Dialectic? *Vordenker*, Summer Edition, 2004.

Russell, B. *The Problem of China.* (New York: The Century Co), 1922.

Sachs, J., Woo, W.T. and Yang, X. Economic Reforms and Constitutional Transition. *Annals of Economics and Finance*, 1(2), 2001, pp. 435–449.

Schumpeter, J.A. *The Theory of Economic Development: An Inquiry into Profits, Capital, Credit, Interest and the Business Cycle.* (New Brunswick and London: Transaction Publishers Co), 1934.

Sheng, H. and Zhao, N. *China's State-Owned Enterprises: Nature Performance and Reform.* Series on Chinese Economics Research. (Singapore: World Scientific Publishing Company), Vol. 1, 2012, p. 408.

Smith, Adam. *Theory of Moral Sentiments.* (London: A. Millar Pub), 1790 (first published 1759)

Smith, A. *An Inquiry into the Nature and Causes of the Wealth of Nations*, 1776. K. Sutherland, ed. (New York: Oxford University Press), 2008, p. 603.

SOEs Realized a Total Sales Volume of More Than RMB 4.2 Billion in 2012, China Net (*zhongguo wang*), January 18, 2013. Available at: http://news.china.com.cn/txt/2013-01/18/content_27732467.htm

Spooner, L. *Natural Law, Or The Science of Justice: A Treatise on Natural Law, Natural Justice, Natural Rights, Natural Liberty, and Natural Society.* (Boston, MA: A. Williams), 1882.

Taylor, J.R. and Calvillo, C.E. Crossing the River by Feeling the Stones: Grassroots Democracy with Chinese Characteristics. *Journal of Chinese Political Science*, 15(2), 2010, pp. 135–151.

Walvoord, J.F. *The Revelation of Jesus Christ.* (Chicago: Moody Press), 1966.

Wang, Z. National Humiliation, History Education, and the Politics of Historical Memory: Patriotic Education Campaign in China. *International Studies Quarterly*, 50, 2008, pp. 783–806.

Wissenbach, U. *Capitalism and the Authoritarian State – the Case of China*, 2008. Available at: http://sorsafoundation.fi/files/2012/07/Uwe_Wissenbach_alus tus.pdf

The World Bank and Development Research Center of the State Council. *China 2030: Building a Modern, Harmonious, and Creative High-Income Society.* (Conference Edition. Washington, DC: The World Bank), 2012.

Wright, G. and Jesse C. The Myth of the Resource Curse. *Challenge*, 47(2), March–April, 2004, pp. 6–39.

Xi, J. *Speech at the Meeting on the Occasion of Celebrating the 30th Anniversary of the Implementation of the Chinese Constitution*, December 4, 2012.

Xi, J. *Speech at the Closing Ceremony of the First Plenary of the 12th National People's Congress*, March 27, 2013.

Xu, M. Statistical Bureau: The Gini Coefficient Was 0.474 Last Year, Falling Gradually From 2008 On. *Xinhua Finance and Economy*, January 18, 2013.

Yang, X. A Comparative Study on Constitutionalism and the System of People's Democracy. *Red Flag Manuscript*, May 22, 2013.

Zhang, B. How Much the SOEs Are Submitting Out of Their Profits. *Caijing Net*, November 15, 2013.

Part II

Economic transformation in China

3 Re-Interpreting the "Chinese Miracle"

China is widely regarded as one of the success stories of globalization, emerging into a giant economy of the 21st century. The success that has been identified is in terms of high and sustained rates of aggregate growth and per capita national income, the absence of major financial crisis and substantial reduction in income poverty. These results in turn are viewed as the consequences of a combination of prudent, yet extensive program of domestic deregulation and global economic integration, as well as a sound macroeconomic management. Hence, it certainly appears that China possesses a "winning recipe" in economic development, which eluded so many countries in the past. A number of analysts have named this the Chinese Miracle, i.e., an economy that has sustained long-term rapid growth for over 30 years, and social scientists have to provide theoretical explanations of the causes of that fact.[1]

A new analytical framework to explain the "Chinese Miracle"

There is an extensive body of literature that attempts to explain the causes of China's miraculous economic growth. We would like to summarize the plentiful explanations available in the literature, and briefly discuss their advantages and disadvantages. The first type of explanation is based on a notion of factor determinism. Lin's (1994) notion of comparative advantage strategy is within the scope of this type, concluding that the "Chinese Miracle" is based on China's comparative advantage, such as cheap labor. From our point of view, however, there are a number of limitations to this explanation. This explanation is only one-dimensional because China's rapid economic development is a function of many institutional factors, leading the way to a multi-dimensional view. As an illustration, China's reform began with the introduction of the rural household responsibility system, which basically has no relationship to comparative advantage, but is pertinent to the property rights and governance reform in rural areas. Anderson (2008) argues that China's high savings rate leads to the "Chinese Miracle." But this is the same as saying the high-level capital factor is the reason for the high growth. Without neglecting its importance, it is obvious that a purely high saving rate doesn't necessarily bring high and sustainable economic growth. If this is possible it depends on whether the savings could be turned into living capital, rather than dead capital (de Soto, 2007). The analysis by Krugman (1994) is of the same type, as it argues that China's growth relies mainly on inputs.[2]

The second type of explanation is based on a notion of government determinism. Many forms of reform strategies, including the theory of comparative advantage, tend to misrepresent the reform process and the causes of economic growth: they wrongly presume government determinism of reform or a government-imposed institutional change, and then they attribute the "Chinese Miracle" to government's performance, or some effective policies of the authoritarian government.[3] Wu (2005) focuses on the causes, background, process and influence on all structural reforms imposed by the government. His opinion on the role of other forces is unknown. Still, this is not enough as the interpretations are one-sided in that they do not involve non-government forces.

The third type of explanation is based on a notion of initial condition determinism. For example, Qian et al. (1993) argue that the structure of Chinese enterprises were of M-form hierarchy (multi-divisional organization structure) before reform, which were different from the U-form hierarchy (unitary system) of the Soviet Union. The specific multi-divisional organization structure of China has thus paved the way for its regional economic development after the reform and opening-up.

The fourth type is based on a notion of intra-Party political competition determinism. For example, Cai (2006) concludes that the "Chinese Miracle" cannot be attributed to political and fiscal decentralization and their subsequent influence, but, on the contrary, the political and fiscal centralization and ultimately, the competition between Beijing's pro- and anti-market fractions have stimulated growth-emphasizing policies. This explanation, however, is logically inconsistent: if a centralized regime is to implement a growth-enhancing market economic policy, it still needs political, administrative, fiscal and economic decentralization. And just like decentralization could not be considered a reason, as the author argues, the internal fractional conflict of top politicians could not either.

In short, there are, among the interpretations, not only the effects of initial conditions and social and market power, but also the roles of the government; not only the domestic causes but also international causes; not only causes on factors of production, producing process and market process, but also causes on institutional arrangements and environments, formal or informal. Thus, there exists a gap in the existing literature which calls for a more comprehensive analysis.

Overall, the different explanations in previous research have suggested a large number of explanatory variables for explaining the Chinese success. However, most of the scholars focus their research on one of these dimensions, such as initial conditions, institutional changes, state and market, etc., and each of these explanations fits the observed facts to some extent but not one of them provides an adequate explanation. It seems unlikely that any single-level variable affords an adequate understanding of the complexity of the causes of the Chinese success, because a joint effect of multiple causal forces shapes the complexity and determines the outcome. A more comprehensive scheme is thus needed to provide a multi-dimensional approach to the problem under investigation. A synthesis created by integrating the key elements of each of the explanations can develop a more comprehensive scheme against which the key causal variables can be located, and thus a more comprehensive explanation can be provided for understanding the Chinese success, because, in a more comprehensive scheme, more is examined and less is assumed.

A synthesis is not only optimal but also achievable. Those explanations do not necessarily compete with each other, given that each of them fits the observed phenomenon to a greater or lesser extent, and that many of the insights and conclusions from different theoretical approaches reflect different sides of an empirical world and are thus part of a unified whole picture of the "Chinese Miracle." Some of the causal factors are structural, some not, some institutional, some political–economic, and others might be mixed. Therefore, different approaches should be considered complementary in explaining the observed phenomena. A combination of the key elements of different approaches into a multi-dimensional analytical framework should be most optimal in explaining the causes of the Chinese success.

Apart from neoclassical economics and regional economics, we should also take into account other theoretical perspectives such as political economy and institutional evolution. The political economy involves new institutional economics, the Austrian School of Economics (Hayek, 1973, 1988, 1998; Papke, 2001), constitutional economics (Buchanan and Tullock, 1965; Brennan and Buchanan, 1980/1985) and the Freiburg School (Eucken, 2001).[4] The new institutional economics involves here mainly North's theory of institutional change, while the theory of institutional evolution mainly refers to Hayek's thought on institutional evolution. We will integrate and modify North's institutional change theory and Hayek's thought on institutional evolution. On this ground we develop our new multi-dimensional framework of institutional change. Also our framework integrates, as an inclusive and encompassing approach, all the existing major approaches to the interpretation of the "Chinese Miracle."

What is needed is to find out a way of integrating various variables into a general analytical framework in which the key elements of different approaches can fit together in a logical explanation.[5] This new multi-dimensional framework is based on the synthesis of North's theory of institutional change and Hayek's theory of institutional evolution, by which the key elements of different approaches can fit together and key variables can be selected in a logical explanation for China's miraculous growth. In the following pages of this chapter, we examine and synthesize some key elements of North's theory and Hayek's theory in such a way as to develop a new multi-dimensional framework.

Since the "Chinese Miracle" is related to its structural reform, in studying what led to the "Miracle," the political economy aspect is inevitably involved. North's theory of institutional change (North, 1990) is mostly involved within the spectrum of new institutional economics. According to North, institutional innovation or change would fuel the increase in productivity and economic growth in the absence of technological change (North, 1968; Chen, 1994). From this perspective, institutional change and technological change are both essential for economic growth. Institutions are the rules of the game of a society or more formally are the humanly devised constraints on the structure of human interaction.

North claims that institutions are composed of formal rules and informal constraints (or informal institutions), and the enforcement characteristic of both. The informal constraints consist of sanctions, taboos, customs, traditions and codes of conduct. Formal rules include constitutions, laws, property rights, etc. Also institutions could be divided into institutional environment and institutional arrangements. By institutional environment we mean a series of political, social and legal rules on which the basis of production, exchange and allocation is constructed; the institutional arrangements, formal or informal, are rules to adjust specific behaviors or relationships (North and Davis, 1994). The institutional change encompasses the creation and alternation of institutions and the way they are changed in time. In this process, the initial conditions become vital. Yet there are problems of path dependence or "lock-ins" standing in the way. According to North, an institutional change consists of five steps: first, to form a primary action group who promotes institutional change; second, to propose the blueprints for alternation of rules; third, to assess and choose from the proposals in conformity with some principles for institutional change; fourth, to form a secondary action group, say, the subordinate group that promotes institutional change; the last, the two groups try together to realize the institutional change (Davis et al., 1971; Chen, 1994).

However, the core of North's works is still the equilibrium theory of neoclassical economics. It only puts emphasis on institutional construction and does not include the effects of institutional evolution. The dichotomy of primary action group and secondary action group is applicable for illustrating stylized comparative static analysis, but not universally useful, especially when it comes to the evolution of formal and informal institutions.

We now turn to a framework of institutional evolution as a modification and supplement for North's framework of institutional change. Hayek's theory of institutional evolution advocates the notion of spontaneous order and embraces perspectives of systems theory and evolution theory.

According to Hayek, spontaneous order is endogenous, the product of human action but not human design (Hayek, 1973). Specifically, this order is a self-generating outcome of the internal organization rather than a product of a deliberate plan, design or construction by some external individuals. For example, the market order or most of the rules of customs come into being via evolution instead of deliberate arrangement or planning, thus they are spontaneous orders. The constructed order is the opposite of spontaneous order. The former describes an imposed and planned order (Hayek, 1973; Papke, 2001), and is always a kind of detailed and deliberately designed order to serve the purposes of the designer. In contrast, a spontaneous order doesn't serve any specific purpose, need not manifest itself to our senses but may be based on purely abstract relations which we can only mentally reconstruct (Hayek, 1973).

The evolutionary rationalism advocated by Hayek is closely linked with Popper's critical rationalism. In accordance with Popper, only through trials and errors, conjectures and refutations can we gradually approximate the truth (Popper, 1972; Hayek, 1988; Engel, 2001). Accordingly, Hayek agrees with Popper's piecemeal social engineering, which allows for trials and errors (Popper, 1945/1992), thus favoring the thought of piecemeal construction rather than total construction (Hayek, 1978b). Now, within Hayek's thoughts we dissect the dichotomy of constructivist rationalism and evolutionary rationalism, from which we abstract three kinds of institutional change: first, total construction-based institutional change (holistic constructivism); second, the spontaneous change of institutions; and third, piecemeal construction-based institutional change. Correspondingly, the dichotomy of spontaneous order and constructed order is substituted by a trichotomy of spontaneous order, total construction order and interim order as a result of the prominent interim order form, which would in fact be called a piecemeal construction order which encompasses many interim forms between the two poles of spontaneous order and total construction order (see Table 3.1).

Table 3.1 Our trichotomy vs. Hayekian dichotomy: types of institutional change, orders and rules

	Hayekian Ideal-Typical Dichotomy	*Authors' Trichotomy*	*Note*
Type of institutional change	Total construction	Total construction of institutions	
		Piecemeal institutional construction	Hayek accepts also "piecemeal social engineering" in Popper's sense
	Spontaneous order	Spontaneous change of institutions	
Types of orders	Constructed order	Total construction order	Hayek refers "constructed order" to "total construction"
		Interim order	
	Spontaneous order	Spontaneous order	
Types of rules	Thesis	Thesis	
	Nomos	Nomos	
		Mixed rules	

Source: The authors.

Under this framework, rules or institutions can be conceived as a mixed trichotomy including the external rules or institutions (Kasper et al., 1998) corresponding to "thesis," internal rules or institutions (ibid.) corresponding to "nomos" and mixed rules, rather than the Hayekian dichotomy of the "thesis" and "nomos." By "thesis" is meant the organizational rules that are deliberately designed according to the will of the organizers or rulers, and serve the special purpose of those special people – they are particular rules rather than general ones (Hayek, 1973). In contrast, by "nomos" we mean rules of just conduct or general conduct that come into being spontaneously during the long-term cultural evolutions in society: or "law" in the strict form by Hayek. The "law" is not a deliberate human design but the result of human action and it includes law of freedom (the common law), tradition, custom and convention.[6]

It is thus clear that our analytical framework enters the dynamic evolutionary theory of institutional change, within which North's concepts of initial state, path dependence, lock-in, action groups are also applicable. This framework follows a conduct–structure–performance approach rather than a structure–conduct–performance approach of neoclassical economics.

We can abstract two criteria from Hayek's theory of order to evaluate the rules and orders: first is the compatibility of the institutional change with the freedom of individuals; second is whether we could make sufficient use of Hayek's division of knowledge (Hayek, 1973). Hayek doesn't mention explicitly these two criteria. Both of them are hidden, but traceable throughout his works. From the viewpoint of economic growth, giving consideration to the two criteria is an indispensable condition for the liberation and release of productive forces and a guarantee for the direction of evolution of the rules and orders in the sense of their improvement. From the constitutional point of view (Buchanan et al., 1965; Brennan et al., 1980, 1985), that is the perspective of rulemaking, these two criteria are of importance. At last, they can be used to make evaluations of institutional change.

Spontaneous and piecemeal construction-based institutional change is an evolutionary and trial-and-error process. This is indeed the reform and opening process in post-Mao China in the past 30 years. China's former planned economy under Mao serves as a good example of the total construction-based institutional change. A planned economy cannot make use of the division of knowledge, and it replaces the different preferences of different individuals with the single preference of the planner in the allocation of resources. It does not provide individuals with freedoms and incentives in pursuit of profit and innovation, denies the aspirations of human nature, and thus results in low productivity and poor efficiency.

Re-interpreting the causes of the "Chinese Miracle"

Here we explain the "Chinese Miracle" by focusing on the underlying institutional change and evolution based on the new multi-dimensional framework, from which the most important components are derived and synthesized: (1) structural forces, (2) institutional factors, (3) political economy, (4) people's choice and (5) elite choice. Given the Chinese context, these key components are made up of a set of favorable initial conditions, a relatively proper reform path, favorable informal institutions, pressure for survival, gradual approach to reform and the existence of multi-action groups. Working in combination, these critical components merge into one main feature underlying China's rapid economic growth and, hence the so-called Chinese Miracle – the liberation of productive forces, i.e., productive forces is liberated from the state planners and designers (Figure 3.1).

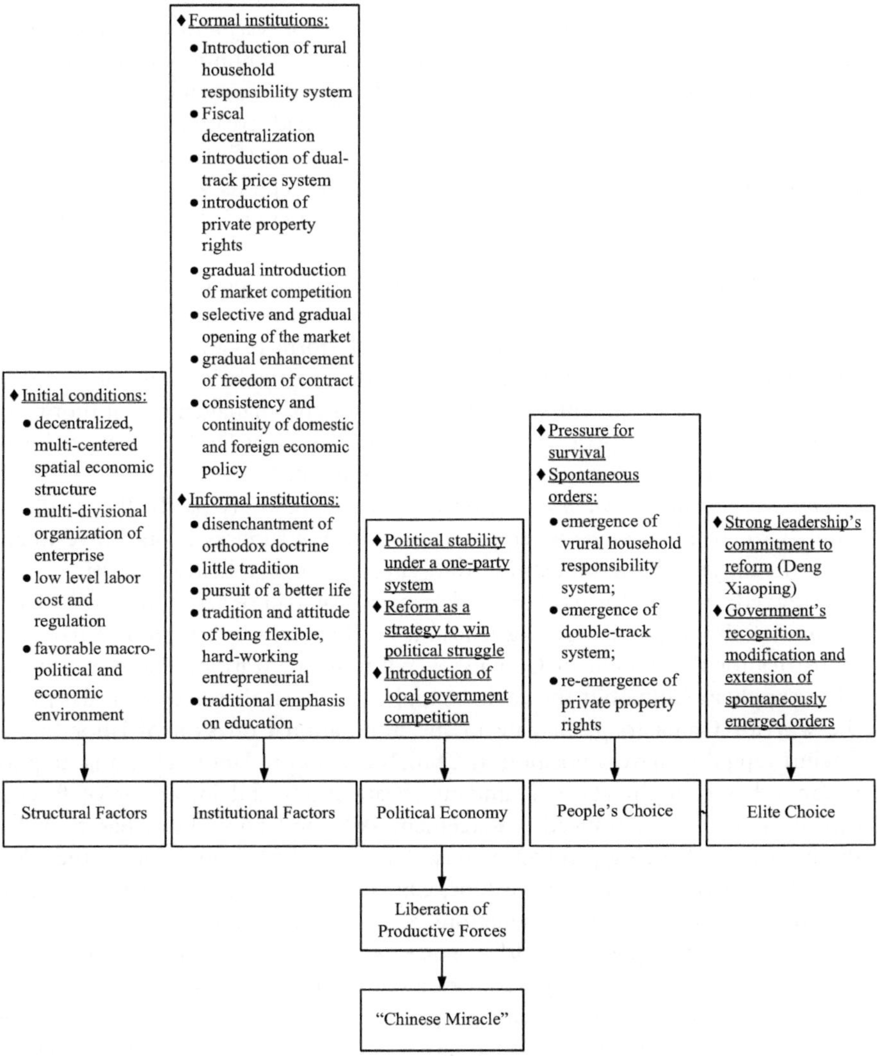

Figure 3.1 Multi-dimensional approach

Source: The authors.

Favorable initial conditions

A developing economy's policy space and its performance over time are constrained by the initial conditions bestowed upon it by nature and an economy's past (Ranis, 1995). In China, favorable initial conditions include decentralized, multi-centered spatial economic structure, M-form organizational structure, low level of labor cost and regulation, and a favorable macro political and economic environment.

Decentralized, multi-centered spatial economic structure: In the era of a planning economy, the central government delivered heavy-industry input to the underdeveloped third-tier regions out of the fear of war, and encouraged self-sufficiency for each province; that is, much of the planning and management authority for economy and investment was delegated to provincial governments (Chen, 2003). In practice, the central planner had created a decentralized, multi-centered spatial economic structure as an unintended consequence of planning, which in turn created conditions for the regions to make use of their own talents and resources to compete with each other and develop after reform and opening-up began in 1978.

Multi-divisional organization: As mentioned above, the enterprises in China prior to reform were of the M-form organizational structure. In contrast, the Soviet Union enterprises were mostly of the U-form (Qian et al., 1993). The structural form of Chinese enterprises provided particularly convenient means for the central government to delegate part of the management authority of the state-owned enterprises to local governments in order for them to boost their motivation for management and development.

Low level of labor cost and regulation: Cheap labor is partly the result of China's catch-up strategy, where consumption was suppressed and investment was encouraged; light industries were suppressed and heavy industries were encouraged; income for workers and farmers was dampened and much of the surplus of the industrial and agricultural production was transferred to heavy industries for the benefit of China's overall industrialization. There was ample labor supply in China but the capital supply was relatively scarce and that paved the way for China to participate in the international division of labor or the foreign capital to have a position in China's division of labor. That a large pool of labor has brought about abundant cheap goods and injections of foreign capital, along with advanced management skills and know-how, has provided the basis for enhancing product quality. There was little regulation of the labor market. That is to say, to some extent, China is one of the world's most flexible countries that put the least regulations on the labor market.

Favorable macro political and economic environment: Since the end of the Cultural Revolution, stability has been a consensus of the political elite as well as the general population despite disagreements on the path of reform or the kind of reform. A favorable macro political and economic environment has been created and maintained for over three decades in the name of stability and reform. The "Chinese Miracle" would be unthinkable without such a favorable environment, which is considered essential for foreign direct investment and business operation in China.

Relatively proper path of reform

China's path of reform is basically one characterized by gradual reform and opening-up. In particular, it includes the adoption of the least resistance path at the beginning of reform, the selective stabilization of currency value, gradual introduction of private property rights and competition, the adoption of open market, gradual approach to freedom of contract and the strengthening of personal and corporate liability, and ensuring the consistency and continuity of economic policy. Although this kind of step-by-step, selectively opening-up approach has been successful, it cannot be considered the key point of the "Chinese Miracle." Rather, it should be pointed out that it liberated the productive forces to some extent. According to general economic theory, it improves the efficiency of resource allocation and expands the production frontier, but still limits further enhancement for resource allocation and thus further expansion of the production frontier.

Adoption of the path with least resistance at the beginning of reform: Choosing the way of least resistance is in accordance with North's theory of institutional change that the expected gain should exceed the expected cost. The rural household responsibility system was initially non-governmental and opposite to national government policy. It was a spontaneous order in the beginning. Rules were mainly what Hayek means by "nomos," with deliberated design of some further rules among the peasants.[7] They were afterwards recognized, modified and extended by the government as formal rules.

Fiscal decentralization: Fiscal contracts were introduced in the early 1980s between the central government and local governments across China, which increased the incentive for local governments to participate in and enhance local economic development. The original design for fiscal decentralization was in line with the Pareto improvement concept in relation to revenues of central government and local governments. However, the strategic actions of the local governments eroded the central government's share of revenue in forms of the so called hiding the wealth among people and the extra-budgetary and extra-revenue system.

The dual-track price system: Local state-owned and collective enterprises, even township and village (collective) enterprises (TVEs) were allowed to be established. At the very beginning, the resources were in the control of state- owned enterprises. Later on, via the dual-track price system which lasted in general until the early 1990s, some resource would be allocated to the market entities as represented by TVEs outside the state-owned enterprises (SOEs) through exchange at higher prices. This was undoubtedly the consequence of the Pareto improvement concept. Also, in the very beginning, the dual-track price system emerged as a spontaneous order of transactions between the SOEs and TVEs, induced by the profit opportunities in market factors (raw materials and resources) and goods. The central government attempted to tackle the transactions and in the end recognized the transactions and thus the dual-track system (Zhang, 2002).

Selective stabilization of the currency value: The overall rate of inflation in China was relatively high before 1994. However, China chose to selectively stabilize its currency value by allowing foreign-invested enterprises, including Sino-foreign joint ventures and cooperative businesses, and wholly foreign-owned enterprises in China to possess foreign exchange certificates which were convertible to foreign currencies. At the beginning of 1994, the new People's Bank Law and new Budget Law eliminated channels for the Ministry of Finance to borrow money or take overdraft from the central bank in order to control price increases. Fiscal surveillance thus matters in controlling price increases. We can see the importance of it in preserving the stability of the currency value. Additionally, capital accounts have been opened restrictedly and selectively over time.[8]

Gradual re-emergence and introduction of private property rights: Private property rights are of great importance (Locke, 1690; de Soto, 2007). The re-emergence of private property rights in China has evolved slowly. In agricultural production, the household responsibility system did not give the farmers private land ownership, but land-use rights. At the early stage of reform, the state-owned enterprises were the main account. But with administrative and fiscal decentralization, collective-owned economy in rural and urban areas, especially township and village (collective) enterprises (TVEs), gained momentum and struggled to compete with the state-owned property rights. Compared with the state-owned economy, collective ownership had advantages over state ownership in that, for instance, personal liability was more visible. From the mid-1980s, the TVEs developed in large scale, and by end of the 1990s, TVEs accounted for half of the country's industrial output; yet local government officials or village cadres took charge of the TVEs and had similar soft budget constraints (Kornai, 1986) as the state-owned enterprises.

The individual industrial and commercial households and private enterprises in China started spontaneously. As a next step, entities with up to seven employees were accepted by government as individual industrial and commercial households. However, the development of such private economy is seen as an evolutionary process that would never stop at this limited scale if productive forces were unleashed. The entrepreneurs for the non-state-owned enterprises were suppressed at an early stage, and were then gradually recognized by the government. In the early 1980s, the rural cottage industries mushroomed, the rural and urban markets enlarged day by day and a large number of specialized households and key households with a certain production scale emerged. Not until 1998 did constitutional amendments give legal status to private enterprises and in the same year the State Council promulgated Provisional Regulations of the People's Republic of China on Private Enterprises. In 1992, the 3rd Plenary Session of its 14th Central Committee of the Chinese Communist Party put forward that economies under various ownership systems would be in a long-term coexistence with public ownership and they would develop together. From then on, China rapidly developed its private sector.

The actual economic development shows that there was an efficiency gap between enterprises with different ownership, with private ownership outperforming others (Liu, 2000, 2004), which then led to two waves of privatization. The first wave took place more or less in the period of 1992–1995, where the reform of state-owned enterprises was characterized by "transforming the operational mechanisms" while the collective enterprises were more of a transition type, involving full or partial privatization. The second wave happened after 1996, when the state-owned enterprises' reform was characterized by establishing a modern enterprises system as well as "managing well large enterprises and adopting a flexible policy towards small ones," and many collective enterprises experienced privatization.

Gradual introduction of market competition: The "Chinese Miracle" is also related to the introduction of market competition. First is international competition. Globalization has brought in international competition, foreign capital, foreign management experience and technology. Hong Kong and Taiwan, especially, have played an important role in this process. Second is the competition between different domestic enterprises, including that between different ownerships and different enterprises.

The unintended introduction of local government competition: At the early stage of reform – after administrative and fiscal decentralization – local governments gained so-called regional property rights (Granick, 1990; Herrmann-Pillath, 1999), which greatly stimulated the incentive to develop the local economy. Local governments began competing for resources and market. This local government competition was introduced as an unintended consequence of the decentralization, yet it has been beneficial to economic development. This kind of decentralization is what Qian and Weingast (1995) define as "market preserving federalism."

The competition among local governments and between local governments and central government sometimes intertwined (Herrmann-Pillath, 1999), providing a vivid picture of the nature of the central government and local governments as "competitive governments" in the Bretonnian sense (Breton, 1998; Herrmann-Pillath, 1999, 2006). For example, the local governments would add benefits for foreign investments beyond the tax benefits central government had agreed to in order to attract foreign investments. Or the local governments would increase subsidies for foreign investments in violation of the central government's uniform requirements.

Additionally, competition among local governments resulted in the privatization of local business (Zhang, 1998). However, the competition also had some negative, unintended results. There were many complaints that, in their efforts to outbid each other in getting foreign investment, local governments were giving too many concessions to foreign investors. There was too much redundancy in what the local governments constructed, and not enough attention to what was needed.

Selective and gradual opening of the market: Ever since the reform process began in 1978, China has opened its foreign capital and domestic capital market selectively and gradually and made use of the international market, including selectively opening some regions, first special administrative regions and then coastal regions. Selective opening of the market has promoted the competition between enterprises of different ownerships, and helped improve the efficiency of the economy as a whole. Additionally, export-orientation facilitated the use of China's comparative advantage in the international division of labor.

Gradual enhancement of freedom of contract: In the planned economy period, there was no freedom of contract; the unified deployment of resources by the government would not solve the problem of innovation and the inability to efficiently aggregate and utilize a large amount of dispersed knowledge within the economy. Economic reform and opening-up has made social forces and market actors organize production and exchange in a better way in order to achieve division of labor and knowledge (Hayek, 1973) via voluntary contracting, which would create more wealth. Only the introduction of private property rights would make a great number of complex contracts possible.

Strengthening individual and corporate liability: The privatization, marketization and emergence of the private sector is the process of enhancing private property rights. The latter means also a process of strengthening individual and corporate liability. The gradual introduction of property rights and freedom of contract has also laid a foundation for strengthening and enforcing individual and corporate liability, which can provide positive impetus to economic growth.

Consistency and continuity of domestic and foreign economic policy: Since the beginning of reform the government authorities have provided a relatively stable policy environment for foreign investment. For example, the commitment on tax concession to foreign investments: income tax was free for the first three years and half for the next five years. For domestic private enterprises, the economic policy and regulations are relatively stable and consistent. However, for small enterprises of special industry, for example, the "five small" enterprises (which are hazardous to the environment), or the enterprises conducting so-called repetitive construction (in fact "repetitive production"), the government has enacted a force-out policy.

The above reform approaches, no matter if they were of the nature of spontaneous order or piecemeal social engineering, rendered in general a higher degree of economic freedom and allowed market actors a larger free space of division of knowledge. In addition, there were also some attempts which reflected a total construction approach but which proved unsuccessful.[9] Also the success of the rural household responsibility system brought about supportive "momentum effects" upon further reforms, for instance, the dual-track system and fiscal decentralization, which brought about effects for the next steps of reforms.[10]

Furthermore, many reform approaches as mentioned above appear to be government-led, but in practice are due to factors both inside and outside of government control. At least until mid-2003, the government had mainly chosen to leave from the economic sector to a certain extent, especially the competitive sector; removed a large number of restrictions, provided a policy and regulations environment that was beneficial for the development of industries and commerce and created and sustained, in most part of the competitive sector, a relatively well-functioning but still "ailing" competition order which has been favorable to performance competition and economic growth. The competition order has provided a large space for bringing into play entrepreneurship in large scale.

Advantageous informal institutions and the pressure for survival

There are informal institutions that are advantageous as well as informal institutions that are disadvantageous to the development of the Chinese economy. The informal institutions and pressure for survival that had been working from before the Chinese Revolution are beneficial for economic growth in China.

Tradition: Tradition in the Chinese culture, as an informal institution within Chinese society, is beneficial for industrial and commercial development. Confucianism is not in favor of politicians and government officials doing business, but does not prevent ordinary people from doing so.[11] The two are reflected in the "great and little tradition," which is inherited from Chinese history. Mencius was even a proponent of an order of exchange, or "catallaxy" in the Hayekian sense (Hayek, 1973), to create the benefits of two sides through exchange. The official ethics and culture involved in the great tradition are mostly ethic requirements, while the ethics and culture within the little tradition are truly internalized, practical informal institutions and rules. Government officials formally stressed agricultural production and restraining commerce, but had to attach importance to and make use of commerce in reality in ancient China.[12]

The pursuit of a better life: Chinese people have always been in pursuit of a better life. This ideology is a kind of informal institution in itself and would help bring into play Chinese entrepreneurship. On the one hand, the Chinese people who believe in Buddhism, as well as many Christians, are in pursuit of the realization in heaven. On the other hand, the Chinese people are pragmatic, seeking mundane satisfaction and better secular life on earth. This attitude among Chinese people, expressed as a kind of commercial culture, was suppressed under the planning era, but has been acting as a motivation for wealth creation after the reform was initiated.

The tradition and attitude of being flexible, hard-working, and entrepreneurial: The pressure of survival in history and the pursuit of a better life have made the Chinese people relatively flexible, hard-working and entrepreneurial. The severe living environments in history and survival pressure have affected people's behavior and helped to shape their hard-working characteristic and pragmatic attitude, which proved beneficial for local economic growth after the reform. Herrmann-Pillath (2007) even argues that the high degree of flexibility and entrepreneurial alertness is the main explanation of the "Chinese Miracle."

Traditional emphasis on education: The Chinese people have a tradition of attaching great importance to children's education. This tradition has formed a relatively well-trained labor force and entrepreneurs in China, with much attention to learning by doing. Culture, tradition of education and the pursuit of a better life have created an informal institutional basis for the emergence of a large number of private entrepreneurs and their bringing into play the entrepreneurship in China after 1978. The pressure of survival and the extension of government's permission (initially tolerance, acquiescence, non-rejection, or even government officials' own involvement) have further promoted the exertion of entrepreneurship. It should be further noted that even the motivation for government officials to reform, and the large-scale investment from entrepreneurs in Hong Kong and Taiwan, has been influenced by the Chinese culture and pro-education tradition, as well as the pursuit of a better life.

However, there is also an ideological obstacle for economic growth – the factor of the official orthodox ideology, which is also a part of informal institutions. This factor attributes to the political lock-in and path dependence in the entire reform process in China. Nevertheless, the realization of the "Chinese Miracle" is the process of overcoming orthodox official ideology that hampers as "thick institutional issue" (Hassink, 2004) the economic growth, and the process of disenchantment of the orthodox official ideology. Here, the survival pressure and the pursuit of a better life that are conducive for economic growth are the key irreversible factors for reform. That is because, along with the reform, officials as well as the people have seen more overall benefits, and the reversal of reform means giving up these benefits.

The gradualist approach of reform

China is often cited as the leading example of a successful gradualist approach to transition from the planned command economy. Chinese reform has demonstrated a different pattern that was characterized by gradual, experimental, phased and partial reform as compared to the former communist countries in Russia and Eastern Europe that were illustrative of a "neoclassical" big bang or radical approach (Guo, 2006). It is a transition without design (Herrmann-Pillath, 2006), and the famous slogan is "crossing the river by feeling the stones." China has experienced a lengthy process of readjusting reform objectives from "a planned economy with some market adjustment," to "a combination of plan and market," and then to "a socialist market economy" (Fan, 1994).

This approach is a double-edged sword. Gradual reform is beneficial for the stability of politics, economy and social order, as well as the stability of regime. According to the Freiburg School (Eucken, 1952), there are many sub-orders within the economic order and social order, and these sub-orders are interdependent with each other in a functioning economic and social order. There is no doubt that this kind of interdependence is the basis for the operation of the whole order. Shock therapy breaks the interdependence between the sub-orders overnight, and since it is hard to run the new sub-orders and establish their interdependence in a short period, the new order as a whole cannot be established and operate in a stable way in a short time and the whole economy would be in severe imbalance. There is no such problem with gradualism, which is in line with the natural rules of development. Additionally, gradual approach allows for the development and evolution of the informal institutions such as culture and ideology. Shock therapy tries to change and adjust informal institutions overnight, which would inevitably experience frustration since informal institutions in general are hard to change or shape in a short period.

The flaw of gradualist reform is that it may be used by the vested interests to impede the process of reform and the stronger the vested interests, or the more of them, the more resistance. And the gradual reform itself could be used as an instrument for corruption since gradualism generally means marginal breakthroughs in changing some existing rules or policies. That kind of breakthrough often involves rent. Also, some interest groups could provide benefits to the government officials in exchange for getting more rent (see Tullock, 1967; Krueger, 1974).

Moreover, the choice of gradualist reform is related to resistance or lack of consensus among decision makers. Most top-down reforms had the pattern of "first experiment and then extend it," and they had no association with the government intention to try and improve, but to preserve the stability of the political regime and to seek their own department interests. Bottom-up reforms often adopt a "first do it and then to be recognized" approach. The reforms often occur spontaneously in an illegal state: they happen first locally and spontaneously, and after becoming a performance benchmark and having constituted a reversed pressure transmission mechanism, the legitimacy of them is eventually recognized, thus providing a basis for their further enforcement. The introduction of rural household responsibility system, dual-track system and private property rights are of that type. Many top-down reforms are also of the "first do and then recognize" approach. Often the experimental units are first permitted, at the boundary of legal and illegal, regular and non-regular actions, and then the achievements are recognized (or denied) and furthered by the government. Such reforms include the reform of state-owned enterprises and township collective enterprises.

Multi-action groups to promote reform and development

Since the reform of the whole economic system involves the reforms of several sub-systems or sub-orders, there is more than one source for pushing forward the reform. Views considering the reform process to be purely top-down or bottom-up are both biased. Both people's choice and elite choice played roles in the overall reform process. And, the action group of pushing forward reform and that of pushing forward economic growth should be differentiated.

In the case of rural household responsibility system reform, mainly the survival pressure resulted in farmers in Fengyang County, Anhui Province, taking risk and spontaneously organizing and implementing the "fixing of farm output quotas for each household." Along with the learning and imitation, the "fixing of farm output quotas for each household" was rapidly spread in Fengyang

County. This reflected a spontaneous order. As a kind of internal order, it was the result of actions of those actors within the system, rather than from the plan, design or construction of outside people. And the operation of it relied on the "nomos" in a Hayekian sense. After the reform and opening-up, the household responsibility system has been formalized and extended with the recognition of government and, hence, become an external piecemeal construction-based order. From the perspective of the pattern but also from the perspective of the two stages: formation of spontaneous order before the extension and the government recognition after the event is in line with North's differentiation on the primary action group (peasants spontaneously implementing contract) and the secondary action group (the government). But considering the development process of the spontaneous order before the extension, even if there were one or several initiators for "fixing of farm output quotas for each household," the shaping of the whole spontaneous order was the result of institutional learning, imitating and innovation, and it is hard to distinguish clearly between the primary action group and secondary action group. In fact, all these action groups had their own aims and each did things in their own ways. This was entirely different to the institutional change with specific aim described in the framework of North's institutional change.

The establishment of some other reform measures was similar to that of the rural household responsibility system, but they had different approaches. Without the recognition by the state, the action group has taken entrepreneur-like measures spontaneously, and from these measures a kind of spontaneous order has evolved, which was then, sometimes after tackling or tolerating, recognized, formalized and extended to one external piecemeal construction-based order (that was given a formal legal position and legal form by the government). This piecemeal construction-based order has taken in the elements of spontaneous evolution, and its formal order is inclined to wander between a piecemeal construction-based order and a spontaneous order. For example, after the reform and opening-up, the development of private enterprises in China was a spontaneous process. As long as the private economy was gradually recognized by the government, the private sector formalized and extended it into a type of piecemeal construction-based order. It should be noted that this piecemeal construction-based order has accommodated elements of spontaneous evolution. Along with the further expansion of the market and private sector, the whole private sector will show more of a spontaneous order.

No doubt, the government has played an important role as an action group as most reform measures were introduced by the government. Examples of such reforms are fiscal and administrative decentralization, selectively preserving a stable currency, gradual introduction of private property rights and competition, selectively opening the market, gradual introduction of freedom of contract, strengthening responsibility and preserving the consistency and continuity of foreign economic policies, and the government's *xiahai* ("go down to the sea") policy that actually encouraged individuals to quit their governmental jobs to start their own business or work in business sectors. These were all piecemeal constructivism orders. The whole process took the form of a "crab-walk path"– one step forward and half a step backward. When the government opened the market, introduced competition, exited from the competitive sector to some degree, it was the private actors within the economy that gained the broad space for free development and promoted economic growth finally leading to the "Chinese Miracle."

Concluding discussion

The rapid economic development and transformation of the Chinese society over the past three decades has been called a "Miracle." The existing explanations are not sufficient to explain China's rapid growth in a comprehensive manner. We re-interpret the causes of China's miraculous growth by developing a new multi-dimensional framework based on North's (1990) theory of institutional change and Hayek's (1973, 1978a, 1988) theory of institutional evolution. This new framework, in turn, is applied in an analytic narrative approach to the Chinese reform experience.[13] To preview the answer, our analysis points out that both Hayekian spontaneous order and Popper's "piecemeal social engineering" played a major role in attaining the "Chinese Miracle." These include favorable initial conditions, a relatively proper reform path, favorable informal institutions, pressure for survival, gradual approach to reform and the existence of multi-action groups.

It is important for China to continue to adopt and improve the set of institutions that have proved successful for maintaining rapid and sustained economic growth and overall development. There are, however, several problems in the Chinese reform process, including lack of labor protection and social securities, severe pollution, violation by arbitrarily taking of farmers' land rights, severe corruption, regional income disparities, potential risk of macroeconomic instability and financial crisis (as a result of overborrowing and misallocation of financial resources), etc. Chinese reform faces a greater difficulty in dealing with core institutional problems, such as preserving the land rights of farmers, breaking up the state monopoly by SOEs, (including the state-owned commercial banks), developing competitive market orders, and preventing the government from intervening in the micro-economic processes. In order to solve these problems, constitutional reforms which Sachs et al. (2000) and later Zhiwu Chen (Li, 2008) suggested should be necessary, since limiting government power and safeguarding individual rights would be involved in political reforms.

There has been a re-emergence of economic thought and the policy of populism, statism, nationalism, as well as dirigisme in the past several years. The economic freedoms of individuals and enterprises, as the basis of "Chinese Miracle," are being eroded. Entrepreneurs' property rights are being deprived more and more quickly (for example, through a large number of labor laws and regulations), economic principles and fiscal and monetary disciplines are being abolished gradually. For instance, the National Development and Reform Commission of the State Council decide, in collaboration with the Central Bank and the China Banking Regulatory Commission, credit policies which should originally be decided by the banks independently. Moreover, the government sets industrial policies as policy priorities, rather than competition policy. A large amount of transfer payments and subsidies have enhanced individual and local dependence on the central state and many people are losing their autonomy and independence. The above-mentioned formal rules or institutions being eroded is not the worst thing. The worst thing is that public awareness of the importance of rule-orientation is losing ground. And after losing these informal institutions, it may take several decades to reshape them, if at all possible.

If property rights protection is not provided, a favorable investment environment and a competitive market order that would enhance performance competition and achieve high efficiency would be lost, the cost for enterprises would inevitably increase, and the technical innovation and industrial upgrading would lag behind. Besides that, many other costs would also increase, such as the increase of disadvantageous supply factors domestic and abroad. If that happens, the "Chinese Miracle" would end much earlier than expected.

Notes

1 From an economic history perspective, a miracle should fulfill four basic conditions: first, the economy should have experienced high growth; second, the high growth should have been sustained over an extended period; third, the economic growth should be stable; fourth, technological development (including the improvement of technological efficiency) should somewhat or largely contribute to the economic growth. For analytic narratives, see Bates et al. (1998).

2 However, some developments, to some degree, support the idea that Chinese economic growth not only relies on inputs, but also on technology and development. In the early stage of reform, i.e., 1979–1992, the growth rate of Total Factor Productivity (TFP) experienced an average annual 1.7 percent rate of growth. This rise in TFP was followed by declining TFP for five consecutive years and did not recover until year 2000. In the entire reform period, the contribution of TFP change to economic growth was 12.7 percent. Purely in terms of the science and technology development in the period from 1991 to 2007, the number of authorized patent applications increased from 24,600 in 1991 to 351,800 pieces in 2007 (Zheng, 2008).

3 See Lin et al. (1994) on imposed institutional change or the corresponding induced institutional change.

4 The neoclassical approach is insufficient. In his book *Structure and Change in Economic History* (New York: W.W. Norton & Co., 1981), Douglass C. North hints at the theoretical incompleteness of property-rights theory, and calls for complementary theories of the state and of ideology. In recognizing this fact, Herrmann-Pillath (1991) proposes a Darwinian framework for the economic analysis of economic change.

5 See Gabriel A. Almond and Laura Roselle, "Model Fitting in Communism Studies," in Frederic J. Fleron, Jr. and Erik P. Hoffmann, eds., *Post-Communist Studies and Political Science: Methodology and Empirical Theory in Sovietology* (Boulder, CO: Westview Press, 1993), p. 62.

6 Deng (2000). According to Blackstone (1765–1769), common law is composed of convention and basic rules whose efficiency is constructed by the judges of the common law courts.

7 This does not affect the nature of the order as a spontaneous one. Vanberg (1994:197) notes that "deliberate intervention in the framework of rules and institutions cannot, per se, be censured to be in irreconcilable conflict with the fundamental principles of a spontaneous order." His notion is based on Hayek's following statement: "While the rules, on which a spontaneous order rests, may also be of spontaneous origin, this need not always be the case . . . and it is at least conceivable that the formation of a spontaneous order relies entirely on rules that were deliberately made. The spontaneous character of the resulting order must therefore be distinguished from the spontaneous origin of the rules on which it rests, and it is possible that an order which would still have to be described as spontaneous rests on rules which are entirely the result of deliberate design" (Hayek, 1973:45).

8 Again, we do not mean this selective policy is recommendable. But at least it was an improvement in terms of liberating and mobilizing productive forces since a stable monetary environment, even if it was selective, did provide a stable expectation for foreign investors.

9 For instance, Premier Zhu Rongji introduced a system of close grain fund circulation and abandoned the right of private grain traders in grain trade in 1998. This was a typical total construction approach. Under such a system, the Agricultural Development Bank of China (ADBC) was solely responsible for disbursing loans to state-owned grain companies which held the exclusive power in purchasing from the hand of farm households and reselling it in the grain market. However, such government action led to unintended consequences: the state-owned grain companies were unable to capture a positive margin by buying low and selling high, and they abused the grain fund for other purposes including investing in housing and hotels. In the end, they were not able to repay loans to the ADBC. In 2004, the ADBC suffered from non-performing loans worth more than RMB 500 billion (Fan, 2004).

10 For momentum effects of the rural household responsibility system upon the dual-track system and those of the latter upon further reforms, see Roland (2000).

11 This point is the result from a discussion with Prof. Carsten Herrmann-Pillath, Sino-German School of Frankfurt School of Finance and Management in March 2008 in Beijing and reflects mainly his opinion.

12 The last chapter of *Shiji (Records of Grand Historian)* is *huozhi* "Biography." By *huozhi* it is meant to pursue wealth and welfare through the production and exchange process.

13 For analytic narratives, see Bates et al. (1998).

Bibliography

The original source of this chapter is: Feng, Xingyuan, Christer Ljungwall, and Sujian Guo. Re-interpreting the "Chinese Miracle", in *International Journal on World Peace* (A SSCI journal), Vol. XXVIII No. 1, March 2011, pp. 7–40.

Almond, G.A. and Roselle, L. "Model Fitting in Communism Studies," in Frederic J. Fleron, Jr. and E.P. Hoffmann, eds., *Post-Communist Studies and Political Science: Methodology and Empirical Theory in Soviet-ology.* (Boulder, CO: Westview Press), 1993, pp. 27–75.

Anderson, J. High Saving Rates Lead to High Growth Rate, the Increase on TFP. *Capital Weekly*, June 9, 2008.

Bates, R.H., Greif, A., Levi, M. and Jean-Laurent, R. *Analytic Narratives.* (Princeton, NJ, and Chichester: Princeton University Press), 1998.

Blackstone, W. *1765–1769: Commentaries on the Laws of England*. Available at: www.avalon.law.yale.edu/subkect_manus/blackstone.sap

Brennan, G. and Buchanan, J.M. *The Power to Tax: Analytical Foundations of a Fiscal Constitution*. (New York: Cambridge University Press), 1980.

Brennan, G. and Buchanan, J.M. *The Reason of Rules: Constitutional Political Economy*. (Cambridge and New York: Cambridge University Press), 1985.

Breton, A. *Competitive Governments: An Economic Theory of Politics and Public Finance*. (New York: Cambridge University Press), 1998.

Buchanan, J.M. and Tullock, G. *The Calculus of Consent, Logical Foundations of Constitutional Democracy*. (Ann Arbor: University of Michigan Press), 1965.

Cai, H. and Treisman, D. Did Government Decentralization Cause China's Economic Miracle? *World Politics*, 58(4), 2006, pp. 505–535.

Chen, D. *The Construction of the Third-tier Region: The Development of the Western Region During the Period of War Preparation, Publishing House of the Party School of the CPC Central Committee*, 2003.

Chen, Y. *Preface for Chinese Version*, in North, D.C. and Davis, L.E. "The Theory on Institutional Change: The Concept and Cause," in Ronald H. Coase, Armen A. Alchian and Douglass C. North, eds., *Property Rights and Institutional Change*. (Shanghai: Shanghai Sanlian Joint Publishing House and Shanghai People's Publishing House), 1994, pp. 266–294.

China Academy of Social Science. Collections of Economics Department, China Academy of Social Sciences. Report on China's Economic Research (2007–2008). (Beijing, Economy and Management Publishing House), 2008.

Davis, L.E. and North, D.C. *Institutional Change and American Economic Growth*. (Cambridge: Cambridge University Press), 1971.

Deng, X. "*The Socialism Should Develop First Productive Force*, Talk with Kenneth David Kaunda, President of Guinea, May 5, 1980," in *Selected Works of Deng Xiaoping*. (Beijing: People's Publishing House), vol. II, 1989, pp. 311–314.

Deng, Z. *A Precondition Commentary on Research on Hayek's Law Theory*. Preface for Chinese Version, in F.A. Hayek. *Law, Legislation and Liberty, Volume I*. (Beijing: China Encyclopedia Press), 2000, pp. 1–69.

Engel, G. "The Pretence of Knowledge – Hayek and Popper's Critical Rationalism," in Gerhard Papke, ed., *Knowledge, Liberty and Order*. (Beijing: China Social Science Publishing House), 2001, pp. 76–108.

Eucken, W. *Grundsätze der Wirtschaftspolitik*, 6th ed. (Tübingen: J.C.B. Mohr, Paul Siebeck), 1952.

Eucken, W. *The Principles of Economic Policy*. (Shanghai: Shanghai People's Publishing House), 2001.

Fan, G. Incremental Changes and Dual-Track Transition: Under-Standing the Case of China. *Economic Policy*, 19, December, 1994, pp. 100–122.

Fan, L. *State Council Released a 'Routine' for the Grain Policy Reform and 500 Billion Yuan Non-performing Loans Are Not Able to Be Recovered*. Dynasty Economy Report, August 20, 2004.

Granick, D. *Chinese State Enterprises: A Regional Property-Rights Analysis*. (Chicago: University of Chicago Press), 1990.

Guo, S. *The Political Economy of Asian Transition from Communism*. (Aldershot, UK: Ashgate), 2006.

Hassink, R. *The Learning Region: A Policy Concept to Unlock Regional Economies from Path Dependency?* Paper Prepared for the Conference Regionalization of Innovation Policy: Options and Experiences, June 4th–5th, Berlin, 2004.

Hayek, F.A. The Use of Knowledge in Society. *American Economic Review*, 35(4), 1945, pp. 519–530.

Hayek, F.A. *Law, Legislation, and Liberty.* (Chicago: University of Chicago Press), 1973.

Hayek, F.A. *New Studies in Philosophy, Politics, Economics and the History of Ideas.* (London: Routledge & Kegan Paul), 1978a.

Hayek, F.A. *The Constitution of Liberty.* (Chicago: University of Chicago Press), 1978b.

Hayek, F.A. *The Fatal Conceit: The Errors of Socialism.* (London: Routledge), 1988.

Hempel, Carl G. *Aspects of Scientific Explanation and Other Essays in the Philosophy of Science.* (New York: The Free Press), 1965.

Herrmann-Pillath, C. A Darwinian Framework for the Economic Analysis of Institutional Change in History. *Journal of Social and Biological Structures*, 14(2), 1991, pp. 127–148.

Herrmann-Pillath, C. Die fiskalische und regionale Dimension des systemischen Wandels großer Länder: Regierungswettbewerb in China und Rußland. *Wittener Diskussionspapiere*, (42), University of Witten/Herdecke, September, 1999.

Herrmann-Pillath, C. An Evolutionary Approach to Endogenous Political Constraints on Transition in China. *Social Science Research Network*, November 29, 2006.

Herrmann-Pillath, C. "Foreword," in Biliang Hu, ed., *Informal Institutions and Rural Development.* (London: Routledge), p. xix.

International Disability and Development Consortium (IDDC). 2004. *Inclusive Development and the UN Convention.* IDDC Reflection Paper, May 2007.

Jha, P.S. *Managed Chaos: The Fragility of the Chinese Miracle.* (New Delhi: Sage Publications), 2009.

Jin, H., Qian, Y. and Weingast, B. Regional Decentralization and Fiscal Incentives: Federalism, Chinese Style. *Journal of Public Economics*, 89(9–10), September, 2005, pp. 1719–1742.

Kasper, W. and Streit, M.E. *Institutional Economics: Social Order and Public Policy.* (Cheltenham, UK and Northampton, MA: Edward Elgar), 1998.

Kornai, J. The Soft Budget Constraint. *Kyklos*, 39(1), 1986, pp. 3–30.

Krueger, A. The Political Economy of the Rent-Seeking Society. *American Economic Review*, 64, 1974, pp. 291–303.

Krugman, P. The Myth of Asia's Miracle. *Foreign Affairs*, 73(6), November/December, 1994, pp. 62–76.

Lakatos, I. *The Methodology of Scientific Research Programmes: Philosophical Papers I.* (Cambridge: Cambridge University Press), 1978.

Li, D. A Theory of Ambiguous Property Rights: The Case of the Chinese Non-State Sector. *Journal of Comparative Economics*, 23(1), 1996, pp. 1–19.

Li, L. A Reconsideration on Reform Path – An Interview with Professor Zhiwu Chen. *Economic Observer Newspaper*, February 16, 2008.

Li, S., Hou, Y., Liu, Y., and He, J. The Analysis on China's Economic Growth Potential and Prospect. *Management World*, (9), 2005, pp. 13–25.

Lin, J. "The Economic Theory on Institutional Change: Induced or Imposed Institutional Change," in *Property Rights and Institutional Change – Property Rights Approach and New Institutional Economics.* Translation Collection. (Shanghai: Shanghai People's Publish House), 2004, pp. 261–264.

Lin, J., Cai, F. and Li, Z. *The China Miracle: Development Strategy and Economic Reform.* (Shanghai: Shanghai People's Publishing House), 1994.

Liu, X. The Effect of Ownership Structure of Industrial Enterprises of China on Differences in Efficiency: An Empirical Analysis of National Industrial Census Data (1995). *Economic Research Journal*, 2, 2000, pp. 17–25.

Liu, X. The Effect of Privatization on China's Industrial Efficiency – An Analysis on National Industrial Census Data (2001). *Economic Research*, 39(8), 2004, pp. 16–26.

Locke, J. *Two Treatises of Government.* (Cambridge: Cambridge University Press), 1990.

North, D.C. Sources of Productivity Change in Ocean Shipping, 1600–1850. *Journal of Political Economy*, 76, 1968, pp. 953–970.

North, D.C. *Institutions, Institutional Change, and Economic Performance.* (Cambridge: Cambridge University Press), 1990.

North, D.C. and Davis, L.E. "The Theory on Institutional Change: The Concept and Cause," in Ronald H. Coase, Armen A. Alchian and Douglass C. North, eds., *Property Rights and Institutional Change.* (Shanghai: Shanghai Sanlian Joint Publishing House and Shanghai People's Publishing House), 1994, pp. 266–294.

Papke, Gerhard, ed. *Knowledge, Liberty and Order.* (Beijing: China Social Science Publishing House), 2001.

Popper, K.R. *Objective Knowledge as an Evolutionary Approach.* (London: Oxford University Press), 1972.

Popper, K.R. *Die Offene Gesellschaft und ihre Feinde.* Band 1: Der Zauber Platons. (Tuebingen: Mohr Siebeck), 1945/1992.

Przeworski, A. and Teune, H. *The Logic of Comparative Social Inquiry.* (New York: John Wiley and Sons), 1979, pp. 20–23.

Qian, Y. and Weingast, B.R. *China's Transition to Markets: Market Preserving Federalism, Chinese Style.* (Stanford: Hoover Press), December 1, 1995.

Qian, Y. and Xu, C. Why China's Economic Reforms Differ: The M-Form Hierarchy and Entry/Expansion of the Non-State Sector. *Economics of Transition*, 1(2), June, 1993, pp. 135–170.

Qin, H. The Formation and Future of Chinese Miracle – My Perspective on the 30 Years since Reform. *Southern China Weekly*, February 22, 2008.

Ranis, G. Another Look at the East Asian Miracle. *The World Bank Economic Review*, 9(3), 1995, pp. 509–534.

Redfield, R. *Peasant Society and Culture: An Anthropological Approach to Civilization.* (Chicago: University of Chicago Press and Cambridge University Press), 1956.

Roland, G. *Transition and Economics.* (Cambridge, MA: MIT Press), 2000.

Sachs, J., Woo, W.T. and Yang, X. Economic Reforms and Constitutional Transition. *Annals of Economics and Finance*, 1(2), 2001, pp. 435–449.

Shan, H. and Shen, K. *Institutions and Growth: Literature Summary and the Experience of China*, November 13, 2007. Available at: www.unirule.cn

Soto, H. de. *The Mystery of Capital.* Translated by Haisheng Yu. (Beijing: Huaxia Press), 2007.

Tullock, G. The Welfare Costs of Tariffs, Monopolies, and Theft. *Western Economic Journal*, 5, 1967, pp. 224–232.

UNIDO. *Productivity in Developing Countries: Country Case Studies.* (China: UNIDO), November 2005.

Vanberg, V.J. *Rules and Choice in Economics.* (London: Routledge), 1994.

Weingast, B.R. The Economic Role of Political Institutions: Market-Preserving Federalism and Economic Growth. *Journal of Law, Economics, and Organization*, 11, 1995, pp. 1–31.

World Bank. *The East Asian Miracle: Economic Growth and Public Policy.* (New York: Oxford University Press), 1993.

Wu, J. *Contemporary Economic Reform in China: Strategy and Implementation.* (Shanghai: Shanghai Fareast Press), 1999.

Wu, J. Understanding and Interpreting Chinese Economic Reform. *Texere*, December 14, 2005.

Zhang, W. "How the Dust Fell onto the Ground?" in Zhaohan Sheng and Depeng Jiang, eds., *Evolutionary Economics.* (Shanghai: Shanghai Sanlian Joint Publishing House), 2002, p. 15.

Zhang, W. and Li, S. Regional Competition and the Privatization of China's State-owned Enterprises. *Economic Research*, 33(12), 1998, pp. 64–71.

Zheng, Y. *Understanding TFP—Several Limitations of Using TFP on Analyzing the Quality of Economic Growth.* China Academy of Social Sciences, June 12, 2008.

Zhou, K.X. *How the Farmers Changed China: Power of the People.* (Boulder, CO: Westview Press), 1996.

Zou, D., ed. *30 Years since China's Reform and Opening-up (1978–2008): The Report on China's Economic Growth and System Reform, No. 1.* (Beijing: Social Sciences Academy Press), 2008.

4 Private sector development as the key to Chinese economic development

In 2010, China became the world's second-largest economy in terms of Gross Domestic Product (GDP) and joined the list of middle-income economies with a per capita GDP of USD 5,432 and 6,100 in 2011 and 2012. However, a number of political, economic and social problems have created a bottleneck in maintaining sustainable economic growth. As has been seen in many other middle-income economies, this can result in a "middle-income trap." To escape this "trap," China must work to improve the efficiency of production factors to maintain high economic growth over an extended period of time. The key is private sector development. This is a necessary step for any country that ultimately wishes to move into the high-income bracket.[1]

The importance of economic freedom

As North (1990) points out, a society's institutional framework seems to play an instrumental role in the long-run performance of its economy. Since then researchers have added economic freedom and other institutional variables to the set of determinants of economic growth. Here, a significant body of research indicates that economic freedom enhances economic growth in the long run.[2] Economic freedom means the degree to which a market economy is in place, where the central components are voluntary exchange, free competition and protection of individuals and property (Gwartney and Lawson, 2002). However, as China continues to develop economically, political and economic freedom of the people does not seem to follow in step. Being the second-largest economy in the world in terms of gross domestic product (GDP) does not mean that the country is the second, fourth or 10th freest economy in the world. Fraser Institute's Economic Freedom of the World (EFW) annual reports show that China's global ranking does not look inspiring. The EFW looks at five important factors such as size of government, extent of regulations and restrictions and openness to global trade.[3] The country ranks 111 out of 157 countries worldwide covered in the EFW 2015 Report (Table 4.1).

The current level of economic freedom may well approximate China's per capita income level but pinpoints the need to expand economic freedom as the economy grows. In this respect it is of particular interest to note that the largest

Table 4.1 Score and global ranking of China in economic freedom

Year of Data	*Overall Score*	*Global Rank*	*Decile*
1995	5.07	96/123	9th
2000	5.75	100/123	9th
2005	6.06	105/153	7th
2010	6.26	120/153	8th
2012	6.39	113/153	8th
2013	6.44	111/157	8th

Source: Economic Freedom of the World 2015 Annual Report.

change – for the worse – happened during the period that included the 2008 global financial crisis. It may be difficult to hasten economic freedom in a one-party state, but the trend is definitely there. Sometimes economic freedom declines, just to inch forward after. At the same time it should be kept in mind that China is neither a market economy, nor a socialist economy, but one featured by strong government interventions and dirigisme in the economy. This has implications for the expansion of economic freedom. In China, currently, the way forward is for the rule of law and market principles to be implemented and respected. That way, the currently limited economic freedom of individuals and private enterprises can be protected and hopefully, be expanded in the future.

The pattern of Chinese development is praised by some China observers as the "Chinese Model." It can be best described as a model of government's preserving a certain degree of economic freedom while maintaining strong political control. This is nothing other than a kind of model of "developmental state" or "East Asian Model." However, the dynamics of Chinese economic growth can be explained by that of the private sector development in China. According to a report released by the Unirule Institute of Economics (Sheng et al., 2012), the SOEs in industrial sectors remained profitable according to the book record between 2001 and 2009, but they actually ran losses during that period of time. The reason is that these SOEs paid very little or even nothing for land and raw materials, paid less in interest on loans, less in taxes and received massive government subsidies. When all of these are put together, the total is greater than the profit on the book. This is clear-cut evidence showing that not the development of SOEs, but that of private enterprises is the key to long-term economic success in China. Of course, government has also a role in economic development in providing a generally favorable economic environment, in which property rights of a changing majority within the society are generally protected, but violated in a selective manner and at cost of a changing minority.

Size and strength of private enterprises in the Chinese economy

Looking back at the short history of China's reform and opening policy since 1978, one can find that the resurgence and development of the private sector has been the key to China's economic success (Feng et al., 2013). With little doubt, private enterprises of all sizes are an important and integral part of the Chinese economy. Whether in terms of sheer numbers or its contribution to GDP, employment or technological innovation (measured by number of registered patents), they far outpace state-owned enterprises. According to statistics, at the end of 2013, China had 12.54 million private companies (*siyingqiye*私营企业) and 44.36 million individually owned businesses (*geti hu*个体户, or *geti gongshang hu*个体工商户). The annual growth rates of their numbers are 23.9 percent and 5.19 percent, respectively (see Tables 4.2 and 4.3).

Based on Tables 4.2 and 4.3, one can calculate the average size of private companies and individually owned businesses. In 2013, an average private company employs 10 employees and holds a registered capital of RMB 3.13 million, while an average individually owned business employs 2.1 employees and holds a registered capital of RMB 54,000.

Table 4.2 Growth of private enterprises, 1992–2013

Year	*Companies*		*Employees*		*Registered Capital*	
	Quantity	*Growth (%)*	*Quantity (10,000)*	*Growth (%)*	*RMB (100 million)*	*Growth (%)*
1992	139,633		232		221	
1995	654,531	51.43	956	47.53	2,622	81.08
2000	1,761,769	16.76	2,407	19.04	13,308	29.37
2005	4,719,500	17.3	5,824	16.08	61,331	27.94
2010	8,455,000	25.61	9,417.6	22.85	192,100	
2011	9,676,800	24.99	10,400	22.13	257,900	34.3
2012	10,857,200	12.2	11,000	5.8	311,000	20.6
2013	12,539,000	15.5	12,500	13.6	393,000	26.4
Annual growth (%)*		23.9		20.9		42.8

Source: The All-China Federation of Industry and Commerce, National Bureau of Industry and Commerce, *China Statistical Yearbook 2011* and *China Statistical Yearbook 2012*.

* Formula used to calculate annual growth rate is based on the level approach: $\bar{x}=\sqrt[n]{\frac{a_n}{a_0}}-1$, in which $\bar{x}$ is annual growth rate, a_n is the value of year n, a_0 is the value of base year and n is the year index number.

Table 4.3 Growth of individually owned business, 1992–2013

Year	*Companies*		*Employees*		*Registered Capital*	
	Quantity (10,000)	*Growth (%)*	*Quantity (10,000)*	*Growth (%)*	*RMB (100 million)*	*Growth (%)*
1992	1,534		2,468		601	
1995	2,529	15.6	4,614	22.2	1,813	37.5
2000	2,571	–18.6	5,070	–18.8	3,315	–3.6
2005	2,463.9	4.8	4,900.5	6.8	5,809.5	14.9
2010	3,452.9	8.0	7,007.6	6.4	13,400	
2011	3,756.5	8.8	7,945.3	13.4	16,200	20.9
2012	4,059.27	8.1	8,454.7	6.4	19,800	22.2
2013	4,436.3	9.3	9,300	10.0	24,000	21.2
Average growth (%)		5.2		6.5		19.2

Source: The All-China Federation of Industry and Commerce, National Bureau of Industry and Commerce, *China Statistical Yearbook 2011* and *China Statistical Yearbook 2012*.

The above two categories alone made up an overwhelming majority of private enterprises (*siren qiye*私人企业), i.e., all the non-public-owned enterprises, *feigong qiye*非公企业. Disregarding the individually owned businesses, privately held enterprises make 79.1 percent of all enterprises settled in China.

In 2013, private enterprises employed 303 million employees, more than four times the number of employees that state-owned enterprises did. Their contribution to GDP was between 50–60 percent; even higher if the "shadow economy" is taken into account. As the non-state sector develops, capital accumulation by non-state enterprises has also increased. As shown in Table 4.5, fixed asset investment by the non-state sector has grown rapidly and steadily.

In terms of scale alone, the number of registered patents among industrial enterprises of scale clearly shows that private enterprises dominate technological innovation. In 2011, the number of patents registered successfully by private enterprises above a designated size totaled 131,986 or 65 percent of all patents. Of these, the number of patents successfully registered by private companies (*saying qiye*) alone was 41,366 or 26.1 percent of the total. This was 2.5 times the total number of patents registered by all three types of state-owned companies (state-owned enterprises, state-owned associated enterprises and wholly state-owned enterprises).

The fast growth of the non-state sector contributes hugely to increases in tax revenue. As shown in Tables 4.4 and 4.5, the two major sources of tax contributions by non-state enterprises come from taxes and additional charges on core business activities and value added taxes, accounting for one third and one half of

Table 4.4 Breakdown of number of enterprises by controlling shareholders, 2012

	Total number	*State-owned*	*Collective*	*Private*	*Hong Kong Macau Taiwan*	*Foreign*	*Other*
Nationwide	8,286,654	278,479	271,295	6,552,049	101,518	109,103	974,210
Percentage	100	3.4	3.3	79.1	1.2	1.3	11.8

Source: *China Statistical Yearbook 2012.*

Table 4.5 Fixed asset investment by industrial state-owned and non-state-owned enterprises (Unit: RMB 100 million)

Year	*A. Fixed Asset Investment by State-Owned Enterprises*	*B. Fixed Asset Investment by Non-State Enterprises (above designated scale)*	*A + B. Total Fixed Asset Investment*
2001	17,606.98	16,607.85	37,213.49
2002	18,877.35	21,171.82	43,499.91
2003	21,661.02	28,996.86	55,566.62
2004	25,027.62	38,482.33	70,477.45
2005	29,666.92	50,682.32	88,773.61
2006	32,963.39	66,176.52	109,998.16
2007	38,706.35	85,263.69	137,323.94
2008	48,704.89	108,716.5	172,828.40
2009	69,692.5	139,418.5	224,598.77
2010	83,316.55	177,597.9	278,121.85
2011	82,494.78	210,273.5	311,485.13
2012	96,220.2	241,992.9	374,694.7
2013	109,849.9	295,039.9	446,294.1

Source: *China Statistical Yearbooks* 2002 to 2014.

total contributions from all entities, respectively. In other words, non-state enterprises contribute the largest amount of value added tax related to export profits, while contributions by state-owned enterprises have been decreasing steadily.

Tax contributions from private enterprises were also higher according to some indexes. While other indexes showed differing results, tax contributions were all higher than that of the state-owned economy. This is due to the fact that much of the tax revenue in China is indirect and tax burdens can be shifted. For instance, state-owned enterprises are concentrated in the upstream portion of many industry chains and hold administrative monopolies, especially over prices,

Table 4.6 Tax contribution and additional charges for core business activities

Year	*Aggregate Tax Revenue*	*State-Owned Enterprises*	*Percentage*	*Non-State Industrial Enterprise*	*Percentage*
2005	2,997.34	1,468.02	48.98%	1,202.4	40.12%
2006	3,746.35	1,724.83	46.04%	1,378.34	36.79%
2007	4,772.08	2,007.26	42.06%	1,504.49	31.53%
2008	6,277.28	2,531.12	40.32%	2,169.94	34.57%
2009	8,995.95	3,113.6	34.61%	2,691.04	29.91%
2010	11,183.11	3,902.53	34.90%	3,471.04	31.04%
2011	12,669.53	2,859.62	22.57%	8,144.63	64.29%

Source: *China Statistical Yearbook on Industrial Economy* 2006 to 2011.

Table 4.7 Value added tax (Unit: RMB 100 million)

Year	*Aggregate Tax Revenue*	*State-Owned Enterprises*	*Percentage*	*Non-State Industrial Enterprise*	*Percentage*
2005	8,520.94	2,278.36	26.74%	4,431.06	52.00%
2006	10,707.16	2,623.71	24.50%	5,721.51	53.44%
2007	13,650.34	3,019.03	22.12%	6,082.07	44.56%
2008	17,690.72	2,544.35	14.38%	8,381.13	47.38%
2009	17,490.2	3,182.22	18.19%	8,471.69	48.44%
2010	22,472.72	3,892.75	17.32%	11,031.94	49.09%
2011	26,302.71	2,829.92	10.76%	10,519.05	39.99%

Source: *China Statistical Yearbook for Industrial Sectors* 2006 to 2011.

which are regularly set at high levels. The lack of demand flexibility for the products and services of these companies means that their tax burdens are easily shifted to downstream private enterprises and consumers, which means that their "tax contributions" should be attributed to the latter (see Tables 4.6 and 4.7).

Problems private enterprises in China are facing

Following survey results, the outlook for private enterprises remains less than positive and has continued to deteriorate in recent years.[4] There are a variety of reasons for this, including systematic problems, market issues and internal management problems. Systematic problems include:

1 The second-class status of private enterprises – under legal and policy regulations, the status of private enterprise remains lower than that of state-owned

enterprises and a similar relationship exists between the state and privately owned economies;

2 Legal security for private enterprises – private enterprises are given less security under the legal system in China as can be seen in the government's restructuring of the coal industry, during which the basic rights of private coal operators were trampled;
3 Frequent changes in the government's macroeconomic policy – specifically for ensuring growth, these almost always infringe upon the rights of private enterprises, which can be seen in policies of credit control and financial repression that led to financing crises for private enterprise;
4 Currency appreciation – this has also affected the production costs and export advantage of many private enterprises in eastern China;
5 Labor regulations – the implementation of a stronger Labor Contract Law, social security regulations and environmental regulations has also increased production and operation costs for companies;
6 Stronger administrative monopolies – the power of administrative monopolies has grown considerably in recent years, taking away the space that private enterprises need to exist and grow;
7 Heavy tax burdens – private enterprises generally face heavier tax burdens than state-owned enterprises;
8 Discretionary corruption – discretionary powers at the local level prevail and often hinder the operations of private businesses.

Market issues constitute another major obstacle and include:

1 A decrease in external demand due to the global financial crisis and the European debt crisis;
2 Multiple trade disagreements between China and trading partners with anti-dumping and other measures taking a toll on the exports of China's private enterprises;
3 Serious overproduction by private enterprises in eastern coastal regions with prices of competitive industrial products going down while the cost of raw materials, labor and other essentials rise, resulting in a crisis for manufacturers in China's eastern coastal regions;
4 The general downturn in the economy has resulted in serious problems of "triangular debt," causing limited levels or lack of liquidity for companies;
5 Regional protectionism is also serious with non-local companies in central and western parts of China finding themselves trapped and threatened;
6 Many companies are faced with industrial transfer or upgrades, but do not have access to sufficient capital. A lack in the development of financial markets has made these transitions even more difficult.

Market access and barriers to liquidity are also still very big problems for private enterprises in China. While access to financial markets for private enterprise has improved in recent years, there are still serious financial barriers. Financial markets still have a strong sense of state control about them. The threshold for private enterprise to create or participate in capital market institutions is high and application requirements are far too strict. This means that there is effectively no market access for private enterprises looking to set up financial institutions in China. While private enterprises are allowed to participate in the creation of village and township banks, the founding institution must be an established commercial bank, meaning that private enterprises have no autonomy even when establishing village and township banks. Recent approval by the government of the establishment of six private commercial banks remains still a pilot reform. For most small and medium private enterprises, the requirements for listing on main-boards, SME (small and medium-size enterprise) boards and growth enterprise boards are all too high. Barriers to financing through enterprise bonds are also very high and limits have been placed on the scale of collective bonds issued by small and medium enterprises.

While barriers that private enterprises face when entering general competitive industries do not seem high on the surface, in real economic terms there is a range of limitations placed on the economic activities of private enterprises. These create a number of barriers to private enterprises looking to enter general competitive industries. These include:

1. Government macroeconomic policies that are not beneficial to the existence or development of private enterprise;
2. Administrative monopolies in land allocation that limit the freedom of private enterprise in land markets;
3. Government tax and subsidy policies that create an environment of unfair competition;
4. Regional protectionism and interest groups that create barriers for private enterprises trying to enter general competitive industries.

In both the educational and health care sectors, there are still considerable barriers to market entry. The government regularly sees these services as part of the public sector, which results in pervasive policy discrimination against private enterprise. Public utilities and traditional monopolies are often turned over to state-owned enterprises, resulting in administrative monopolies. However, the Chinese government is now encouraging private participation in public utilities, partially due to the fact that local government has piled up massive debt and needs to attract private capital to offset that debt.

Very rarely are all aspects of these monopolized sectors fully open and even if they are mostly open, there is still a "glass ceiling" that prevents private enterprises from truly entering into these industries. Those that do get in often ultimately find themselves pushed out at a later date. In the petroleum industry, there are cases in which the government has allowed private enterprises to import crude oil, but these imports must still be incorporated into the production plans for China's two major state-owned oil companies. If they choose not to, they will be denied permission to ship or even refine their product within China. To make things even more difficult, the state-owned oil companies are generally reluctant to refine oil imported by these private companies and refuse to incorporate the crude oil into their existing plans. Private companies that do get their crude oil refined are further limited in terms of the volume that can be refined and retail locations to sell their refined products.

New policies relating to private sector development

While there is a general worsening in the state of private enterprises, external support has actually increased. Generally, implementation directives for the "New 36" benefit private enterprise. These were released gradually in the period before June 2013, however, many of the directives are not specific enough and many of the articles still lack the strength they need to be enforced. Many implementation directives include the phrase "what should be done" as well as conflicting instructions on what can be carried out and what cannot, which requires even more specifics before they can be put into practice. However, the overall intention of these directives is positive. The "Decision of the 3rd Plenary Session of the 18th Communist Party of China Central Committee" (hereafter "Decision") in 2013 and the resolution of the National People's Congress in March 2014 continued this positive direction, especially in terms of financial reforms, despite the major barriers that remain in general principles, which will be discussed throughout this book.

China's government treats private enterprise very differently from developed market economies. In developed economies, there is no express limit on market entry for private enterprises and denial of access is always the exception. Granting market access to state-owned enterprises is also an exception and must be approved by passage of a law. State-owned enterprises are in general not permitted to compete with private companies and their functions are specified, permitting them to function in a supplementary capacity outside of competitive and profit-driven sectors. This is known as the principle of subsidiarity. The "New 36" and its implementation directives have specified how and to what extent private enterprise is allowed to enter previously inaccessible industries. Meanwhile, state-owned enterprises are allowed to do as they please without being restricted by the principle of subsidiarity. The Decision supports the development of a mixed ownership economy in the sense that state-owned enterprises and private enterprises are encouraged hold equity in each other, but this is a double-edge sword for the development of the private sector and further jeopardizes this principle.

China's economy is currently closer to dirigisme, somewhere between a market economy and a planned economy. When dealing with the productive force of the private sector, the government has in general opted to set up barriers rather than let go that force. This behavior is rooted in the excessive discretionary power of governmental agencies and excessive government interference, which are not beneficial to the existence or development of private enterprise. An appropriate anecdote here would be the story of the mythical figure Gun, the father of Yu the Great, who tried to build bigger dams on the base of existing dams to stop terrible flooding, but he failed to prevent flood disasters and was put to death. Yu the Great inherited his father's charge and chose instead to remove some parts of existing dams to allow and ease the flow of the waters, letting them flow naturally, ultimately providing even greater protection. He succeeded where his father had failed and is remembered throughout history for his great contribution. China's economy is very similar to the flooding in this story, and must similarly provide room for the flow of the natural productive forces of private enterprise, and not try to contain it.

Necessary turn of development paradigm

A policy that allows for private enterprise, bringing market forces into full play, would ultimately be expressed in the creation and maintenance of a competitive order that is based on performance. Walter Eucken, a key figure of the Freiburg School in Germany, believed that the function of the state was to create and maintain a competitive order and act within the framework of the "Rechtsstaat," i.e., rule of law. The constituent principles of competitive order include a functioning price system; stability of currency value (primacy of monetary policy); an open market (freedom of access and exit); private property; liabilities (to one's obligations and actions); freedom of contract and constant economic policy (which focuses on keeping such a competition order). These seven constituent principles were generally implemented and realized during the period of the post-war reconstruction and in the early years of social market economy in Germany. Germany's "economic miracle" is closely related to the comprehensive maintenance of this competitive order, especially in how its constituent principles were upheld.

China's economic success since reform and opening are to a certain extent due to a selective and forced implementing of the core principles of such a competitive order. China was only recently added to the list of the world's middle-income countries and still faces many problems. Some say that China has fallen or is falling victim to the "middle-income trap." If China is to make it out of the "middle-income trap" and become a high-income country, it must free up productivity to ensure that the maximum return on investment is achieved for all factors of production. This can only be achieved by creating, maintaining and adhering to the constituent principles mentioned above and guaranteeing an efficient competitive order, which will in turn ensure the long-term development of private enterprise.

Of course, private enterprises also have internal problems that must be solved. Some private enterprises are using international standards to strengthen internal management, but most still have a good number of issues in internal management, including property rights structures, corporate governance as well as management of human resources, financing, accounting, production and marketing. Some of China's entrepreneurs are relatively uneducated (this is also seen at high levels of state-owned enterprises, but most of these individuals are government appointed officials and not entrepreneurs). These kinds of issues can often affect the growth of private enterprise, its reputation, its ability to source financing and other operational capabilities. For instance, banks pay special attention to whether financial management in private enterprises is handled properly. If a private enterprise does not adhere to standard bookkeeping and accounting practices, banks will not be able to assess the actual financial situation of the company and may lack sufficient basis to issue loans. However, in a competitive order that emphasizes performance-oriented competition, this type of competition can serve to weed out the weak from the strong among private enterprises. Under this type of competitive order, the government ensures competition, not the existence of particular competitors.

Gross Domestic Product (GDP) growth in the first three quarters of 2012 was 8.1 percent, 7.6 percent and 7.4 percent, respectively. This was the first time that the second quarter fell below 8 percent and caused concern in the government, which lowered interest rates twice (June 8 and July 6, 2012) in an attempt to stimulate the economy. The expansionist fiscal policy of the government in basic infrastructure, in conjunction with the lowering of interest rates, means that meeting GDP growth rate goals of 7.5 percent for the year as proposed at the "Two Meetings" (that of the National People's Congress and that of the China People's Political Consultative Conference) in March 2012 was not a problem. However, the lowering of interest rates did not encourage banks to lend more to private enterprise. It actually made them more wary. But this did not preclude some of the stronger companies from obtaining capital through banks and "re-lending" it to private enterprises through other channels. Of course, the drop in interest rates did lighten the burden on some private enterprises that have been lucky enough to get loans and made it possible for such companies to survive and grow.

Generally, lower interest rates have been effective in stimulating economic growth. But sometimes there can be a delay before stimulus can completely take effect. This is why even though the government has lowered interest rates and adjusted its monetary policy, the actual draw on GDP has not been very large. It's very clear why the government has simultaneously implemented a fiscal stimulus package to speed up the start of large-scale projects that will have far-reaching effects and will drive growth. Increasing fiscal investment is a tactic the government uses every time growth tends to slow. Oftentimes, the government will also issue policies that are beneficial to the growth of private enterprise. However, the difference is that fiscal policy expansion is often carried out without hesitation, while policies related to private enterprise are nearly always implemented with incredible resistance and difficulty. For example, the "New 36" issued in 2010 were to provide market access to private enterprises, but as of 2013 these regulations were still not fully implemented.

The above-mentioned combinations of expansionist monetary and fiscal policies in the era of the former leadership are classic Keynesian dirigisme, which in the long term is rooted in discretionary decision making and ignores the reworking of industry structures as well as the maintenance and strengthening of private enterprise. Prior to early 2013, under former Premier Wen Jiabao, GDP growth had continued to rely on fiscal expansion to reach targeted levels. However, this practice created an unhealthy cycle that exacerbated the government's debt burden, which opted to increase control by pushing forward "renationalization" pushing out private investment, which delayed structural change. Over time, the number of infrastructure projects the government can throw money at will decrease. Steel, roads, railways, airports and water works projects implemented by previous governments have had little effect on the lives of the average person. Marginal return continued to decrease driving private investment away as they were only permitted to provide temporary employment for parts of a project. However, this delayed structural reforms of the economy.

The slowing of economic growth is simply an expression of overall change, while the structural problems that lurk behind it, a legacy left behind by the former government, are much more serious. The huge numbers of private manufacturing companies in eastern China are concentrated in narrow, traditional competitive industries. Other industries have been taken over by companies with administrative monopolies. The real estate industry has been suppressed by the government through volume and credit controls. The long-term lackluster performance in the stock markets is also related to this. In general competitive industries such as shoes or textiles, prices continue to drop, while costs are rising across the board. This is especially true in terms of labor costs, social security costs and environmental pressures, which push up the price of raw materials. With external demand dropping off and the appreciation of the RMB, many private enterprises are finding it hard to stay in business. Private enterprises also generally lack experience and technical know-how when trying to transition or upgrade. While central and western China will be able to absorb some manufacturing, the cost of labor is increasing rapidly there as well. This means that many private manufacturers in eastern China that are unable to transition or upgrade will end up closing and laying-off their workforce. If we then look at the number of workers waiting to enter the labor market, the situation seems even more dire. The new government must start change now, giving Chinese private enterprises the room they need to survive and thrive. Some solutions would help improve the situation for manufacturers in eastern China and then could be expanded into central and western China where costs are lower. The first change that must be made is to lower taxes. Lowering taxes doesn't have to be just a stop-gap measure; it could also pave the way to a low-tax regime.

Structural change in China's economy cannot be delayed any longer. Sufficient space must be given to major market entities for them to grow and develop, driving structural change through self-organization. Financial and economic controls must also be loosened, while at the same time strengthening protection of property rights, the development of service industries, vocational education, technological development and urbanization. These are all key. Among these, technological development is what will define China's position in the global "division of labor." However, this can only be accomplished with financial and economic deregulation as well as an increased protection of property rights.

Lao-tzu is known for having said, "Ruling a country is like cooking a small fish." The Tang Dynasty Emperor Xuanzong expounded on this, saying the fish cannot be moved around too much in the pot or it will fall apart; as with a large country, the people must be handled delicately in order to ensure a successful rule. This is indeed the time for a change in China's economic model. Control through discretionary power must be abandoned and true rule of law must be put into practice. The key to this is the establishing and maintaining of a performance-oriented and rule-based competitive order as described above.

Concluding discussion

In summary, the only way out of an all-out crisis is to boost overall economic freedom, promote private sector development, and better protect the property rights of individuals and private entrepreneurs. Policies should include the introduction of an independent judiciary that guarantees citizens the ability to protect their property rights against government discretion, local democracy to increase government responsibility and fiscal transparency, privatization of SOEs and state-owned banks, free market entry of non-state enterprises in all economic sectors and the financial sector, new public management which allows more private participation in public infrastructure, and land reform which at the very least allows land transfers at fair market prices and enforces land allocation based on due process and proper compensation.

Notes

1 With respect to the concept of economic freedom Robert Lucas, the 1995 Nobel laureate, has stated, "Once you start thinking about economic growth, it is hard to think about anything else." (www.fraserinstitute.org)
2 See for example, Justesen, M. (2008).
3 To a large degree, the EFW measure is an effort to identify how closely the institutions and policies of a country correspond with the ideal of a limited government, where the government protects property rights and arranges for the provision of a limited set of "public goods" such as national defense and access to money of sound value, but little beyond these core functions. In order to receive a high EFW rating, a country must provide secure protection of privately owned property, even-handed enforcement of contracts, and a stable monetary environment. It also must keep taxes low, refrain from creating barriers to both domestic and international trade, and rely more fully on markets rather than government spending and regulation to allocate goods and resources.
4 See Feng, Ljungwall and He (2015).

Bibliography

Eucken, W. *Grundsaetzeder Wirtschaftspolitik*. (Bern and Tübingen: Francke Mohr), 1952.

Feng, X. Local Government Debt and Municipal Bonds in China: Problems and a Framework of Rules. *The Copenhagen Journal of Asian Studies*, 31, 2013, pp. 23–53.

Feng, X., Ljungwall, C. and Guo, S. Re-interpreting the Chinese Miracle. *International Journal on World Peace*, 28, 2011, pp. 7–40.

Feng, X., Ljungwall, C. and He, G. *The Ecology of Chinese Private Enterprises*, Series on Chinese Economics Research. (Singapore: World Scientific Publishing Company), Vol. 11, 2015.

Feng, X., Ljungwall, C. and Xia, Y. *Protection of Property Rights as a Key to Economic Success in China*. In the 2013 Report: International Property Rights Index. Available at: www.internationalpropertyrightsindex.org

Gwartney, J. and Lawson, R.A. *Economic Freedom of the World: 2013 Annual Report.* (Vancouver: Fraser Institute), 2002, p. 275.

Justesen, M. The Effect of Economic Freedom on Growth Revisited: New Evidence on Causality from a Panel of Countries 1970–1999. *European Journal of Political Economy*, 24(3), 2008, pp. 642–660.

North, D.C. *Institutions, Institutional Change, and Economic Performance.* (Cambridge: Cambridge University Press), 1990.

Sheng, H. and Zhao, N. *China's State-Owned Enterprises: Nature, Performance and Reform,* Series on Chinese Economics Research. (Singapore: World Scientific Publishing Company), Vol.1, 2012, p. 408.

The World Bank and Development Research Center of the State Council. *China 2030: Building a Modern, Harmonious, and Creative High-Income Society.* (Washington, DC: The World Bank), 2012.

Wu, Y. Chinese Economic Reform in a Comparative Perspective: Asia vs. Europe. *Issues and Studies*, 38(4)/39(1), 2003, pp. 93–138.

Zhu, J. Local Developmental State and Order in China's Urban Development during Transition. *International Journal of Urban and Regional Research*, 28(2), 2004, pp. 424–447.

5 Capital freedom

Evidence from China's provinces

China's economy has been liberalized to a notable degree since the late 1970s. Annual growth in GDP has averaged 9.7 percent over the period 1980–2014, leading to a more than 12-fold increase in real GDP per capita. Several scholars such as Gregory et al. (2000) and Dorn (2004) have made the case for improved economic freedom (EF) as a means for promoting this development.[1] In consideration of the high importance attributed to EF, the Fraser Institute began in 1996 publishing the *Economic Freedom of the World* (EFW) Report, which presents an EF index today covering 141 nations.[2] China, the world's second-largest economy, has low ratings but has made tremendous strides toward more EF over the course of reform. As measured by the Fraser Institute in its 2014 Report, China's rating (chain-linked) increased from 3.74 in 1980 to 6.20 in 2012, while its ranking (chain-linked) dropped from 92 to 96.[3]

Nonetheless, despite these considerable improvements in the scores of EF, a number of problems affecting them and its ranking exist in China. Since 1978, factors such as different natural endowments, diversified local economic cultures, territorial competition and unbalanced regional development strategies, have led to an uneven level of economic development and marketization, including significant differences in financial development, and free movement of capital across China (Fan et al., 2001; Feng, 2010; Feng et al., 2011). Other, more visible constraints are related to economic dirigisme, administrative complexities, insufficient protection of property rights, bureaucratic inefficiency and corruption (Lu, 2000; Manion, 2004; Feng et al., 2015).

While economic freedom generally refers to the freedom of individuals, there is a necessity to measure individual and corporate capital freedom (CF), which can be regarded as one dimension of economic freedom and reflects individual and corporate freedom to hold, access, utilize and move capital in an economy. This specific angle is very important in China since this can be an indicator not only for the level of protection of property rights of individuals, but also for how favorable the environment for the survival and development of private enterprises in an economy is. It touches the core section of economic life: the section that combines the capital, labor and land and transforms them into goods and services that everyone needs for one's survival and development. As a consequence, Cathay Institute for Public Affairs (CIPA) has developed a specific index to measure capital freedom (CF), at the provincial level. The Provincial Capital Freedom Index for China (PCFIC) approximates regional disparities in the level of capital freedom, and allows us to track changes over time.

Concept and importance of capital freedom

The term "capital freedom" originated from a 2003 article by James A. Dorn, titled "Capital Freedom for China." He references it to the abolishment of the RMB peg to the dollar and full RMB convertibility. This term has to be defined in relationship to the concept of economic freedom. According to the Economic Freedom of the World 2014 Annual Report, the cornerstones of economic freedom include: "(1) personal choice, (2) voluntary exchange coordinated by markets, (3) freedom to enter and compete in markets, and (4) protection of persons and their property from aggression by others" (Gwartney et al., 2014, p. 1).

Capital freedom is one dimension of economic freedom. By incorporating the standard definition of capital as given by Samuelson (2001), where capital is one of the three factors of production input (land, labor and capital), into the CF concept, one can identify four dimensions, also four cornerstones of capital freedom: (1) freedom to hold capital, (2) freedom to access capital, (3) freedom to utilize capital and (4) freedom to move capital.

Freedom to hold capital involves the protection of fundamental property rights of the individuals in terms of possessing the capital. Freedom to access capital implies that there should exist a functioning financial market that is open to individuals and firms and is able to meet their effective demand of financial services. Freedom to utilize capital implies the freedom to enter and exit competitive sectors, public utilities and the financial market. Freedom to move capital refers to freedom of interregional and international capital mobility.

There has been a huge bundle of literature justifying EF. First, EF is conducive to economic development. Gaining new importance in growth theory, the basic link between that of the free movement of labor and capital and that of economic growth can be traced to Adam Smith's *The Wealth of Nations* in 1776, which set forth two linked and indispensable conditions to be met if the model he described were to work: free movement for all in the system; free competition among all; there must be no monopolies or combinations in restraint of trade or limiting entry into new fields and government-granted privileges for a favored few. Smith also argued against the many government restrictions and regulations of that time, which he saw as preventing the free movement of men and capital throughout the economy that was necessary for prosperity and growth (Montgomery, 1982). A number of recent empirical studies suggest that EF may be important in explaining cross-country differences in economic performance (Hanke et al., 1997; De Haan et al., 1998; Gwartney et al., 1999; Sturm et al., 2001; Doucouliagos et al., 2006; De Vanssay et al., 2007). Notably, De Haan et al. (2000) conclude that more EF fosters economic growth, but that the level of freedom is not related to growth.[4]

In other words, they argue that more economic freedom will bring countries more quickly to their steady state level of economic growth, which is irrelevant to the degree of EF. While there is scholarly debate about the exact nature of these relationships, the results are uniform: measures of EF relate positively with economic growth (De Haan et al., 2006). Thus, both theory and empirical evidence support the hypothesis that a free flow of production factors is not only a basic feature of the market but also a fundamental guarantee for bringing the advantages of the market economy into full play. Second, EF not only relates to freedom in economic affairs, but also to personal and political freedom. Just as Hayek (1944, p. 13) said: "We have progressively abandoned that freedom in economic affairs without which personal and political freedom has never existed in the past." As long as EF is justifiable, CF is also justifiable, because CF is an integrated core part of the EF.

Composition of provincial capital freedom index for China

The CF index draws on the *Economic Freedom of the World Report* and is concerned with measuring the changes made in four major areas: (1) government and institutions, (2) economy, (3) money supply and financial development, and (4) marketization level of the financial market. These areas have 21 components and are then combined into one general index providing information on the overall scores and sequence of the relative level of CF of the respective province.[5]

In order to ensure the comparability of the scores in different years, we set the base year for individual indicators (in this report, the base year is 2001), with the maximum and the minimum values of each individual indicator in the base year set as 10 and 0, respectively. This means that, with respect to each individual indicator, the province with the highest degree of CF in the base year has a value of 10, and the province with the poorest CF has a value of 0. Then, the scores of other provinces in the base year are determined according to the values of respective indicators to form corresponding individual indicators.

Following the theoretical relationship between index value and the degree of CF, the formulas calculating indicator scores are classified into two categories. When the value of an indicator is of positive correlation with the degree of CF, the score of the index will be calculated with the first formula. That is, the higher the original value is, the higher the score will be, and the higher the degree of CF represented by the respective indicator will be. For example, the score of the indicator "efficiency of judicial system" is calculated as follows (Equation 5.1):

$$\text{Score of the } i^{\text{th}} \text{ indicator} = \frac{V_i - V_{min}}{V_{max} - V_{min}} \times 10$$

V_i refers to the original value of the ith indicator of a region, V_{max} refers to the largest one of the original value of all the 30 regions relevant to the ith indicator in the base year (2001), and V_{min} refers to the smallest one. When the original value of an indicator is of negative correlation with the degree of CF, the score of the indicator will be calculated with the second formula. That is, the higher the original value is, the lower the score of the indicator will be, and the lower the degree of capital freedom embodied by the indicator will be. For example, the score of the indicator "inflation rate" is calculated as follows (Equation 5.2):

$$\text{Score of the } i^{\text{th}} \text{ indicator} = \frac{V_{max} - V_{min}}{V_{max} - V_{min}} \times 10$$

Through the above treatment, the scores are in positive correlation with the degree of CF. The higher the score is, the higher the degree of CF will be; and the lower the score is, the lower the degree of CF will be.

With a view to ensure the comparability of the indicator scores of provinces with the previous years so as to reflect the progress in CF, we adopt the following formula (applicable to positive-correlated indicators) when calculating the scores of individual indicators of the years following the base year (Equation 5.3):

$$\text{Score of the } i^{\text{th}} \text{ indicator in year } t = \frac{V_{i(t)} - V_{\min(0)}}{V_{\max(0)} - V_{\min(0)}} \times 10$$

The subscript (t) represents the year of the calculation, and the subscript (0) represents the base year. The following formula is adopted when calculating the negative-correlated indicators after the base year (Equation 5.4):

$$\text{Score of the } i^{\text{th}} \text{ indicator year } t = \frac{V_{\max(0)} - V_{i(t)}}{V_{\max(0)} - V_{\min(0)}} \times 10$$

The maximum and the minimum scores of individual indicators in non-base years are allowed to be bigger than 10 or smaller than 0. For example, when the score of "share of the non-state industry in total production value of the total industry" of a province in 2001 is 10 (the highest proportion among the 30 provinces and regions), and the proportion in 2002 is further elevated, breaking its own record in 2001, then its score in 2002 will be higher than 10.

In order to avoid interferences of subjective and random factors, similar to what the Fraser Institute adopts in its EFW Report, we don't use the Principal Components Analysis to determine weights of the individual indicators in the respective areas. The greatest advantage of this method lies in its objectiveness. That is, the weights are determined based on the features of the data themselves but not subjective judgments. However, a main problem is that weights of various factors change over time, and this will render CF indexes in different years incomparable with one another thus complicating cross-year analysis. Besides, affected by the accuracy of statistical data and other factors, individual weights generated may deviate from the normal scope.

In view of the above, we calculate CF indexes with the Arithmetic Average Method, following the Fraser Institute's approach. The rationale for using this method is that when an index system is composed of variables that contain sufficient information, different variables are replaceable by one another to a certain extent. Under such a circumstance, the size of weight (within a certain scope) no longer has important influence on the results of ranking. To test its significance, we calculated CF indexes for the period 2001–2005 using both Principal Components Analysis and the Arithmetic Average Method. The results show that the ranking retrieved from the two methods fit closely with each other. Table 5.1 lists the indexes used to construct the Provincial Capital Freedom Index for China.

Table 5.1 Composition of capital freedom index

Name		*Category*
1.	**Government and Institutional Factors**	Area Index
1.a.	Share of Market Allocation of Resources (Percentage of Government Expenditure to GDP)	Component
1.b.	Percentage of Government Subsidies to Enterprises to GDP	Component
1.c.	Non-Tax Burden of Enterprises	Component
1.d.	Local Protectionism	Component
1.e.	Legal Protection (Efficiency of Judicial System)	Component
2.	**Economic Factors**	Area Index
2.a.	Ratio of Number of Enterprises to Population	Component
2.b.	Size of Non-State Sector	Component
2.b.1.	Share of the Non-State Industry in Total Production Value of the Total Industry	Sub-Component
2.b.2.	Share of the Non-State Sector in Total Capital Construction Investment	Sub-Component
2.c.	Share of Foreign Investment in GDP	Component
3.	**Money Supply and Financial Development**	Area Index
3.a.	Percentage of Total Deposits to GDP	Component
3.b.	Rate of Inflation	Component
3.c.	Standard Deviation in Rate of Inflation	Component
3.d.	Share of Return from Assets of Urban Households in Their Total Disposable Income	Component

Name		*Category*
3.e.	Share of Cash Held by Urban Households in Their Total Disposable Income	Component
3.f.	Number of Bank Cards per Capita	Component
4.	**Marketization Level of Financial Market**	Area Index
4.a.	Competition among Banks and Other Financial Institutions	Component
4.a.1.	Percentage of Deposit with Non-State Financial Institutions to Total Deposit	Sub-Component
4.a.2.	Percentage of Loans for Non-State Enterprises to Total Loans Granted by Financial Institutions	Sub-Component
4.b.	Stock Market	Component
4.b.1.	Share of Number of Non-State Controlled Listed Companies in Total Number of Listed Companies	Sub-Component
4.b.2.	Share of Number of Tradable Stocks in Total Number of Stocks	Sub-Component
4.b.3.	Share of Non-State Controlled Listed Companies in Total Assets of All Listed Companies	Sub-Component
4.b.4.	Share of Non-State Controlled Listed Companies in Total Funds Raised in Stock Market by All Listed Companies	Sub-Component

Source: The authors.

Scores and rankings of provincial capital freedom in China

After constituting the indicator system for the CF index, we cannot measure it with existing data. The index covers all provinces, municipalities directly under the Central Government, and autonomous regions but Tibet. Tibet is excluded due to lack of data. Hong Kong and Macau are excluded due to their specific position. Data are mainly collected from the National Bureau of Statistics and People's Bank. Values of indicators "non-tax burden of enterprises," "local protectionism" and "legal protection" (efficiency of judicial system) are survey findings of NERI and were made available by it.

The overall ranking of provinces over the period 2006–2011 from high to low is given in Table 5.2. Zhejiang is the clear winner in this respect and has positioned itself as number one for six consecutive years. Shanghai, Jiangsu, Guangdong and Beijing also perform particularly well altering their positions between the top five. Guizhou, Gansu and Qinghai position themselves at the other end of the scale, ranked number 28, 29 and 30 in 2011.

A slightly different picture is given by the relative changes in CF scores over the six-year period, as given by Table 5.3. First, and in parallel with the most recent estimate by the Fraser Institute, the results suggest that combined CF suffered a setback in 2008 as compared to 2007 and 2006. Accordingly, China – in

Table 5.2 Provincial ranking of capital freedom, 2006–2011 (base year = 2001)

Rank	*2006*	*2007*	*2008*	*2009*	*2010*	*2011*
1	Zhejiang	Zhejiang	Zhejiang	Zhejiang	Zhejiang	Zhejiang
2	Shanghai	Jiangsu	Guangdong	Shanghai	Shanghai	Shanghai
3	Guangdong	Guangdong	Jiangsu	Jiangsu	Beijing	Jiangsu
4	Jiangsu	Shanghai	Shanghai	Guangdong	Jiangsu	Beijing
5	Beijing	Beijing	Beijing	Tianjin	Guangdong	Guangdong
6	Tianjin	Hainan	Fujian	Fujian	Fujian	Fujian
7	Shandong	Tianjin	Tianjin	Liaoning	Tianjin	Tianjin
8	Fujian	Shandong	Hainan	Beijing	Liaoning	Liaoning
9	Hainan	Fujian	Liaoning	Hainan	Hainan	Chongqing
10	Liaoning	Liaoning	Shandong	Shandong	Chongqing	Hainan
11	Chongqing	Chongqing	Chongqing	Chongqing	Shandong	Shandong
12	Sichuan	Sichuan	Sichuan	Sichuan	Sichuan	Sichuan
13	Xinjiang	Xinjiang	Inner Mongolia	Inner Mongolia	Hubei	Hubei
14	Anhui	Anhui	Hubei	Hubei	Inner Mongolia	Inner Mongolia
15	Hebei	Inner Mongolia	Hunan	Jilin	Anhui	Anhui
16	Inner Mongolia	Hubei	Jilin	Hunan	Jiangxi	Jilin
17	Hubei	Hebei	Hebei	Guangxi	Jilin	Jiangxi
18	Guangxi	Shanxi	Guangxi	Anhui	Hunan	Hunan
19	Hunan	Hunan	Anhui	Henan	Yunnan	Henan

20	Ningxia	Guangxi	Yunnan	Hebei	Guangxi	Guangxi
21	Shaanxi	Jilin	Henan	Yunnan	Henan	Yunnan
22	Shanxi	Henan	Jiangxi	Jiangxi	Hebei	Hebei
23	Henan	Yunnan	Shanxi	Ningxia	Ningxia	Ningxia
24	Qinghai	Ningxia	Ningxia	Shanxi	Shanxi	Shanxi
25	Jilin	Qinghai	Heilongjiang	Shaanxi	Shaanxi	Shaanxi
26	Jiangxi	Jiangxi	Shaanxi	Heilongjiang	Xinjiang	Xinjiang
27	Yunnan	Shaanxi	Xinjiang	Xinjiang	Heilongjiang	Heilongjiang
28	Heilongjiang	Heilongjiang	Guizhou	Guizhou	Guizhou	Guizhou
29	Gansu	Guizhou	Qinghai	Qinghai	Gansu	Gansu
30	Guizhou	Gansu	Gansu	Gansu	Qinghai	Qinghai

Source: The authors.

Table 5.3 Overall scores of capital freedom, 2006–2011 (base year = 2001)

Region	*2006*	*2007*	*2008*	*2009*	*2010*	*2011*	*Period Relative Changes**
China	6.19	6.25	6.08	6.29	6.49	6.86	0.67
Beijing	7.65	7.54	7.38	7.36	8.54	8.77	1.12
Tianjin	7.14	7.21	7.31	7.74	8.01	8.40	1.26
Hebei	5.87	5.89	5.71	5.70	5.65	5.92	0.05
Shanxi	5.48	5.79	5.35	5.21	5.37	5.73	0.25
Inner Mongolia	5.84	5.98	6.05	6.36	6.40	6.58	0.74
Liaoning	6.88	6.89	7.05	7.51	7.75	7.94	1.06
Jilin	5.29	5.62	5.74	6.02	6.00	6.44	1.15
Heilongjiang	5.04	4.83	4.93	5.10	5.12	5.39	0.35
Shanghai	7.95	7.78	8.05	8.49	8.65	9.14	1.19
Jiangsu	7.90	8.15	8.07	8.37	8.53	8.84	0.94
Zhejiang	8.93	8.97	8.83	9.25	9.58	10.05	1.12
Anhui	5.94	5.98	5.58	5.81	6.11	6.45	0.51
Fujian	7.04	6.98	7.37	7.64	8.02	8.57	1.53
Jiangxi	5.29	5.39	5.37	5.65	6.02	6.32	1.03
Shandong	7.05	7.03	6.79	6.99	7.13	7.34	0.29
Henan	5.34	5.62	5.48	5.75	5.90	6.30	0.96
Hubei	5.82	5.96	5.95	6.31	6.47	6.76	0.94
Hunan	5.59	5.72	5.77	5.91	5.97	6.30	0.71
Guangdong	7.90	8.13	8.22	8.33	8.28	8.71	0.81
Guangxi	5.62	5.71	5.64	5.81	5.92	6.29	0.67
Hainan	6.96	7.46	7.05	7.21	7.54	7.73	0.77
Chongqing	6.48	6.51	6.45	6.85	7.22	7.83	1.35
Sichuan	6.20	6.27	6.13	6.48	6.82	7.28	1.08
Guizhou	4.28	4.40	4.13	4.18	4.35	4.75	0.47
Yunnan	5.24	5.51	5.50	5.68	5.95	6.27	1.03
Shaanxi	5.51	5.23	4.82	5.11	5.22	5.67	0.16
Gansu	4.32	4.04	3.79	3.88	3.87	4.42	0.1
Qinghai	5.31	5.43	4.02	3.91	3.78	4.19	-1.12
Ningxia	5.55	5.44	5.03	5.29	5.42	5.77	0.22
Xinjiang	6.13	6.14	4.69	4.82	5.13	5.62	-0.51

Source: The authors.

*Positive/negative numbers in the last column indicate a rise/decline in the relative degree of capital freedom over the 2006–2011 period.

2008 – followed a global trend of declining economic freedom. This declining trend was reversed in 2009 when China reached a combined score of 6.29. This was further improved in 2011 reaching a combined score of 6.86. Fujian's relative change of 1.53 over the six-year period is unmatched. Qinghai had the worst development in relative terms over the six-year period experiencing a decline (–1.12).

A main reason for the lower combined CF score in 2008 is the negative change reflected by government and institutional factors, while there were signs of improvements in the level of marketization in financial markets. The pattern is similar at the provincial level, where 28 out of 30 provinces had a negative impact coming from government and institutional factors alone, closely followed by the level of marketization in financial markets. Similarly, improvement in both combined and provincial CF in 2009 over previous years is related to positive changes in government and institutional factors.

Concluding discussion

As a result of the high importance attributed to EF, this chapter introduces a provincial capital freedom index for China. CF can be seen as one core dimension of EF and has a special focus on individual and corporate freedom to hold, access, utilize and move capital. The provincial capital freedom index is used to analyze the degrees of provincial CF, their relative differences and changes annually. The chapter discusses the ground-laying interpretation and importance of CF. It shows that China's overall CF score has been still low and there are huge differences in scores and rankings of the overall CF index, respective areas and indicators of Chinese provinces. Since all these findings are open to the public, local governments can be made aware of progress of and hindrances to CF, and advantages and shortages in this field in their respective provinces. Local government leaders who are far-sighted can make their endeavors to overcome their shortages, enhance their advantages, and thus shape their competitive edge in territorial competition in China. This would be conducive to the shaping of a performance-based competition order, which is essential to boost overall economic development across China.

Notes

1 See also, J.Y. Lin. *Economic Development and Transition: Thought, Strategy, and Viability* (New York: Cambridge University Press, 2009).

2 Another index is the NERI Marketization Index in China developed by Fan et al. (2001), which measures the economic freedom for Chinese provinces. It was developed by the National Economy Research Institute (NERI) in 2003, based on the methodology developed by the Fraser Institute calculating its Economic Freedom of the World index.

3 This refers to China's combined score of economic freedom (chain-linked) as measured by Fraser Institute EFW 2014 Report (Gwartney et al., 2014), e.g., their latest available results. If unadjusted, China's scores for respective areas in 2012 are as follows (the world ranking is given within parenthesis): size of

government: 3.64 (121); legal structure and security of property rights: 5.52 (71); access to sound money: 8.03 (77); freedom to trade internationally: 6.95 (70); regulation of credit, labor and business: 6.86 (69).

4 See, De Haan et al. (2006) for an excellent survey on economic freedom indexes and economic growth.

5 See, De Haan et al. (2006) for a critical review of economic freedom indexes.

Bibliography

De Haan, J., Lundstrom, S. and Sturm, J.-E. Market-oriented Institutions and Policies and Economic Growth: A Critical Survey. *Journal of Economic Surveys*, 20(2), 2006, pp. 157–191.

De Haan, J. and Siermann, C.L.J. Further Evidence on the Relationship between Economic Freedom and Economic Growth. *Public Choice*, 95, 1998, pp. 363–380.

De Haan, J. and Sturm, J.-E. On the Relationship between Economic Freedom and Economic Growth. *European Journal of Political Economy*, 16, 2000, pp. 215–241.

De Vanssay, X., Hildebrand, V. and Spindler, Z.A. Institutional Foundations of Economic Freedom: A Time-Series Cross-Section Analysis. *Constitutional Political Economy*, 16(4), 2007, pp. 327–346.

Dorn, J.A. Capital Freedom for China. *Asian Wall Street Journal*, September 9, 2003.

Dorn, J.A. Trade and Human Rights: The Case of China. *The Cato Journal*, 16(1), 2004, pp. 77–98.

Doucouliagos, C. and Ulubasoglu, M. Economic Freedom and Economic Growth: What Difference Does Specification Make? *European Journal of Political Economy*, 22, 2006, pp. 60–81.

Fan, G. and Xiaolu W. *NERI's Index of Marketization of China's Provinces: 2000 Report.* (Beijing: China Economy Publishing House), 2001.

Feng, X. *Local Government Competition in China: Paradigms, Analytical Framework and Empirical Study.* (Nanjing: Yilin Press), 2010.

Feng, X., Ljungwall, C. and He, G. *The Ecology of Chinese Private Enterprises*, Series on Chinese Economics Research. (Singapore: World Scientific Publishing Company), Vol. 11, 2015.

Feng, X. and Shoulong, M. *Capital Freedom in China: The 2014 Report.* (Beijing: Huaxia Press), 2014.

Feng, X. and Yeliang, X. *The CIPA Index and Analysis of Corporate Capital Freedom in China.* (Beijing: Huaxia Press), 2008.

Gregory, N., Tenev, S. and Wagle, D.M. *China's Emerging Private Enterprises, Prospects for the New Century.* (Washington, DC: International Finance Corporation), 2000.

Gwartney, J., Hall, J. and Lawson R. *Economic Freedom of the World: 2010 Annual Report.* (Vancouver: The Fraser Institute), 2010.

Gwartney, J., Lawson, R. and Hall, J. *Economic Freedom of the World: 2014 Annual Report.* (Vancouver: The Fraser Institute), 2014.

Gwartney, J., Lawson, R. and Holcombe, R.G. Economic Freedom and the Environment for Economic Growth. *Journal of Institutional and Theoretical Economics*, 155, 1999, pp. 643–663.

Hanke, S.H. and Walters, S.J.K. Economic Freedom, Prosperity, and Equality: A Survey. *The Cato Journal*, 17(2), 1997, pp. 117–146.

Lin, J.Y. *Economic Development and Transition: Thought, Strategy, and Viability.* (New York: Cambridge University Press), 2009.
Lu, X. Booty Socialism, Bureau-Preneurs, and the State in Transition: Organizational Corruption in China. *Comparative Politics*, 32(3), April, 2000, pp. 273–294.
Manion, M. *Corruption by Design: Building Clean Government in Mainland China and Hong Kong.* (Cambridge, MA and London: Harvard University Press), 2004.
Montgomery, J. Adam Smith's Economics of Freedom. *The Freemen*, January, 1982, pp. 47–54.
Samuelson, P.A. and Nordhaus W.D. *Economics.* (Boston, MA: McGraw-Hill), 2001.
Sturm, J.-E. and De Haan, J. How Robust Is the Relationship between Economic Freedom and Economic Growth Really? *Applied Economics*, 33, 2001, pp. 839–844.

Part III

Fiscal transformation in China

6 Fiscal federalism

A refined theory and its application in the Chinese context

China's economic restructuring over the last three decades is exceptional by world standards. It started with the introduction of economic reform in 1978 when China began to shift its economic policies toward greater openness and market orientation. Since 1978, the annual growth in Gross Domestic Product (GDP) has averaged 9.7 percent leading to a more than 12-fold increase in real GDP per capita. Several scholars such as Qian and Weingast (1996), and Xu and Zhuang (1998) have made the case for fiscal decentralization as a means of promoting this development.[1] Indeed, if defined in terms of fiscal expenditure, China is among the most decentralized economies in the world with roughly 70 percent of budgetary revenue spent by local governments as compared to 32 percent in OECD countries (Wong, 2005).

On the discussion of China's intergovernmental relations, several scholars argue that a federalist approach has been adopted in China (Zheng, 2007), although neither a federalist tradition nor a constitution stipulating a federalist approach has existed. Earlier work by Bahl (1999) argues, "China is not a federal country, but its public financing system has features of a fiscal federalism" (p. 128). Herrmann-Pillath and Zhu (1998) in an in-depth analysis show that China has experienced a transition to federalism. Roland (2000) follows this by concluding that China's intergovernmental relations conform to fiscal federalism in Western countries. Others, such as Wong and Bhattasali (2003), point out that China's fiscal system shares the same characteristics as that of a federal system, while Tsai (2004) further suggests that an evolving fiscal federalism is envisaged in China, and Krug et al. (2004) describe the Chinese fiscal system as de facto federalism.

Despite the interpretation of China's fiscal system either as a system with many similarities to, or some deviations from, fiscal federalism in Western countries, or as de facto fiscal federalism, the development in intergovernmental relations over the past 15 years in China suggests a reverse direction. The central government has regained its upper hand in revenue collection while letting local governments compete for lucrative central grants. Central government revenue as a share of aggregate income increased from 22 percent in 1993 to 51 percent in 2010, while expenditure responsibilities have been remarkably decentralized to sub-national governments (see Figure 6.1).

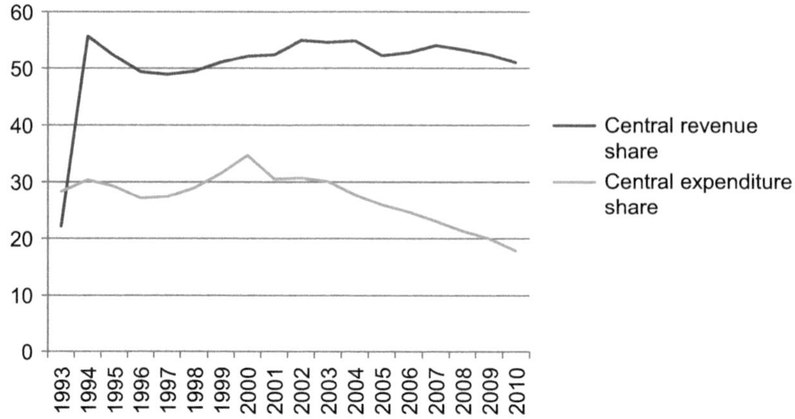

Figure 6.1 Central government share of total budgetary revenue and expenditure
Source: *China Statistical Yearbook 2011*.

In addition to fiscal recentralization on the revenue side, political centralization has been intensified, with more direct political control over regions, including more fiscal extractions from rich regions, and with energetic fiscal transfers to poor regions. Huang (1996) points out that political control through provincial leaders being appointed by the center is an important tool with which the central government can demand compliance from local governments. Fiscal extractions and central transfers tend to aggravate political control.

Despite the rich literature on fiscal federalism and related topics in China, the studies have not captured the most recent development in central–local fiscal relations and the unfolding changes at the local level. This chapter attempts to narrow that gap by addressing two sets of important questions related to fiscal federalism in the Chinese context: first, to what extent do Chinese central–local fiscal relations conform to fiscal federalism in Western literature? Second, what type of fiscal federalism corresponds to the Chinese situation and what policies should the Chinese government pursue in the future?

Prototypes of fiscal federalism

This section offers a critical and in-depth review and evaluation of the important elements of current knowledge and theoretical development of fiscal federalism, with a goal to develop and introduce a refined prototype of fiscal federalism that may be applicable to the Chinese political context.

First generation of fiscal federalism

The first generation theory of fiscal federalism was originally developed and introduced as a sub-field of economics by Musgrave (1959) and Oates (1972).[2]

This theory focuses on the assignments of fiscal responsibilities among various government levels and the functions of the public sector (see also King, 1984; Bird, 2009). According to Oates (1998, p. xiv.), "The basic theory of fiscal federalism lays out in a general way a normative framework for the assignment of fiscal functions to different levels of government and the appropriate fiscal instruments for carrying out these functions." Fiscal federalism is about understanding which functions and instruments are best centralized and which are best placed in the sphere of decentralized levels of government (Oates, 1999). The theory of fiscal federalism emphasizes assignments of revenues and expenditures among governments in order to improve the welfare of society, and is largely based on Musgrave's suggestion of the three main functions of the government: resource allocation, income distribution and macroeconomic stabilization (see Musgrave, 1959; Oates, 1972; Musgrave and Musgrave, 1984):

> *Allocation function*: National governments may provide public goods benefiting the total population in the country while local governments produce social goods for their constituencies.[3]
>
> *Distribution function*: Redistribution should be conducted by the national government given that spillover effects may render local governments' redistribution function ineffective.
>
> *Stabilization function*: Fiscal and monetary policies should be coordinated by the national government in order to maintain economic stabilization.

Groenendijk (2002) further argues that the theory of fiscal federalism can be applied to a wide variety of countries, such as unitary, federal and confederate systems. Therefore, although a country is not legally defined as federalism, it can adopt the principles of fiscal federalism in practice. Moreover, according to Sharma (2005a), fiscal federalism contains some guiding concepts for the structure of intergovernmental relations while fiscal decentralization is only related to power devolution among governments. Sharma (2005b) further clarifies that due to the difference of political environments in federal and non-federal countries, fiscal decentralization may devolve into distinct types of arrangements while fiscal federalism may require very similar arrangements.

The first generation of fiscal federalism, or the traditional theory of fiscal federalism, has some deficiencies in reality. First, the assumption of a benevolent government is flawed (Montinola et al., 1995). The theory views the government as a benign body always considering the welfare of society. However, the conjecture may not be accurate. As compared with the traditional theory of fiscal federalism, federalism theory itself nevertheless presumes a selfish government; thus it needs checks and balances.[4] In addition to the assignments of responsibilities between the national government and local governments, Dye (1990) argues that federalism is the creation of "opposite and rival" interests among governments. Nevertheless, the traditional theory of fiscal federalism with a benign government assumption considers less about checks and balances among governments.

Second, the first generation of fiscal federalism discounts the benefits of overlaps in intergovernmental relations. Competition among local governments is overlooked. Dye (1990, p. 12) points out the fiscal federalism "largely ignores the political problem of controlling Leviathan." Fiscal federalism advocates a clear assignment of government responsibilities to a given government level. Therefore, competition within and between levels of government is unnecessarily and unreasonably curtailed. Hollander (2009) argues that many countries endeavor to eliminate the overlap and duplication among different tiers of government. When responsibility assignments become less debatable in practice, nonetheless, checks and balances between national and local governments become ineffective. Citizens cannot appeal to other government authorities due to failure in one level of government. We concur with the argument raised by Hollander because competition among governments is an effective instrument to correct policy failure and promote good public services.

Third, the first generation of fiscal federalism posits a strong capacity of higher authorities. As noted by Dye (1990), fiscal federalism has an inherent tendency of centralization. This is closely linked to the presumption of a benevolent government. If a higher authority can do more efficiently than a lower one, the relevant competence tends to be assigned to the higher one. However, local citizens in a jurisdiction might prefer local autonomy and prevent this competence assignment out of political considerations thus assuming control of both legislative and executive powers.

Finally, the first generation of fiscal federalism may complicate our understanding over intergovernmental relations in some countries. Some countries may be misunderstood as federal countries because these countries adopt the arrangement of fiscal federalism. It is revealing in the case of China. As noted by Huang (1996), the personnel system in China is very centralized. Put simply, chief executives at various levels are de facto appointed by high authorities and nominally elected by their constituencies. In public finance, local governments also highly rely on central grants to make ends meet (Guo, 2008). Thus, although intergovernmental relations in some countries resemble traditional settings of fiscal federalism, the differences are still substantial.

Second generation of fiscal federalism

A significant modification of the theory of fiscal federalism has taken place since the days of Musgrave and Oates. In second-generation fiscal federalism, the postulation of a benign government is replaced by a self-serving government assumption. In order to improve public governance, new theories on fiscal federalism, or the second generation of fiscal federalism (Oates, 2005), devote great attention to both the benefits and the motives of fiscal federalism. Basically, they caution about an assertive central government and favor the practice of empowering local governments with more power and responsibilities.

Following Qian and Weingast (1997), second-generation theory has been inspired by two theories. Embedding these theories, fiscal decentralization is much favored by the second-generation theorists. First, Hayek (1945) suggested that because local governments have more knowledge about their population's preferences, they are in a better position to provide public services effectively. Thus, local governments should shoulder the main responsibilities of public services. Second, citizens' sorting process presses local governments to respond to local needs as noted by Tiebout (1956). This argument posits that citizens may move out from localities that provide inferior public services while collecting high taxes. Those places that match citizens' preferences mostly will be the destination due to the sorting process. "Votes with feet" create great pressure on local governments to respond to various needs since citizens' taxes are important sources of government revenues. The sorting process and inter-jurisdictional competition are beneficial for a better government. Thus, local governments should be empowered to perform effectively and reduce the possibility of sorting out.

Based on the above assumptions, central governments should constrain themselves to a limited area, such as macroeconomic management and policing the common market within the country. More important, many believe that empowering local governments may enhance the accountability and transparency of the governmental system (see Hankla, 2009). As citizens are more capable to collect information about the performance of local governments and impose sanctions on them through a sorting process or election systems, fiscal decentralization is beneficial to improve accountability, which is critical to quality governance.

Among others, "market-preserving federalism" can be regarded as one of the most important theories contributing to the second generation of fiscal federalism. China's experience in intergovernmental relations becomes a focus of the second generation of fiscal federalism. Qian and Weingast (1997) view China as a model of "market-preserving federalism." In the view of some second-generation theorists, "market-preserving federalism" will protect the market from being encroached by the government. Thus, although the Chinese government does not have a constitutional arrangement governing central–local relations, the model adopted by China is better than those applied in federal countries such as India and Brazil (Montinola et al., 1995; Martinez-Vazquez and Rider, 2006).

Following Montinola et al. (1995, p. 55), "market-preserving federalism" should satisfy the following conditions:

- A hierarchy of governments with a delineated scope of authority (for example, between the national and sub-national governments) exists so that each government is autonomous within its own sphere of authority.
- The sub-national governments have primary authority over the economy within their jurisdictions.
- The national government has the authority to police the common market and to ensure the mobility of goods and factors across sub-government jurisdictions.

- Revenue sharing among governments is limited and borrowing by governments is constrained so that all governments face hard budget constraints.
- The allocation of authority and responsibility has an institutionalized degree of durability so that it cannot be altered by the national government either unilaterally or under pressure from sub-national governments.

According to Montinola et al. (1995), the Chinese situation fits squarely with "market-preserving federalism." First, local governments in China have primary authority over economic affairs at the local level. It renders local governments more adaptive to local market and citizens' preferences. Second, excessive discretion of the central government was seriously constrained. Local governments have more autonomy over local affairs; at the same time, many local officials are more accountable to their constituencies than to the central government. Third, fiscal decentralization leads to the uprise of regional economic powers or even "regional property rights" (Granick, 1990), which strengthen inter-jurisdictional competition and cooperation. As noted by Montinola et al. (1995, p. 69), "these limits seem to endow the reforms with a degree of durability, making reversal more costly, if not impossible."

Similar to the Tiebout sorting, although the Chinese government lacks a clear guideline for protecting civil rights, inter-jurisdictional competition in China makes local governments responsive to the demands of investors, and ultimately to those of citizens (Jin et al., 1999). This is more evident when the mobility of goods and factors across jurisdictions has become intensified in recent years. Thus, the Chinese experience is a perfect case for illustrating the theories of fiscal federalism, especially those proposed by the second-generation theorists.

Many scholars further compare "federalism" in Russia and China. Due to different structures of fiscal decentralization, China is viewed as "market-preserving federalism" as noted, while Russia is depicted as market-distorting or market-hampering federalism (Dethier, 2000; Eckardt, 2002). Zhuravskaya (2000) notes that revenue sharing among regional and local governments in Russia yields limited incentives for local governments to improve revenues because the increments in revenue will accrue to regional governments instead. Thus, local governments were keen to toe the line of higher authorities. Furthermore, the industrial structure in Russia is more concentrated than in China. Thus, inter-jurisdictional competition is less intensive in Russia.[5]

Without free speech and rule of law, China still has impressed the world with decades of phenomenal and stable economic growth. This is largely due to the liberation of productive forces, or the increase in economic freedom and the guarantee by an authoritarian regime of a relatively secure environment for production and commerce, to which the Chinese-style intergovernmental fiscal relations in effect made a significant contribution (Feng et al., 2011).

Although the theory of "market-preserving federalism" is correct in pointing out the advantages of the Chinese fiscal system, it signals confusing information that China develops a federal system superior to some Western countries and, hence, a caveat is in order: the decentralization of economic and fiscal systems in China occurs in a politically unitary country with the central government imposing a centralized personnel control over local authorities. Decentralization in China was initiated with a top-down approach, not explicitly with a bottom-up approach and citizen participation; hence, Chinese-style decentralization is significantly distinct from many of the worlds' existing federal systems.[6]

Furthermore, the theory of "market-preserving federalism" neglects the issue of the sources of government power. It stressed economic and fiscal decentralization. Decentralization is nonetheless different from vertical and horizontal separations of power, or even checks and balances between central and local governments. In many cases, decentralization alone makes no sense. Instead, protecting individual rights of citizens is crucial to ensuring a well-functioning government and making decentralization, power separation and checks and balances effective. To some extent, freedom and liberty is much more fundamental than decentralization and vertical and horizontal power separations.

In addition, not all the five components of "market-preserving federalism" exist in China. For example, a trend in China is that national governments receive increasing revenue while leaving heightened responsibilities for local governments to handle (World Bank, 2007). It can be justified in part because a fiscally strong central government may manage macroeconomic issues much better. Thus, vertical revenue sharing is unavoidable. "Market-preserving federalism," nonetheless, takes limited revenue sharing for granted.

More generally, second-generation theories of fiscal federalism are not immune from criticism. For example, many argue that the sorting process (Tiebout, 1956) may not exist in reality. This situation is especially acute in developing countries where mobility of citizens may not be allowed by governments (Bardhan, 2002). In addition, many argue that decentralization alone may not improve public governance. Instead, decentralization may increase corruption and public misadministration at the local level (Smoke, 2006). Thus, additional mechanisms, for instance, local fiscal democracy, seem to be needed for decentralization to play a constructive role.

Refined fiscal federalism

The debate over fiscal federalism in the past decades has led up to some general principles for separating responsibilities between governments. Table 6.1 demonstrates the eight principles of fiscal federalism as defined by Brown and Jackson (1990).

In general, the normative principles of fiscal federalism put forward by Brown and Jackson (1990) are instrumental for assigning government responsibilities. Nevertheless, some should be modified. First, the principle of subsidiarity, which underlies all the above eight normative principles, should be added. This principle in a narrow sense implies that one should leave the lowest layer of government to excise a competence before considering taking it over (Kasper et al., 2000). Meanwhile, the principle in a broad sense means that the government doesn't have to take over a function if the society or market can do it better.

Table 6.1 Eight principles of fiscal federalism

Principles	*Description*
Diversity	Communities may have diversified needs of public services; thus, the federal system should allow flexibility for different localities in fiscal arrangements.
Equivalence	The benefits of public services are spatial. The nationwide defense system benefits the entire population in the country while some local services such as street lighting are strictly limited to small communities. The costs should be borne by residents who benefit directly from given public services.
Centralized redistribution	Finance ministries at the national level should carry out the redistribution function, such as progressive taxation and national grants. Local redistribution may not be effective.
Locational neutrality	Disparities in fiscal policy in different localities may affect economic activity. Therefore, different taxation should be discouraged in reality.
Centralized stabilization	Policies such as macroeconomic stabilization should be handled by national governments because local governments have no effective policy instruments to promote macro-policy in general.
Correction of spillovers	Spillovers among jurisdictions discourage local governments to improve their public services; therefore, higher-level authorities should interfere with local authorities only when needed.
Minimum provision of essential public services	Although various governments have distinct fiscal capacity, basic public services should be guaranteed in every jurisdiction in a country. That is, a minimum level of public services such as education and health care should be provided to every citizen no matter where she/he resides.
Equalization of fiscal position	Closely related to minimum provision of essential public services, some degree of fiscal equalization should be promoted in a given country. Regional disparities in fiscal capacity cannot be eliminated completely; thus, national transfers are needed to mitigate the problems of discrepancies between fiscal capacity and expenditure needs.

Source: Brown and Jackson (1990).

The reason why we add this principle is that it can also cover other fields, which are subject to this principle but not yet necessarily covered by these principles. For instance, many state-owned enterprises (SOEs) and state-owned banks (SOBs) operate in competitive and profitable sectors, thus crowding out private investments. According to this principle, the government should remove itself from these sectors. Another example is again related to the first example. The eight traditional principles don't deal with whether a SOE or SOB should be administered by central or local governments. However, according to the principle of subsidiarity, they are to be privatized and it is out of question to discuss which layer of government should administer them.

In addition to the principle of subsidiary, the principle of protecting individual rights should be incorporated, which is again the basis of all the other eight principles. As noted before, one of the shortages of fiscal federalism theories is that the sources of government power have been overlooked. Checks and balances between central and local governments are not sufficient to ensure a well-functioning, people-oriented government. Protecting individual rights, despite seemingly not close to intergovernmental management, is actually the ultimate goal of federalism. In fiscal federalism, this principle can be the fundamental principle among all. By restricting government power and preventing fiscal prolificacy, the principle of protecting individual rights is critical in realizing the benefits of fiscal federalism. According to this principle, a violation of property rights in the form of excessive fiscal extraction or reckless fiscal behaviors must be prohibited. It applies to the violation of property rights in the form of misallocation of fiscal resources to the creation and expansion of SOEs and SOBs in competitive and profitable sectors, not to mention assigning the extracted revenues to different layers of government.

Apart from the above two principles, some of the eight principles need to be further modified in order to improve their real-world validity. For example, the principle of locational neutrality disapproves of the differential taxation in various localities. However, modest differences in taxation may be encouraged because this will facilitate inter-jurisdictional competition, which is vital to curb local predatory behaviors, and should be considered as a balance to the principle of locational neutrality and adopted in combination with the latter. Brown and Jackson (1990) suggest that macroeconomic policy should be carried out by the national government. We concur with this judgment in general. Nevertheless, the principle of centralized stabilization also has some deficiencies. For one thing, this principle may not be applicable to mega-states like China with a huge territory and large population, with some provinces being larger in both size and population than many European countries. With regional macroeconomic conditions differing significantly, provincial governments definitely have capacity, and the need to conduct parts of macroeconomic policy. In the same vein, the principle of centralized redistribution should not be emphasized strictly. Regarding the case in China, the social security systems are decentralized. Provincial governments can initiate and carry out fiscal transfers among their jurisdictions. The accounts for social insurances can be mutually accepted and made transferrable, rather than centralized.

Correction for spillovers may not need to be conducted by higher authorities as well. Adjoining jurisdictions can make arrangements to solve the negative aspects of spillovers. It is increasingly common to see that local governments cooperate to address some shared concerns in China. Second, it may not be effective and responsive if higher authorities provide public goods and services to avoid spillovers. For example, pollution control has a spillover effect on other localities. Centralized coordinated pollution control, however, does not always result in an improvement in the environment since many local governments often develop some countermeasures. Therefore, we argue that the principles of centralized redistribution and stabilization can be replaced by a ***principle of relatively centralized redistribution*** and a ***principle of relatively centralized stabilization***. Furthermore, locational neutrality should be combined with an additional principle, that of tax competition.

If the above newly added and modified principles can be strictly implemented, the favorable effects of fiscal federalism would be materialized. We call this type of fiscal federalism *refined fiscal federalism*. As shown in Table 6.2, refined fiscal

Table 6.2 Principles of three models of fiscal federalism

No.	*Traditional Fiscal Federalism*	*Revised Principles of Fiscal Federalism*	*Refined Principles of Fiscal Federalism*
1	Diversity	Diversity	Diversity
2	Equivalence	Equivalence	Equivalence
3	Centralized redistribution	Relatively centralized redistribution	Relatively centralized redistribution
4	Locational neutrality	Locational neutrality	Locational neutrality of central tax, together with local tax competition
5	Centralized stabilization	Relatively centralized stabilization	Relatively centralized stabilization
6	Correction for spillovers	Correction for spillovers	Equalization of fiscal position
7	Minimum provision of essential public services	Minimum provision of essential public services	Minimum provision of essential public services
8	Equalization of fiscal position	Equalization of fiscal position	Equalization of fiscal position
9	X	X	Tax competition
10	X	X	Principle of subsidiary
11	X	X	Protecting individual rights, implicitly including some principles of fiscal democracy

Source: The principles of traditional fiscal federalism are retrieved from Brown and Jackson (1990), while those of revised fiscal federalism are retrieved from Qian and Weingast (1997), Oates (2005) and Weingast (2005).

Note: X denotes "non-existent."

federalism includes the following principles: diversity, equivalence, relatively centralized redistribution, locational neutrality, relatively centralized stabilization, equalization of fiscal position, minimum provision of essential public services, equalization of fiscal position, tax competition, the principle of subsidiarity and the principle of protecting individual rights. The first eight principles are developed from the traditional or general fiscal federalism theory while the last three crucial principles are additional. These three additions are not only reflective of the reality of Chinese fiscal federalism but also are theoretically justified and derived from relevant general theories, such as theories of tax competition, good governance and public service delivery. Tax competition between and among states is inter-jurisdictional and intergovernmental contests under federalism, aiming at attracting direct or indirect foreign investment, high-value human resources and other state-favored industries in the era of globalization, which contribute to state policy innovation, creating comparative advantage, stimulating economic growth and leading to good governance of the public budget (Martin, 1940; Oates, 1972; Wilson, 1986; Devereux et al., 2007; Jacobs et al., 2010). Governance requires "horizontal" bargaining and coordination, rule of law, transparency, accountability, responsiveness, inclusiveness and meaningful citizen participation. Public delivery service also requires meaningful and informed "citizen participation" in the conduct of public affairs and public service delivery (Chen, 2001; Batley, 2004; Demmers, 2004; Surendra and Abraham, 2004; Shah, 2005; Jing and Savas, 2009; UNESCAP, 2009).

Refined fiscal federalism comes with a few critical implications. First, refined fiscal federalism is an updated version of the first and second generations of fiscal federalism. It not only covers but also modifies the core theory attached to fiscal federalism. Three crucial components, e.g., that of tax competition, subsidiarity and protection of individual rights, are added in order to improve the theoretical and practical strengths of fiscal federalism.

Second, refined fiscal federalism attaches significant attention to power sources of federalism. That is, federalism serves to protect individual rights and basic freedom while containing the power of the government. This point is particularly essential in many developing countries, as authoritarian regimes tend to ignore individual rights while maintaining a de facto federalism. In many cases, intergovernmental management may simply turn into collusions among national and local governments in developing economies.

Third, refined fiscal federalism encourages horizontal cooperation as a solution to many intergovernmental disputes. As noted before, one of the great weaknesses of the first generation theory of fiscal federalism is that central coordination is viewed as the best choice for addressing intergovernmental problems. However, taking the principle of subsidiarity into consideration, horizontal coordination or outsourcing of some public service delivery (such as wastewater treatment) can be an efficient priority solution.

We categorize a given country into a specific type as shown in Table 6.3, without blurring federalism and fiscal federalism. Constitutional and economic efficiency are added in the table to show the performance of a given fiscal

Table 6.3 Fiscal arrangements

Type / country	*Type of Federalism in Country*	*Definition*	*Performance*
1	Refined fiscal federalism	Conforms equally to principles of refined fiscal federalism. In addition, the country is a federal system.	Highest level of constitutional and economic efficiency
2	De facto refined fiscal federalism	Conforms to the principles of refined fiscal federalism, but is not a federal system	Highest level of constitutional and economic efficiency
3	Traditional fiscal federalism	Conforms to all principles of traditional fiscal federalism but without principles 9, 10 and 11. In addition, the country has a legal framework of fiscal federalism.	High level of constitutional efficiency. Highest level of economic efficiency
4	De facto traditional fiscal federalism	Conforms to all principles of traditional fiscal federalism while a legal framework of fiscal federalism and principles 9, 10 and 11 are absent	High level of constitutional efficiency. Highest level of economic efficiency
5	Quasi-traditional fiscal federalism	Conforms to most principles of traditional fiscal federalism while principles 9, 10 and 11 are absent	Low level of constitutional and economic efficiency
6	Non-fiscal federalism	Does not conform to the principles of fiscal federalism	Lowest level of constitutional and economic efficiency

Source: The authors.

relation. Constitutional efficiency is “related closely to the whole discussion about the efficiency or efficacy of rules as opposed to discretionary actions” (Buchanan, 2004), whereas the term “constitution” is meant as “a set of rules that is agreed upon in advance and within which subsequent action will be conducted” (Buchanan and Tullock, 1962). Accordingly, the constitutional efficiency can be defined in our context as the efficiency of the rules, which is attainable if following all these principles of refined fiscal federalism. Without the proposed three additional principles of federalism, the constitutional efficiency would not be able to be attained. Economic efficiency is what the traditional fiscal federalism is designated for. It is defined as what is standard in public finance theory, i.e., allocative efficiency or “Pareto efficiency” (Musgrave, 1959). The fiscal federalism is designed to best realize the three above-mentioned main functions of government, i.e., allocation function, redistribution and stabilization function (Musgrave and Musgrave, 1984) by best assigning fiscal instruments to various layers of government (Oates, 1999). It is also the inevitable instrument to attain the implied combination of efficiency and equality of a fiscal federalism system. However, without the proposed three additional principles of fiscal federalism, such economic efficiency cannot be attained.

From Type 6 to Type 1, both constitutional and economic efficiency ascend. Economic efficiency is at the highest level amongst Type 1, 2, 3, and 4 while constitutional efficiency is at the highest level amongst Type 1 and 2.

In accordance with Table 6.3, refined fiscal federalism performs best since both constitutional and economic efficiency are at the highest level. De facto traditional fiscal federalism, although it conforms to all principles of traditional fiscal federalism, lacks some fundamental principles such as subsidiary and protection of individual rights. As will be pointed out later, the Chinese fiscal system qualifies as a quasi-traditional fiscal federalism, in which most traditional or general principles of traditional fiscal federalism can be found while principles 9 and 11 are absent. Thus, both constitutional and economic efficiency is low.

De facto traditional fiscal federalism should conform to all principles of traditional fiscal federalism while both a legal framework of fiscal federalism and principles 9, 10 and 11 are not available. In the case of China, intergovernmental fiscal relations cannot satisfy all conditions of traditional fiscal federalism. In addition, principles 10 and 11 are to a great extent absent in China.

Fiscal federalism in the Chinese context

We argue that quasi-traditional fiscal federalism is a much closer reality in China since the early 1980s, as fiscal arrangements conform to most principles of traditional fiscal federalism except principles 9, 10 and 11 as noted in Table 6.3.

It is important to note that in China, fiscal decentralization is only one side of the coin. China adopted a decentralized system in the 1980s, which was fundamentally altered in 1994. Since then, China has adopted a combination of revenue centralization and expenditure decentralization. Two concrete objectives of the 1994 fiscal reform were to increase the central share in the total fiscal revenue and the ratio of fiscal revenue to GDP. The central government has ultimate authority over all the important issues related to fiscal policy while local governments have some degree of autonomy in daily fiscal management. Table 6.4 illustrates the situation.

In greater detail there exists some kind of bureaucratic bargaining and coordination between central and local governments in China. For instance, the level-by-level management governs the vertical intergovernmental relationships wherein the central government lays down the principles with regard to fiscal relations between the central and provincial governments. Provincial governments then make decisions over fiscal systems within their jurisdictions. Local governments may bargain with the central government for financial resources and preferential policies through some informal channels. However, the Party

Table 6.4 Assignment of responsibilities in the Chinese government

Type	*Formal System*	*De Facto System*
Fiscal management	Centralization combined with administrative and fiscal decentralization. Level-by-level management over personnel and fiscal management. The center lays down the regulations over fiscal relations among central and provincial governments while leaving sub-national governments to determine fiscal arrangements in their jurisdictions.	Provincial governments enjoy substantial discretion over fiscal managements in their jurisdictions. Some degree of checks and balances between the central and local governments, but not formally recognized
Taxation power	Tightly controlled by the national government	Local governments alter both tax base and tax rate through various ways to attract investments; local governments impose also extra fees or cost apportion on individuals and firms, collect land transfer revenue and raise debts.
Power of collecting fees and special funds	Tightly controlled by higher authorities such as central and provincial governments. Ultimate power held by the central government	Beside the approved, locally imposed fees and special funds, local governments collect non-approved fees (system-external revenue) and impose cost apportion for local projects.
Tax revenue	Central and shared taxes are collected by the central government while local governments receive local taxes. Fee collection concentrated at provincial, municipal and county levels	Local governments maximize those revenues, which go to local coffers.
Responsibility and provision of services	Defense and foreign affairs are provided by the central government.	Local governments involved in foreign affairs. Costs of defense are partly borne by local governments.
	Cross-provincial road construction and maintenance are provided by the central government. The construction of across-regional roads within the respective province is provided by the provincial government. Municipal and county roads are provided by municipal and county governments. The central government provides subsidies to local road construction.	County and township governments put numerous resources on road construction, partly through budgetary, partly extra-budgetary channels (including land transfer revenue), debt financing and even illegal cost apportion.

Type	*Formal System*	*De Facto System*
	Public utilities are provided by local governments.	Budgetary and extra-budgetary revenue (including land transfer revenue), debt financing and even illegal cost apportion are used as financing channels.
	Primary and secondary education and health are provided by city and county governments. Higher education is partly provided by central government, partly by local governments.	For primary and secondary education, city and county governments provide the bulk of the services. Central and provincial government provide fiscal transfers.
	Social security in general provided by prefecture-level city governments or county-level governments. Social security for personnel of the central government and central-level state-owned enterprises is provided by the central government.	No difference to formal institution. Central government and provincial governments provide subsidies for various social insurance schemes. Significant parts of many social security funds were often utilized for other purposes and governments have to refill them.
	Policy subsidies to enterprises are provided by central and provincial governments.	No difference to formal institution

Source: The authors with reference to *China Fiscal Yearbook* and data provided by the Ministry of Finance of the PRC, various years.

and the central government in China forbid collective bargaining arrangements or resistance by provincial governments against the center (Ma, 1995).

The institutional setting of the Chinese fiscal system entails both central control over local governments and some degree of local autonomy in an informal fashion. The Organic Law of Local People's Congresses and Local Governments stipulates that lower governments should abide by decisions and orders made by higher authorities. The term is nonetheless vague so that local governments, more often than not, create some circumvention to mitigate the burdens imposed by higher authorities.

Although taxing power is formally controlled by the central government, local governments alter both the tax base and tax rate through various means in regard to local taxes and locally collected shared taxes. Local governments also have an informal taxation power related to fees and funds collected by them. More recently, local governments have piled up substantial local debts through local government financing vehicles. Nevertheless, almost no local government will go bankrupt in China partly due to the fact that the central government has to bail out local governments in reality. The latest development is that the central government will help clean up local debt totaling RMB 2–3 trillion in order to avoid more disastrous consequences of local debt defaults (Reuters, 2011).

It is argued that decentralization on the expenditure side is exceptionally high in China, and far exceeds the international standard (World Bank, 2002). However, this also suggests a substantial autonomy of local governments as well as excessive responsibilities imposed on local authorities. Nevertheless, statistics over expenditure by central and local governments attest to dysfunctions of intergovernmental fiscal management in China. The central government, in recent years, has increasingly issued unfunded mandates, such as nationwide civil service pay raises, improvements in education and health provisions, to local governments; thus, local fiscal burdens have become increasingly large (Wong, 2005). The fiscal position of local governments has been tremendously alarming thus far. In response to local complaints, the central government heightened fiscal transfers to local governments, especially those in the Central and Western Region. Both the general and earmarked transfers have increased rapidly since the 1994 fiscal reform. However, the share of general transfers in accordance to prevailing international definitions has lagged behind the share of earmarked transfers until now. The consequences of enlarged central transfers are that the ministry control over local expenditure (see Wu, 2013) has been enhanced since earmarked transfers instead of general transfers readily impose central intervention on local governments. More central mandates combined with central transfers indicate the intensification of central control over fiscal policy in China. Despite some improvements during the economic reform, the Chinese fiscal system still conforms mostly to the quasi-traditional fiscal federalism. The economic and constitutional efficiencies are low in this system, and thus need to be improved in the future.

Table 6.5 summarizes the Chinese fiscal system in comparison to different prototypes of fiscal federalism. Although some view China as an ideal type of market-preserving federalism, the Chinese central – local fiscal relations are still far from the revised or refined principles of fiscal federalism discussed earlier.

Brown and Jackson (1990) argue that a successful federal system should be able to respond to diversities of various regions, suggesting that local governments may have substantial autonomy in local affairs. In China, a unitary fiscal system was imposed by the central government to govern intergovernmental fiscal relationships between the central government and provincial governments. However, there is some degree of fiscal discretion in an informal fashion, as mentioned above. Meanwhile the center allows an institutional diversity across Chinese regions below the provincial level. Echoing Brown and Jackson (1990), refined fiscal federalism suggests that a relatively centralized redistribution is desirable. In the case of China, the relatively centralized redistribution is partially applied with reference to provincial or prefectural, or county-level governments, who, for example, assume responsibilities over a unified management of social security funds. The central government is responsible for the central social security fund addressing central government officials and employees of centrally

Table 6.5 Fiscal federalism and the Chinese situation

Traditional Fiscal Federalism	*Revised Fiscal Federalism*	*Refined Fiscal Federalism*	*Chinese Situation*
Diversity	Diversity	Diversity	Unitary system imposed on sub-national governments. Provincial governments have discretion in local affairs.
Equivalence	Equivalence	Equivalence	Partial equivalence
Centralized redistribution	Relatively centralized redistribution	Relatively centralized redistribution	Partially realized. Areas, such as social security, are locally financed and distributed.
Locational neutrality	Locational neutrality of central tax, together with local tax competition	Locational neutrality of central tax, together with local tax competition	Central government unable to maintain locational neutrality of central taxes as different tax rates are set across regions and special economic zones
Centralized stabilization	Relatively centralized stabilization	Relatively centralized stabilization	Centralized stabilization exists. Local conditions make relative centralized stabilization possible.
Correction for spillovers	Correction for spillovers	Equalization of fiscal position	Weak equalization of fiscal position and correction for spillovers
Minimum provision of essential public services	Minimum provision of essential public services	Minimum provision of essential public services	Minimum provision of essential public services
Equalization of fiscal position	Equalization of fiscal position	Equalization of fiscal position	Unsatisfactory equalization of fiscal position; wide disparities among provinces
X	X	Tax competition	Existent, not transparent
X	X	Principle of subsidiarity	Partially realized
X	X	Protection of individual rights. Implies inclusion of principles of fiscal democracy	Improving but still unsatisfactory

Source: The authors.

Note: X denotes "non-existent."

controlled state-owned enterprises. A system of mutual acceptance and convertibility of local social security systems is in progress.

Other inadequacies in Chinese intergovernmental fiscal relations include wide fiscal disparities among provinces. Hence, the principle of equalization of fiscal position has been far from being implemented despite substantial central transfers in recent years. Central transfers mitigate the problem of fiscal disparities to some extent, but transfers per se are not without flaws. Mounting central transfers lead to some harmful negative consequences: some governments in the western region in China make great efforts in rent-seeking for winning central transfers and central projects, while overlooking local institutional development, and a positive business and investment climate. In addition, the protection of individual rights is rather problematic in China. Extra fiscal burdens imposed on enterprises and individuals are widespread at the local level, which are called the "three arbitraries," including arbitrary fees, arbitrary fines and arbitrary apportionments (Lin, 2002; Gong, 2006). It means that enterprises and individuals should not only pay formal taxes to the state, but also additional fees to satisfy local governments or cadres' personal needs.

China's central–local fiscal relations have been marked by perpetual changes amidst economic restructuring. Fiscal decentralization on the expenditure side has been paralleled by centralization on the revenue side since 1994. China's intergovernmental fiscal relations are not without controversies; intergovernmental fiscal relations are interpreted as either market-preserving federalism or de facto fiscal federalism. There are marked differences between the formal system and de facto system. More important, although significant progress has been made, reforms in the fiscal system have not developed into an efficient and effective system of intergovernmental fiscal management.

There is not an optimal system of intergovernmental fiscal management or a set of rules governing the decentralization process that could fit all situations. Yet, there are key elements in the design of a fiscal system that fosters both constitutional and economic efficiency, such as the decentralization of fiscal powers and resources accompanied by relevant responsibilities as well as strengthening the fiscal capacity of various levels of government.

Concluding discussion

Based on an updated version of first- and second-generation fiscal federalism, this chapter develops a refined fiscal federalism framework that modifies the core theory. Here, the principle of tax competition is added as a complement to the principle of locational neutrality along with the principles of subsidiarity and individual rights, as the latter two are fundamental principles of fiscal federalism. Refined fiscal federalism attaches significant attention to power sources of federalism wherein federalism serves as the defender of individual rights and basic freedom while containing the power of predatory government. Refined fiscal federalism also encourages horizontal cooperation as a solution to many intergovernmental disputes.

Refined fiscal federalism should perform best in terms of constitutional efficiency and economic efficiency. This is particularly clear when compared to the quasi-traditional fiscal federalism in today's China. Thus, refined fiscal federalism is both a logical and desirable direction in the next step of Chinese fiscal reforms. It may not be feasible to move on all these fronts simultaneously. What is essential, however, is that the direction is clear, a starting point is correctly identified, reform programs are consistent and the government should persevere with further reforms.

Notes

1 The structure of a country's intergovernmental fiscal relation plays a crucial role in shaping the conduct and performance of sub-national governments, which, in turn, has a potentially important influence on a country's economic growth (Martinez-Vazquez and Rider, 2006).
2 See Weingast (2009).
3 Musgrave and Musgrave (1984, p. 9) argue "although social goods are available equally to those concerned, their benefits may be spatially limited."
4 For the definition of federalism, see Stanford Encyclopedia of Philosophy (2010).
5 A dispersed industrial structure stimulates inter-jurisdictional competition in China. This was an unintended consequence of the "Third Front" Project between 1964 and 1973. This point benefited greatly from the discussion of Xingyuan Feng, one coauthor of this paper in 2004 with Professor Herrmann-Pillath. Also see Xiao et al. (2011).
6 At the end of the Cultural Revolution, the political, economic and social system was close to collapse in China. Under such strong pressures, the central government devolved part of its fiscal and economic power to local governments to motivate them to rehabilitate, stabilize and strengthen local economic development. At the same time, some farmers organized themselves to implement a household responsibility system under strong pressure for survival in the Xiaogang Village of Fengyang County, Anhui Province. This system was thus a spontaneous order at the outset and later recognized and extended by the central government (Feng, 2002).

Bibliography

The original source of this chapter is: Feng, Xingyuan, Christer Ljungwall, Sujian Guo, and Alfred M. Wu. Fiscal Federalism: A Refined Theory and Its Application in the Chinese Context, in *Journal of Contemporary China* (A SSCI Journal), Vol. 22, Nr. 82, 2013, pp. 573–593.

Bahl, R.W. *Fiscal policy in China: Taxation and Intergovernmental Fiscal Relations.* (South San Francisco: The 1990 Institute), 1999.

Bardhan, P. Decentralization of Governance and Development. *Journal of Economic Perspectives*, 16(4), 2002, pp. 185–205.

Batley, R. The Politics of Service Delivery Reform. *Development and Change*, 35(1), 2004, pp. 31–56.

Bird, R. *Fiscal Federalism*, 2009. Available at: www.urban.org/uploadedPDF/1000529.pdf

Brown, C.V. and Jackson, P.M. *Public Sector Economics*, 4th ed. (Oxford: B. Blackwell), 1990.

Buchanan, J.M. Constitutional Efficiency and the European Central Bank. *The Cato Journal*, 24(1–2), 2004, pp. 13–17.

Buchanan, J.M. and Tullock, G. *The Calculus of Consent, Logical Foundations of Constitutional Democracy.* (Ann Arbor: University of Michigan Press), 1962.

Chen, G. China's Nongovernmental Organizations: Status, Government Policies, and Prospects for Further Development. *The International Journal of Not-for-Profit Law*, 3(3), 2001. Available at: http://www.icnl.org/research/journal/vol3iss3/art_2.htm

Demmers, J., Fernandez, J. and Hogenboom, B., eds. *Good Governance in the Era of Global Neoliberalism: Conflict and Depolitisation in Latin America, Eastern Europe, Asia and Africa.* (London: Routledge), 2004.

Dethier, J. *Governance, Decentralization, and Reform in China, India, and Russia.* (Boston, Dordrecht and London: Kluwer Academic Publishers), 2000.

Devereux, M., Lockwood, B. and Redoano, M. Horizontal and Vertical Indirect Tax Competition: Theory and Some Evidence from the USA. *Journal of Public Economics*, 91, 2007, pp. 451–479.

Dye, T.R. *American Federalism: Competition Among Governments.* (Lexington, MA and Toronto: Lexington Books), 1990.

Eckardt, S. *Russia's Market Distorting Federalism: Decentralisation, Governance, and Economic Performance in Russia in the 90s*, 2002. Available at: http://www.oei.fu-berlin.de/politik/publikationen/AP42.pdf

Feng, X. *EU and Germany: The Way to Address the Regional Disparities* (in Chinese). (Beijing: zhongguo laodong shehuibaozhang chubanshe), 2002.

Feng, X., Ljungwall, C. and Guo, S. Re-interpreting the 'Chinese Miracle'. *International Journal on World Peace*, XXVIII(1), 2011, pp. 7–40.

Gong, T. Corruption and Local Governance: The Double Identity of Chinese Local Governments in Market Reform. *The Pacific Review*, 19(1), 2006, pp. 85–102.

Granick, D. *Chinese State Enterprises: A Regional Property Rights Analysis.* (Chicago: University of Chicago Press), 1990.

Groenendijk, N. *Fiscal Federalism Revisited.* Paper Presented at Institutions in Transition Conference Organized by IMAD, Ljubljana, Slovenia, 2002.

Guo, G. Vertical Imbalance and Local Fiscal Discipline in China. *Journal of East Asian Studies*, 8(1), 2008, pp. 61–88.

Hankla, C.R. When Is Fiscal Decentralization Good for Governance? *Publius: Journal of Federalism*, 39(4), 2009, pp. 632–650.

Hayek, F.A. The Use of Knowledge in Society. *American Economic Review*, XXXV(4), 1945, pp. 519–530.

Herrmann-Pillath, C. and Zhu, Q. Stille Föderalisierung oder kalte Desintegration? – Zum institutionellen Wandel des chinesischen Steuerstaates. *WeltTrends, Zeitschrift für internationale Politik und vergleichende Studien (Hrsg.)*, Nummer 21, 1998, pp. 103–130.

Hollander, R. Rethinking Overlap and Duplication: Federalism and Environmental Assessment in Australia. *The Journal of Federalism*, 40(1), 2009, pp. 136–170.

Huang, Y. *Inflation and Investment Controls in China: The Political Economy of Central-local Relations during the Reform Era.* (Cambridge, England and New York: Cambridge University Press), 1996.

Jacobs, J., Ligthart, J. and Vrijburg, H. Consumption Tax Competition among Governments: Evidence from the United States. *International Tax and Public Finance*, 17, 2010, pp. 271–294.

Jin, H., Qian, Y. and Weingast, B.R. *Regional Decentralization and Fiscal Incentives: Federalism Chinese Style*, 1999. Available at: www-econ.stanford.edu/faculty/workp/swp99013.pdf

Jing, Y. and Savas, E. Managing Collaborative Service Delivery: Comparing China and the United States. *Public Administration Review*, 69(s1), 2009, pp. s101–s107.

Kasper, W. and Streit, M.E. *Institutional Economics: Social Order and Public Policy.* (Cheltenham: Edward Elgar Publishing), 2000.

King, D.N. *Fiscal Tiers: The Economics of Multi-Level Government.* (London: Allen and Unwin), 1984.

Krug, B., Zhu, Z. and Hendrischke, H. *China's Emerging Tax Regime: Devolution, Fiscal Federalism, or Tax Farming?* (ERIM Report Series Reference No. ERS-2004–113-ORG), 2004.

Lin, S. Too Many Fees and Too Many Charges: China Streamlines Fiscal System, in John Wong and Lu Ding, eds., *China's Economy into the New Century: Structural Issues and Problems.* (Singapore: Singapore University Press), 2002, pp. 182–192.

Ma, J. Modeling Central-Local Fiscal Relations in China. *China Economic Review*, 6(1), 1995, pp. 105–136.

Martin, J.W. Tax Competition between States. *Annals of the American Academy of Political and Social Science*, 207, 1940, pp. 62–69.

Martinez-Vazquez, J. and Rider, M. Fiscal Decentralization and Economic Growth: A Comparative Study of China and India. *Indian Journal of Economics & Business*, Special Issue China & India, 2006, pp. 29–46.

Ministry of Finance. *China Fiscal Yearbook.* (Beijing: Zhongguo caizheng zazhishe: Journal of China State Public Finance), 2007.

Ministry of Finance Website. 2011. Available at: www.mof.gov.cn

Montinola, G., Qian, Y. and Weingast, B.R. Federalism, Chinese Style: The Political Basis for Economic Success in China. *World Politics*, 48(1), 1995, pp. 50–81.

Musgrave, R.A. *The Theory of Public Finance: A Study in Public Economy.* (New York: McGraw Hill), 1995.

Musgrave, R.A. and Musgrave, P. *Public Finance in Theory and Practice.* (New York: McGraw-Hill Book Company), 1984.

National Bureau of Statistics of China. *China Statistical Yearbook.* (Beijing: China Statistic Press), 2010.

Oates, W.E. *Fiscal Federalism.* (New York: Harcourt Brace Jovanovich), 1972.

Oates, W.E. *The Economics of Fiscal Federalism and Local Finance*, Wallace E. Oates, ed., (Cheltenham and Northampton: Edward Elgar Publishing), 1998.

Oates, W.E. An Essay on Fiscal Federalism. *Journal of Economic Literature*, 37(3), 1999, pp. 1120–1149.

Oates, W.E. Toward a Second-Generation Theory of Fiscal Federalism. *International Tax and Public Finance*, 12, 2005, pp. 349–373.

Qian, Y. and Weingast, B.R. China's Transition to Markets: Market-Preserving Federalism, Chinese Style. *Journal of Policy Reform*, 1, 1996, pp. 149–185.

Qian, Y. and Weingast, B.R. Federalism as a Commitment to Preserving Market Incentives. *Journal of Economic Perspectives*, 11(4), 1997, pp. 83–92.

Reuters. *China to Clean Up Billions in Local Government Debt.* June 2, Available at: www.reuters.com/article/2011/05/31/us-china-economy-debt-idUSTRE74U3CO20110531, 2011.

Roland, G. *Transition and Economics: Politics, Markets, and Firms.* (Cambridge, MA: MIT Press), 2000.

Shah, A. *Public Services Delivery*. (Washington, DC: The World Bank), 2005.

Sharma, C.K. When Does Decentralization Deliver? *The Dilemma of Design, South Asian Journal of Socio-Political Studies*, 6(1), 2005a, pp. 38–45.

Sharma, C.K. The Federal Approach to Fiscal Decentralization: Conceptual Contours for Policy Makers. *Loyola Journal of Social Sciences*, XIX(2), 2005b, pp. 169–188.

Smoke, P. "Fiscal Decentralization in Developing Countries: Theory and Practice," in Y. Bangura and G.A. Larbi eds., *Public Sector Reform in Developing Countries: Capacity Challenges to Improve Services*. (New York: Palgrave Macmillan/ UNRISD), 2006, pp. 195–227.

Stanford Encyclopedia of Philosophy. 2010. Available at: www.plato.stanford.edu

Surendra, M. and Abraham, B. *Good Governance, Democratic Societies and Globalization*. (New York: Sage Publications), 2004.

Tiebout, C. A Pure Theory of Local Expenditures. *Journal of Political Economy*, 64, 1956, pp. 416–424.

Tsai, K.S. Off Balance: The Unintended Consequences of Fiscal Federalism in China. *Journal of Chinese Political Science*, 9(2), 2004, pp. 7–26.

UNESCAP. *What Is Good Governance*, 2009. Available at: http://www.unescap.org/pdd/prs/ProjectActivities/Ongoing/gg/governance.asp

Weingast, B.R. Second Generation Fiscal Federalism: The Implications of Fiscal Incentives. *Journal of Urban Economics*, 65(3), 2009, pp. 279–293.

Wilson, J.D. A Theory of Interregional Tax Competition. *Journal of Urban Economics*, 19(3), 1986, pp. 296–315.

Wong, C.P.W. *Can China Change Development Paradigm for the 21st Century*. Working paper FG 7, 2005/03. (Berlin: Stiftung Wissenschaft und Politik), 2005.

Wong, C.P.W. and Bhattasali, D. *China: National Development and Sub-National Finance* (in Chinese). (Beijing: zhongxin chubanshe), 2003.

World Bank. *China National Development and Sub-National Finance*, Report N.22951-CHA, (Washington, DC: The World Bank), 2002.

World Bank. *China Improving Rural Public Finance for the Harmonious Society*. (Washington, DC: The World Bank), 2007.

Wu, A.M. How Does Decentralized Governance Work? Evidence from China. *Journal of Contemporary China*, 22(81), 2013, pp. 379–393.

Xiao, C., Sun, J. and Ye, Z. The Evolution of the Regional Economic Development Strategy of China. *Learning and Practice*, 7, 2011, pp. 5–11.

Xu, C. and Zhuang, J. "Why China Grew: The Role of Decentralization," in Peter Boone, Stanislaw Gomulka and Richard Layard, eds., *Emerging from Communism: Lessons from Russia, China, and Eastern Europe*. (Cambridge: MIT Press), 1998, pp. 183–212.

Zheng, Y. *De Facto Federalism in China: Reforms and Dynamics of Central-local Relations*. Series on Contemporary China. Vol. 7, 2007.

Zhuravskaya, E.V. Incentives to Provide Local Public Goods: Fiscal Federalism, Russian Style. *Journal of Public Economics*, 76(3), June, 2000, pp. 337–368.

7 Local government debt and municipal bonds in China

Problems and a framework of rules

Administrative and fiscal decentralization in the early 1980s led to the formation of strong local political interests and to a certain degree of regional and local autonomy with relatively hard budget constraints for local governments (Herrmann-Pillath and Feng, 2004; Jin et al., 2005)[1] However, it took place under a system of authoritarian government, including both the central government and local governments. The decentralization gave rise to fierce competition among local governments in China (Li et al., 1998; Feng, 2010). And the close link between local government revenue and expenditure provides strong incentives for local governments to drive local economic development. Although China is formally a unitary system, government behavior can be well described by employing a "competitive governments" paradigm (Breton, 1996; Herrmann-Pillath, 1999; Herrmann-Pillath and Feng, 2004) or a "competitive authoritarianism" paradigm (Levitsky and Way, 2013).[2]

Local state developmentalism has led to rapid industrialization and urbanization across China, which have progressed at breakneck speed since 1996. During both processes, local governments have been faced with increased financial pressure and a widening gap between revenue and expenditure. Accordingly, local governments, especially at the city and county level, have faced continually increasing debts. This problem became much more serious after a rapid expansion of local government debt took place with the central government's launch of the stimulus package in 2008. It has caught the attention of the government and society. More and more people are looking at problems of near unrestrained debt financing behavior, low fiscal transparency and high fiscal risks of local governments. "Municipal bond" issuances as part of actual or hidden local government debts have become increasingly visible. The enforcement of a suitable framework of rules regulating local debt financing, including "municipal bond" issuance, has become necessary in this situation.

Almost without exception, the existing literature on local government debt in China mainly deals with the size, growth, causes and risks of local government debt. However, because of the adoption of a proactive debt financing strategy never seen before and encouraged by the central government, as well as the rapid increase in the size of local government debt since 2008, the literature on the empirical assessment of the level of fiscal risks of local governments prior to that year has become less relevant. Given the lack of transparency of local debt financing, up-to-date and in-depth empirical studies are still in the early stages, mainly focusing on some particular dimensions of local government debt. For instance, He and Man (2011) assess the size, growth, causes and risks of interest-bearing debts of local government investment and financing vehicle companies of Chinese provinces. Their study shows that the fiscal risks in some provinces are relatively high in terms of the ratio of debt balance to local budgetary revenue. However, the assessed debt constitutes only a part of local government debt, thus an incomplete reflection of the overall situation of debt financing of local governments. Yu and Wei (2012) estimate the total size of government debt in 2010. Lu (2012) analyzes quite systematically the problems of local government vehicle companies in China. As a supplement to the empirical assessments, additional analyses are made from a political economy perspective. Brennan and Buchanan (1980, 1985) elaborate on government behavior with self-interest maximizing models and derive some necessary constitutional rules for "taming" the government from a theoretical perspective of constitutional economics. Feng and Li (2005) and Zheng (2012) adopt such a perspective to elaborate the self-interest-oriented "leviathan" features of local governments in debt financing in China and problems with the lack of democracy and fiscal surveillance, and identified their negative effects on the private sector development of local China.[3] In summary, there is still a lack of a balanced analysis of the local government debt and the issuance of "municipal bonds" from both the political economy and public finance perspectives.[4] Without such an analysis, we are less likely to get deep insights into the problems of local government debt and to identify rules regulating local governments' debt financing behavior.

Local government debt in China: the current situation

There are a number of different definitions of local government debts in China. The first is a narrow one: actual government debt when total expenditure exceeds total revenue of local governments. Therefore, local government debt can be interpreted as the difference between the total local expenditure and the total local revenue of a local government, where the total local expenditure includes the budgetary, extra-budgetary and system-external expenditures and total local revenue includes the budgetary, extra-budgetary and system-external revenues.[5] This definition includes many types of debts, such as government loans from businesses or banks, short-term intergovernmental loans, debts owed to construction companies or teams for public works projects, etc.

However, local governments in China must also take on the debt for projects of companies that are directly or indirectly under them. Therefore, a broader definition of government debt should also include part or all of such debt. Unless otherwise stated, local government debt in China in this chapter should be understood in the context of this second, broader definition. The "Budget Law" of China explicitly provides that:

> Local budgets at various levels shall be compiled according to the principles of keeping expenditure within the limits of revenue and maintaining a balance between revenue and expenditure, and shall not contain deficits. Except for where provided by law or State Council regulation, local governments shall not issue local government debt bonds.
>
> (Article 28)

The "General Lending Provisions" and "Guarantee Law" of China also prohibit local governments from taking loans from banks. However, local governments deal with deficit financing through their projects or companies, or some subordinate public institutions such as public schools or hospitals and are able to find ways to issue openly or covertly, directly or indirectly, a large amount of debt and this phenomenon has become increasingly common. The whole process lacks transparency. The debt financing problem has become more serious since 2008 with the global financial crisis, when the central government released an RMB 4 trillion stimulus package and allowed local governments to engage in deficit financing proactively by taking out large loans from banks to invest mainly in infrastructure projects. This set the stage for the emergence of a large number of local financing vehicle companies (*difang rongzi pingtai gongsi*, hereafter referred to as "financing vehicle companies") connected to local governments.

Statistics from the China Banking Regulatory Commission show that as of May 2009, there were 8,221 financing vehicle companies at the provincial, prefecture and county levels registered in China. Of these, 4,907 were registered at the county level. The 2010 Report on Regional Financial Operations of the People's Bank of China shows that by the end of 2010, there were over 10,000 financing vehicle companies established by local governments, up 25 percent over 2008. Of these financing vehicle companies, 70 percent were at the county level or below. According to the audit report of the National Audit Office (2011), there were in total 6,576 financing vehicle companies at the provincial, prefecture and county level in 2010.

These financing vehicle companies have been quickly established by local governments through the allocation of land, equity shares, fees and national bonds and have a level of capital or cash flow that allows them to carry out financing. When needed, they can also act to supplement funds from general fiscal revenue and land revenue, and even provide direct or indirect government credit guarantees. These companies use various methods to bring financing capital into their regions, then transfer it to public enterprises or institutions for projects of varying degrees of profitability, including urban infrastructure projects.

Financing vehicle companies usually appear as urban construction investment companies (*chengtou gongsi*). They may also be called "urban development" and "urban financing" companies. The operational structure of financing vehicle companies is shown in Figure 7.1. These companies are always fully owned or

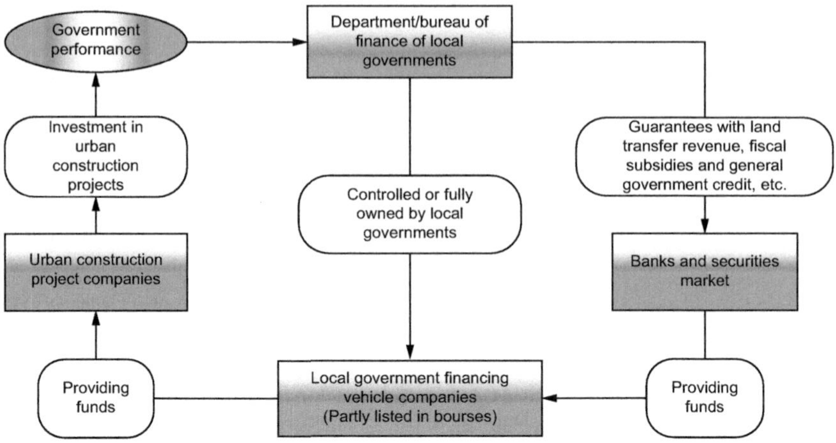

Figure 7.1 Operating model of local government financing vehicle companies
Source: The authors.

controlled by local governments. Some are even listed on stock exchanges. Local governments use land transfer revenue, fiscal subsidies or even government credit as guarantees for financing vehicle companies looking to obtain loans, or issue "urban investment bonds" to financial organizations or other investors on securities markets. These financing vehicle companies then take the funds that they have collected and invest them in urban construction projects. However, these projects often cannot repay the loans that fund them. The responsibility for repaying these loans thus falls on the local governments, which implies that if a large-scale debt crisis emerges, the ones ultimately responsible are taxpayers at the local level or possibly even at the national level. Under this backdrop, debt accumulated by financing vehicle companies continues to grow. The 2010 data deserves special attention since several sources revealed different data for the first time. Based on the comparison between them, one can estimate the overall debt size of local governments or even the whole government system more precisely than before.

Figure 7.2 shows the scale of interest-bearing debt held by 340 of these companies that issued urban investment bonds in China from 2006 to 2009. These data include short- and long-term loans, interest payable and bonds payable held by them. The size of interest-bearing debt of these companies increased rapidly from RMB 4.79 trillion in 2008 to RMB 7.97 trillion in 2009, reflecting the central government's new policy of encouraging local governments' deficit financing through their financing vehicle companies.

Local governments' debt financing levels have increased rapidly up to now. Figure 7.3 shows the incomplete size of local governments' direct debt, revealed by various government departments. It increased from RMB 8.3 trillion in 2010

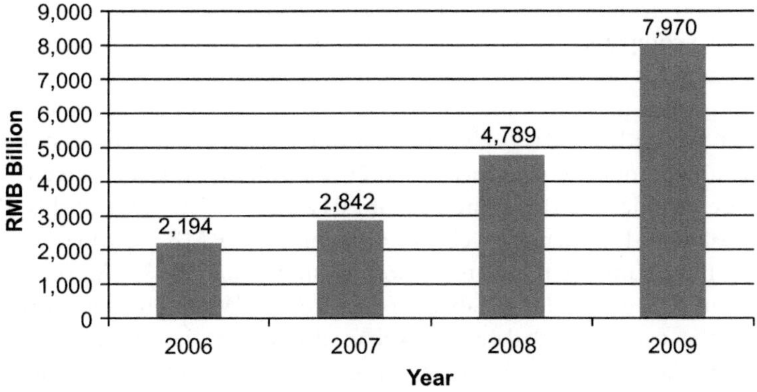

Figure 7.2 Amount of interest-bearing debt held by financing vehicle companies, 2006–2009

Source: He and Man (2011).

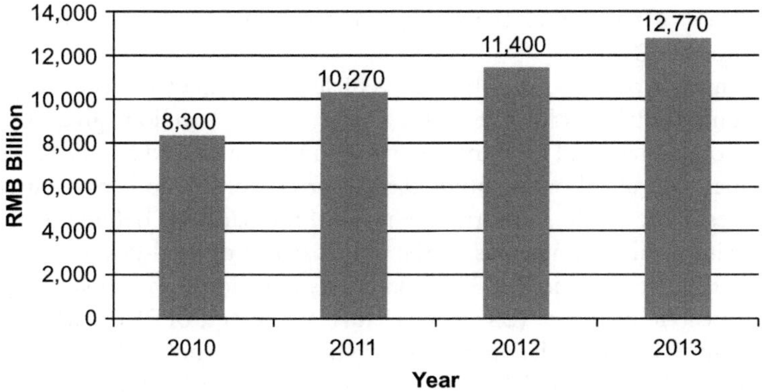

Figure 7.3 Amount of direct debt of local governments, 2010–2013

Sources: National Audit Office (2011); Yang (2013).

Note: The 2010 data includes the direct debt held by all financing vehicle companies audited by the National Audit Office (2011). The data of 2011–2013 are revealed or predicted by the State Asset Supervision and Administration Commission (Yang, 2013). These government departments reported only a narrowly defined debt size of a part of vehicle companies, while the debt size of the remaining part has been kept hidden resulting in an underreporting of the actual direct debt size of vehicle companies. Therefore, the data in Figure 7.3 are incomplete.

to RMB 11.4 trillion in 2012. According to the data revealed by the China Banking Regulatory Commission, bank loans alone held by financing vehicle companies amounted to RMB 9.2 trillion by the end of 2012 (Netease Finance, 2013a), while the debt balance of urban investment bonds, mid-term notes and short-term financing notes, private targeted financing instruments and asset-backed notes of financing vehicle companies reached RMB 2.5 trillion (Zhang, 2013). This does not include the direct debt held by government departments, construction project companies, units for public services such as public schools and hospitals and payables for construction teams or companies.

In the following, we can estimate the total debt of local governments in China at the end of 2012. The total amount of direct and indirect debt held by local governments was at least RMB 25.11 trillion, or 48.35 percent of Gross Domestic product (GDP) at the end of 2012 (Table 7.1). Out of this, the total balance of loans for financing vehicle companies was RMB 9.2 trillion, according to the China Banking Regulatory Commission (Shi, 2013). According to the calculation based on the databank provided by Wind Financial Information System, the total debt balance of urban investment bonds, mid-term notes, short-term financing notes, private targeted debt financing instruments and asset-backed notes was RMB 2.5 trillion (Zhang, 2013). Because of the strict regulations of the China Banking Regulatory Commission and the Securities Commission, local governments increasingly rely on funds from trust fund borrowings, which are off-balance-sheet, and often request repurchase agreements as repayment guarantees. According to the China Trust Business Association, the balance of trust fund borrowing totaled RMB 0.5 trillion at the end of 2012 (Xu, 2013).

The amount of borrowing by non-vehicle government project companies or public units can be estimated to be at least RMB 3 trillion, given that many project companies of all levels not only use funds transferred by financing vehicle companies, but also borrow funds directly from banks and other sources. This is a low estimate by the authors. The ratio of the narrowly defined debt balance of financing vehicle companies to the debt balance of local government departments and institutions in the 36 jurisdictions at various levels that were audited by National Audit Office (2013) was 1.8:1 at the end of 2012, which is much lower than 3:1, the underlying ratio of China as a whole adopted here.[6] This also implies that non-vehicle borrowing could eventually reach around half of the direct debt of financing vehicle companies across China, i.e., as high as around RMB 5 trillion. The total payables for construction companies or teams or other units, and the balance of contingent debt can be estimated to be at least RMB 3.04 trillion for both, if taking only 20 percent of the above sum of direct debt as the basis for estimation. Hidden debt related to retirement insurance totalled RMB 2.23 trillion.[7] The balance of local government bonds (*difang zhengfu zhaiquan*) was RMB 650 billion at the end of 2012, according to Ministry of Finance statistics. Township-level government liabilities totaled RMB 830 billion in 2010 (Yu and Wei, 2012). We take this figure as the estimated debt size of township-level governments at the end of 2012, while at the village level, the direct debt is estimated as RMB 120 billion. Villages are not legally governments, but here their function and operation is similar to self-governing entities as seen in the West. According to the report of the Team of the Project on "Research on Problems with County and Township Level Government Finance in China" (2005), the average net debt balance of each

Table 7.1 Estimates of local government liabilities in China at the end of 2012 (RMB trillion)

Type of Liability	*Amount*	*Scope*	*Description*
Total loans of financing vehicle companies	9.2	Direct debt	Data provided by the China Banking Regulatory Commission (Shi, 2013).
Total debt balance of urban investment bonds, mid-term notes, short-term financing notes, private targeted financing instruments and asset-backed notes of financing vehicle companies	2.5	Direct debt	Calculation based on Wind Financial Information System (Zhang, 2013). The balance of urban investment bonds and mid-term notes is RMB 1.44 trillion (Li, 2013).
Trust fund borrowings (*xintuo zijin*) of local governments	0.5	Direct debt	Statistics of China Trust Business Association (Xu, 2013); including those of financing vehicle companies and local government departments and institutions.
Other borrowings of local government departments or institutions	3.0	Direct debt	Low estimate by author.
Payables of local governments for construction companies or teams	3.04	Direct debt	Low estimate of around 20% of the above total direct debt of local governments.
Contingent debt held by local governments	3.04	Contingent debt	Hidden guarantees by local government, low level of estimation of 20% of the above total debt of local governments excluding the payables.
Hidden debt related to retirement insurance	2.23	Hidden debt	Wang (2013).
Local government bonds	0.65	Direct debt	Ministry of Finance data.
Estimated township-level government debt	0.83	Direct or contingent debt	Yu and Wei (2012).
Estimated village liabilities	0.12	Direct or contingent debt	Authors' estimate.
Total	25.11		
Percentage of GDP	42.35%		

Source: China Banking Regulatory Commission; China Trust Business Association; Li (2013); Ministry of Finance; Yu and Wei (2012); Wang (2013); Xu (2013); Zhang (2013); and authors' estimates.

village was RMB 200,000 in 2002. The number of administrative villages was over 600,000 in 2012, according to the Ministry of Civil Affairs. Taking this average debt size as the base and disregarding the growth rate and a reduction in the number of villages through mergers, the total village net liabilities are estimated to be at least RMB 120 billion in 2012.

For comparison, Standard Chartered (2013) estimated the current amount of the outstanding debt of financing vehicle companies is in the range of RMB 14–15 trillion, some 30 percent of Chinese GDP at the end of 2012. Our estimate of the debt is larger. Such a comparison is not very meaningful since it is unclear how Standard Chartered defines local government debt in China.

Table 7.2 estimates the total debt held by the central government and local governments in China, which is around RMB 44.89 trillion, taking 86.44 percent of GDP at the end of 2012. This does not include contingent liabilities held by the central government. For comparison, the International Monetary Fund (IMF, 2013) released an estimate of the total "augmented debt" of the Chinese government, including the central government and local governments, which totaled nearly 50 percent of China's GDP in 2013. Fewer forms of government debt are included in the definition of the "augmented debt." According to the IMF's explanation, augmented government debt not only includes the debt of a general government, but also captures borrowing by LGFVs (local government financing vehicle companies) through market

Table 7.2 Estimated debts of central and local governments in China at the end of 2012 (RMB trillion)

Type of Debt	*Amount*	*Description*
Local government debt	25.11	See Table 7.1.
Central government domestic debt	7.67	Ministry of Finance statistics
Central government foreign debt	0.08	Ministry of Finance statistics
Central government policy financial bonds	7.84*	*China Urban and Rural Finance Daily* (2012)
Central government debt related to the transfer of non-performing loans to asset management companies	1.4	Yu and Wei (2012)
Department of Railways liabilities	2.79	Netease Finance (2013b)
Total government debt	44.89	
Percentage of GDP	86.44%	

Sources: *China Urban and Rural Finance Daily* (2012); Ministry of Finance; Netease Finance (2013b); Yu and Wei (2012); and estimates included in the previous table.

* This amount is the balance to December 24, 2012.

financing channels. As in other countries, it excludes liabilities of regular SOEs and other state entities as well as contingent liabilities, such as NPLs in the banking sector, policy bank loans and pension liabilities. At the same time, it measures gross debt only, and so excludes government assets (IMF, 2013).

Characteristics and problems of local government debt

While there are currently many types of local government debt, there are two rough categories that can be identified based on levels of local government activity in debt financing. The first is active debt financing, which comes from the need for capital to fund local construction and economic development. The other is passive debt financing due to excessive fiscal pressure, leaving governments without any other choice but to borrow money and go into debt. This also includes other passive liabilities caused by the bankruptcy of state-owned enterprises, losses from guaranteed projects and the takeover by local governments of financial repayment responsibilities. There are essential differences in their causes, characteristics and impact on the local economy. The first type is a general liability and can have a positive impact on the local economy. This type of liability can be standardized in the form of municipal bonds. However, the second type is incurred due to hidden deficits and bad debts. This should not be replaced by issuing municipal bonds. In general, local government debt has the following characteristics:

1 The overall debt level of local governments is already very high and will further increase in the coming years. The total amount of the debt balance of local governments rose rapidly after 2008 and reached a record high of 42.35 percent of Chinese GDP at the end of 2012, as shown in Table 7.1. According to the estimate by the National Audit Office (2011), which encompasses only a narrowly defined debt size of a part of vehicle companies, local governments' ratio of total debt balance to their total regular budgetary revenue was 70.45 percent across the whole country, and it even exceeded 100 percent in 78 prefecture-level cities and 99 counties (or county-level cities or districts) at the end of 2010. The ratio of direct debt to the consolidated local budgetary revenue (including fiscal transfer) of 10 out of 36 audited local governments exceeded 100 percent at the end of 2012, with 188.95 percent as the highest ratio (National Audit Office, 2013). The central government and local governments have not taken measures to reduce debts, and they have kept expanding their spending, so that the overall trend will be a further rise in the debt levels of local governments.
2 The debt levels differ significantly from one region to another. According to He and Man (2011), the levels of total interest-bearing debt of financing vehicle companies of Chinese provinces differed widely in 2009: the ratio of total debt balance of financing vehicle companies to local governments' total regular budgetary revenue ranged from 0.11 in Guizhou Province to 12.42 in Jiangsu Province.

3 The debt structure is multi-leveled and complex. This is mainly due to remaining historical issues and the many reforms that have been implemented over the past nearly two decades. Local government debts can be grouped into six categories based on their characteristics (Fan et al., 2001; He and Man, 2011; Wang, 2013). The six categories are:

  a Debts held by local governments, their functional departments and associated entities for public services such as public schools and hospitals. This includes loans from international financial organizations, on-lending funds raised by the Ministry of Finance by issuing treasury bills (*guozhai zhuan dai zijin*), local government bonds issued by the Ministry of Finance on behalf of local governments or by local governments themselves, loans from domestic financial institutions and loans from other units or individuals;
  b Debt guaranteed directly or indirectly by local governments;
  c Dead debt caused by losses incurred by local government-owned companies such as grain companies, or payables of local governments such as unpaid salaries and benefits, and outstanding payments for local government procurements;
  d Debt not directly owed by local governments, but by local government-owned trust and investment companies, banks or local financing vehicle companies;
  e Debt resulting from failed local state-owned enterprises and the takeover by local governments of financial repayment responsibilities such as the case of local government closing down Rural Cooperative Funds (*nongcun hezuo jijinhui*) by order of the central government in 1999;
  f Hidden debt related to retirement insurance. Categories c, e and f involve passive debt financing. Other categories are involved with both active and passive debt financing.

4 The funds raised are mainly used for local construction projects. Of the local spending of RMB 3,643.4 billion audited by the National Audit Office (2013), 92.14 percent was used for construction projects in transport, public utilities, education, culture, science, health care, agriculture, water conservation, environmental protection, affordable housing and land take and reserve.

5 More and more debt is raised through financing vehicle companies, especially by taking bank loans and issuing urban investment bonds. The total amount of local government bonds issued by the Ministry of Finance on behalf of local governments and by several local governments themselves as pilot measures has also increased. According to the National Audit Office (2013), 78.07 percent of the debt balance of the audited 36 local governments was loans, and 12.06 percent was bonds at the end of 2012.

Debt financing was discouraged by the central government before the outbreak of the global financial crisis, explicitly encouraged by the central government in 2009, and tolerated by it to maintain a strong stimulus to the economy.[8]

However, some measures were taken to control fiscal risks related to local government debt, mainly by standardizing the operations of financing vehicle companies and strengthening the loan control and the control of issuance of urban investment bonds.[9] However, both loan balances and amount of urban investment bonds keep increasing. Local governments also resort to other types of financial services, such as off-sheet financial services of banking institutions and trust products to meet their demand for additional funds. In addition, the central government imposed upon local governments the task of building 36 million apartments for low-income people in the framework of the government's affordable housing program across China within the 12th planning period (2011–2015). This has led to greater fiscal pressure on local governments and the necessary tolerance by the central government of local governments' debt financing on a vast scale.

The following problems can be identified with the debt financing of local governments:

1. There is a lack of transparency in local governments' debt financing. During the period prior to the mid-1990s, when fiscal affairs were managed independently, local debt mainly comprised open debts like unpaid accounts, the issuing of bonds and bank loans. Since the implementation of the Budget Law, released in 1994, a large part of debt has become hidden or contingent. In recent years, not only has open debt greatly increased, hidden debt has also steadily risen. For example, loans and financing through financing vehicle companies since 2008 are a type of open debt. Hidden debts mainly include contingent liabilities and unpaid costs such as salaries, work expenses, venue costs, roadways and bridges.
2. A part of the debt is not fully covered by guarantees or collaterals (He and Man, 2011; National Audit Office, 2013). In addition to the debts of financing vehicle companies, some guarantors provide guarantees for debt held by other companies. If there is a default with these other companies, the real value of the guarantees provided for the debt held by a vehicle company will be affected. There are also often cases where the same collateral (for instance, the use right of a piece of land) is repeatedly provided to back several debts owed to different creditors (so-called *yi wu duo ya*).
3. The assets of a significant part of financing vehicle companies are relatively poor and the registered capital of many financing vehicle companies is insufficient, unlawfully paid in, partly falsified or partly diverted for other uses. By the end of 2012, out of the 223 financing platform companies of the 36 audited local governments, there were 94 companies possessing assets of RMB 897.592 billion that are not or not easily realizable, accounting for 37.60 percent of their total assets. Of these, five have registered capital of RMB 56.19 billion that is not in place; six companies reported assets amounting to RMB 37.107 which did not exist; and local governments of three provincial capital cities injected unqualified capital totaling RMB 4.553 billion in the form of parks, roads and other public assets

(National Audit Office, 2013). Around one sixth of all the financing vehicle companies had problems related to false or insufficient capital registration or improper use of registered capital in 2010 (Nie, 2013). Taking Liaoning Province as an example, in over one third of the 184 financing vehicle companies in that province, part of their registered capital was false in 2010, and the income of 100 of them was insufficient to cover the repayment of debt and interest in the same year (Li, 2011).

4 It is pervasive that local governments provide indirect or implicit guarantees for the debt repayment or provide some subsidy in case of a default with a local government-related debt (Cao, 2013; Yang, 2013).

5 The repayment of local government debt relies heavily on land transfer revenue and new borrowings and the repayment pressure is considerable (National Audit Office, 2011, 2013). According to the National Audit Office (2011), local governments of 12 provinces, 307 cities and 1,131 counties guaranteed repayment of 37.96 percent of the assessed local government debt from their land transfer revenue in 2010. Of the debt payable in 2010, 54.65 percent was repaid from funds raised by new borrowings. According to the National Audit Office (2013), at the end of 2012, the ratio of direct debt repayments to consolidated local budgetary revenue (including fiscal transfer) of the audited governments of 13 provincial capital cities exceeded 20 percent, with 38.01 percent as the highest ratio at the end of 2012; the debt/asset ratio of 68 of the above-mentioned 223 financing vehicle companies of the 36 local governments exceeded 70 percent. Furthermore, the income of 151 out of the 223 financing vehicle companies was insufficient to repay the principal and interest due in 2012. According to the National Audit Office (2011), the period of 2012–2013 was the beginning of the peak period for local debt coming into repayment. The total debt to be repaid by financing vehicle companies should have been at least RMB 1.84 trillion in 2012 and will be at least RMB 1.22 trillion in 2013. This is a huge challenge for these financing vehicle companies.

6 The default rate has been increasing since 2010. According to the National Audit Office (2011), one fifth of the 6,500 financing vehicle companies on its list registered a loss at the end of 2010. Some defaults occurred already in 2010. The default rate of local governments in four prefecture-level cities and 23 counties exceeded 10 percent. According to the National Audit Office (2013), the default rate relating to the repayments of the consolidated debt (including direct debt, guarantees and other related debt) of the above-mentioned 36 audited local governments was 0.75 percent at the end of 2012, up 0.48 of a percentage point from 2010. The default rate of the governments of two audited provincial capital cities exceeded 10 percent, with the highest reaching 16.36 percent at the end of 2012. According to the National Audit Office (Nie, 2013), the ratio of repayments based on new borrowing exceeded 55 percent among 358 out of the more than 6,500 financing vehicle companies, and the default rate of around 150

exceeded 16 percent in 2011. Such repayment arrangements are almost a synonym for hidden defaults. Consequently, news reports on defaults that took place in 2012 are just the tip of the iceberg.[10]

7 There is a lack of effective control by both the central government and local citizens of local governments' debt financing behavior that is characterized by a continuous expansion of the debt size with accumulating fiscal and financial risks.

Apart from some technical issues, a large share of the above-mentioned problems can be traced back to a series of institutional shortcomings in the governmental system of China.

1. There is a lack of local democracy in fiscal decision making, including decisions on debt financing and in the management and supervision of fiscal affairs. The power of local governments is not restricted by local citizens, but rather selectively restricted by the central government that is facing a problem of asymmetric information in its supervision of local governments' behavior.
2. Chinese local Party and government leaders are appointed rather than actually elected, so they are more responsible to the upper level of Party organs and government than to local citizens.[11]
3. In general, one of the most important criteria to measure the performance of local government leaders is still the economic performance of their jurisdictions (Figure 7.1), and good economic performance in terms of a high GDP growth rate is essential for their careers.[12] Investment in infrastructure is a key factor in attracting investment in local industries.[13]
4. The term of office of local government leaders is five years and they are not liable for the debt repayment after their leave.
5. Fiscal revenue has been centralized since the 1994 fiscal reform, which leads to strategic actions by local governments, including the large-scale sale of land use rights and deficit financing. The 2008 global financial crisis allowed more leeway for local governments to raise more debt.

The above analysis shows that the fiscal and financial risks have been mounting. It would be fatal to underestimate their threat to fiscal and financial stability in China. This partial loss of control has brought about and exacerbated debt and could lead to widespread financial crises that are already brewing. The new borrowings used for old debt repayments and the defaults that have occurred up to now are clear-cut signals of a looming fiscal crisis. Since most of the borrowings are money from banks or the interbank market, the looming fiscal crisis has already spread over to financial risks in the banking sector. The banking sector has already accumulated a relatively high non-performing loan (NPL) rate because of local government debt financing. However, the NPLs are mainly hidden behind new loans after loan restructuring. The whole process is a dangerous trip toward a fatal collapse of the financial system.

Chinese economic growth has slowed since 2011. Given the high level of local government debt, the new leadership has distanced itself from launching a new stimulus package that would lead almost inevitably to a fiscal and financial crisis. In addition, the real level of existing local government debt still needs to be clarified and it is a ticking time bomb. That is why the National Audit Office, in August 2013, started a new round of audits of local government debt, aimed at thoroughly checking on the local debt situation.

Management and characteristics of urban investment bonds and local government bonds

As shown in Table 7.1, local governments currently use mainly bank capital in their deficit financing, while urban investment bonds and local government bonds are secondary. However, urban investment bonds and local government bonds deserve special attention since bond issuance and management are essential to ensure transparency of local government debt, if bonds are standardized and become their major debt financing channel. Municipal bonds are a common, internationally accepted method of issuing local government debt. This kind of debt instrument is not limited to municipal governments and includes bonds issued by all levels of government below the national level. In general, municipal bonds cannot be used to cover regular budgetary deficits of local governments and can only be used for specific purposes. First, they are used to make up for differences in tax revenue and expenditure or to resolve problems caused by temporary fiscal operations. Second, they are used to provide financial support for various public capital investment programs such as the maintenance of public works, building of schools, water drainage systems, etc. Third, they are used to support and subsidize programs that spur local development and improve the lives of local residents, including the building of industrial parks, parking lots, etc. (Fisher, 1996).

In a broad sense, municipal bonds refer to bonds issued by local governments or other authorized agencies and guaranteed by local governments. Funds collected are mainly used for the construction of local public infrastructure. In mature economies such as the United States, municipal bonds usually have four specific characteristics (Ba and Xing, 2009): they are issued by the local government or an authorized agency thereof; the collected funds are used for the construction of public infrastructure at the municipal/local level; there is a diverse range of sources for repayment; and they enjoy special tax-free exemptions. It is necessary to compare urban investment bonds and local government bonds with the standard municipal bonds in the world and look into the features of these two kinds of Chinese "municipal bonds."

Urban investment bonds

Urban investment bonds are issued as enterprise bonds by financing vehicle companies that are owned or controlled by local governments in China. The first such company was founded in 1992 in Shanghai city, and the first urban investment

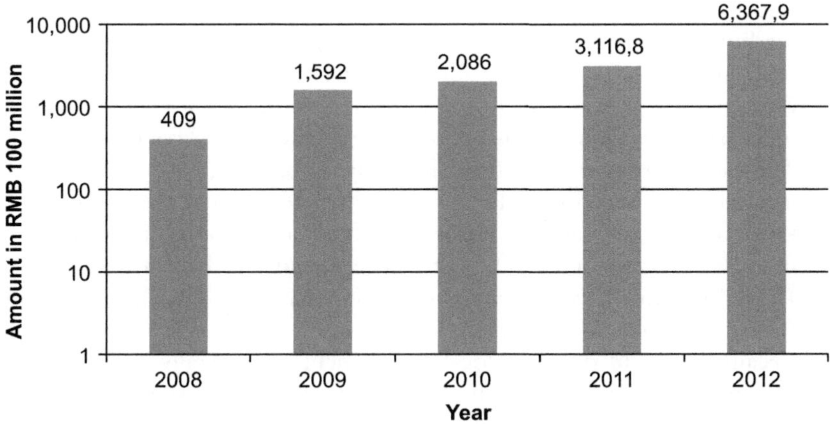

Figure 7.4 Amount of newly issued urban investment bonds in China, 2008–2012
Sources: Zhao (2010), China Industry Research Net (2012), Yang (2013), Zhang (2013).

bond was issued by a financing vehicle company in Chongqing city in 2012. In the period 2008–2012, the total amount of urban investment bonds issued was around RMB 1.36 billion (see Figure 7.4). They basically meet the standards for municipal bonds, but are not tax free. Urban investment bonds can be regarded as "quasi municipal bonds." The funds raised are used for the building of public infrastructure. In this regard, the financing vehicle companies are in fact similar to subordinate departments of local governments, companies in which they have controlling shares or agencies of local governments. Local governments also provide them with hidden guarantees. Therefore, local governments and financing vehicle companies can be regarded as a single entity with mutual obligations.

Urban investment bonds are transacted in the interbank debt market. The explosion of urban investment bonds is related to the increasing rate of urbanization and even more so to the demand of local governments for the expansion of their spending in the face of the global financial crisis. Urban investment bonds issued in 2009 totaled RMB 159.2 billion, while the amount issued in 2012 reached a record high of RMB 636.79 billion (Figure 7.4).

The operation of the urban investment bonds has the following general characteristics:

1 They are issued by financing vehicle companies, which are in fact issuing them on behalf of the local government.
2 While urban investment bonds are issued as enterprise bonds, they actually function as municipal bonds.
3 Local governments provide hidden guarantees, which means that if there is the risk of defaulting, the local government will step in and provide assistance and bailouts.

4 The cost of financing is higher than the average level for enterprise bonds. According to research by He and Man (2011), the average coupon rate for bonds issued by financing vehicle companies from 2006 to 2009 was 5.72 percent, while the rate for enterprise bonds of the same period was 5.63 percent. The explanation for this is that the higher cost of financing for urban investment bonds reflected the market actors' concern about risk.
5 The capital brought in by financing vehicle companies is generally used by local governments for public infrastructure projects and the company itself is not actually obligated to repay the debt. The party responsible for repayment is the work unit or the local government to which it belongs.
6 Urban investment bonds and the entities that issue them are not subject to local democratic processes.
7 Because the debt owed by local governments is generally rather large, the risk of defaulting is also high. This makes the risk of defaulting on urban investment bonds also relatively high.

Local government bonds

The experiment with the issuance of local government bonds started in 2009. The total balance of local government bonds was RMB 650 billion at the end of 2012, which makes up only 2.6 percent of the total debt of local governments in China. Most local government bonds are issued by the Ministry of Finance on behalf of local governments. The Ministry charged an issuance fee at a rate of 0.5 percent and 1.0 percent of the face value of the bonds issued in 2012. Only Shanghai, Zhejiang, Guangdong and Shenzhen are part of a trial self-issuing pilot program begun in 2012. The government bonds issued by trial provinces or cities are fixed-rate bonds with a term structure of three years or five years and made up 50 percent of all bond issuances approved by the State Council. Local governments below these levels of government do not have access to this financing instrument. But the provinces or cities that receive funds through the above issuance of local government bonds are allowed to on-lend the funds to lower levels of government. All of the local government bonds are to be repaid by the Ministry on behalf of these local governments. It is obvious that local governments lack local autonomy and local democracy in the whole process, which makes them only "quasi municipal bonds." The central government is still in control of any payment crisis that may result from its issuing these bonds on behalf of local governments or issuing them by local governments themselves since the central government is in charge of repayment on behalf of all the relevant local governments.

The major characteristics of local government bonds are as follows:

1 The introduction of local government bonds used a central government "top-down" format, but its motivation comes from local governments' need to issue bonds. The Ministry of Finance has played a key role in this area.

2 The central government emphasizes that it is acting as an agent to control the risk of bonds and ensure against default.
3 The amount of bonds that can be issued has been increasing, but is still limited. It has increased from RMB 200 billion in 2009 to RMB 350 billion in 2013.
4 Currently, only provincial-level governments and Shenzhen as a special economic zone is allowed to issue local government bonds directly. However, the issuance has not been extended to all levels of local government, including the various levels of government under them.
5 The overall operations lack local autonomy and local democracy. However, it will be difficult to use the current top-down control mechanism as a springboard to true municipal bonds. Local democracy is needed to turn this kind of bond into true municipal bonds.

Rules for local government debts and bond issuance

As the local governments' debts have been mounting to a critical level since 2008, increasing local fiscal transparency and restricting local governments' behavior has also become a necessity. Management of revenue and expenditure, including the power to issue debt for financing, is one of the competencies that local governments should have under the tax sharing system. Local government debts are a reality and the causes are complex. Simply forbidding local governments to raise debts by issuing debt bonds, or not giving local governments full status to issue Local Government Debt and Municipal Bonds in China and repay their own debt bonds will not effectively stop local governments from collecting fees and raising debts in other ways. Quite the opposite, it will push these fee collections and debt financing activities out of the formal fiscal system, not only breeding illegal practices, but also threatening financial stability and China's macroeconomic balance. Allowing and standardizing taxation and debt financing, including the issuing by local governments of municipal bonds, is the only way to solve current problems at their root.

Allowing local governments to issue municipal bonds simply requires clear limits on use and supervision. Once a certain scale is reached and it is cost effective, this is the most effective way to legalize current local government debt practices and make them more transparent and standardized. To a great extent, not only will this relieve the fiscal pressure felt by local governments, it will also allow China's strict bond regulation system to make these types of programs more transparent and standardized (An and Wang, 2000; Gu, 2000; Xu, 2001; Wei, 2004). As the content of this chapter does not cover the entire debt issuing system, we simply attempted to analyze what has been said thus far and listed a few of the major problems facing local governments' bond issuance. Based on this, we can now propose basic policies from a constitutional and regulatory perspective. The main focus will be on clarifying the whole necessary institutional framework and local government responsibilities, and strengthening rule-based constraints, thus preventing uncontrolled expansion of local debts to which no one is held accountable.

1 A proper political reform is needed to constrain local government behavior. This would consist of:

Enforcement of a constitutional reform and public participation: The Constitution, fiscal constitution or any other basic law should clearly stipulate the power of local governments to manage public affairs, collect taxes and arrange expenditures. This will strengthen the sense of responsibility that governments feel to the people within their jurisdiction. In terms of municipal bond issuance and other fiscal decision-making processes, it will strengthen channels through which the public can participate. When organizing funding for and implementation of major municipal construction projects, it may also be advisable to have a referendum or hearing on the matter.

Introduction of local autonomy and democracy: This can help standardize the handling of local government debts, urban investment bonds and local government bonds. It can force local governments to arrange their expenditure based on local citizens' preferences and the competencies of local governments. They can then raise funds based on need, through both taxation and debt issuance. Local autonomy refers to self-determination and self-governance by local citizens in the provision of local public goods and services, which differs from any idea of political independence or separation.

2 Strict rules of fiscal surveillance, auditing and supervision should be established and followed:

Strengthening fiscal surveillance: The core of the current problem is the uncontrolled expansion of local government debt, which may also be the biggest risk of allowing local governments to openly issue debts. Even if a number of measures could be conceived of to hedge this type of risk, the best policies must also have clear debt ceilings for each level of government at a higher legal level (ideally at the constitutional level). An example of this would be the local setting of upper limits based on the ratio of local government debt to local GDP or local fiscal revenue (these upper limits could be further divided into those for an emergency and general situations within the respective jurisdictions).

Auditing and supervisory regulation: Strict accounting procedures and standardized accounting records should also be put into place to allow for independent fiscal audits. There is also a need for a national committee to develop regulations on municipal bonds that place limits on the actions of local governments. These regulations would also deal with the underwriting of municipal bonds, broker–dealers and banks.[14]

3 A set of concrete fiscal rules for local government debt financing, including municipal bond issuance, should be established and enforced:

Uses of municipal bonds and reasons for their issuance: Considering the lack of standardization in the operations of local governments in China as well as their wide range of responsibilities, it is necessary to strictly limit the uses of municipal bonds and the reasons for their issuance, especially in issuing bonds to balance budget deficits. One possibility is the establishment of conditions for bond issuance, allowing local governments to issue bonds only if the overall debt levels and the budget deficits are kept within a certain range, for instance, for three consecutive years. Furthermore, authorization to issue bonds would be revoked for the following fiscal year should the government incur a large fiscal deficit. In considering the difficulty of external supervision and the possibility of local governments deliberately using funds for other purposes, one option when first issuing municipal bonds could be to only allow local governments to issue revenue bonds with clear-use purposes (as in the building of a local roadway) instead of general obligation bonds. As local democratic fiscal procedures improve, this could be relaxed to include general obligation bonds.

Debt issuing entities and procedures: To change the current chaos of governments, their various departments and even companies or public service units under their charge (such as public schools and hospitals), so that debt raising is predictable and transparent, only a single or relatively limited number of specified entities would be authorized to issue debt (i.e., government financial departments). Procedures for issuing debt must be standardized by law, including methods for application, approval, credit rating, commissioned agencies and public placement. The forced proportional distribution of debt must also be prohibited. Purchasing qualifications should also be more closely controlled, prohibiting administrative work units and companies with a certain portion of state-owned assets from purchasing, to prevent covert proportional distribution.

Internal controls and external supervision: Due to the difficulty of quickly establishing a democratic system that can respond to the preferences of local residents in the short term, a plausible option for internal control is to strengthen the power of the local people's congress. Requirements can be put in place that a single bond or a series of bonds to be used for a specific project of a certain scale must go through hearings and be approved by the people's congress (and consultative committee). External supervision is usually carried out by financial authorities, but as a transitional measure, the supervisory powers of higher levels of government and the people's congress could be strengthened. This can be done in such a way that local debt issuances above a certain scale must be approved by a higher level of government or the people's congress, based on a minimum standard. They can also be required to submit periodic reports on the state of the debt, its market price and efficiency.

Procedures for passing on debt to a new administration: When a new administration comes in or major officials are replaced, a major audit of debt must be carried out. The scale of the debt issued during a term and the efficiency of its use during a certain period of time after that term has ended should be included in the evaluation of the Party or government official in office when the debt was issued. This could, to a certain extent, prevent excessive debt due to shortsightedness.

Repayment of debt: To ensure that the principal and interest on debt is paid in a timely manner, a repayment fund should be established that holds a portion of revenue periodically placed in the fund from projects funded by municipal bonds. An order of priority for sources of loan repayment should also be established, setting a ceiling and ratio for the amount of tax revenue to be used for their repayment. Laws should also be passed that clearly define under what financial circumstances or what kind of revenue situation for a specific project constitutes a payment crisis. This could prevent local governments from deliberately not paying debts. Currently, government bankruptcy is not a feasible option (this would increase the moral risk that governments face). One option may be to extend payment periods or allow governments to make partial payments, which would eliminate the idea that a government will get off on a fluke. This would leave some risk in place and prevent investors from ignoring risk and investing too much.

Joint responsibility between governments: Currently, lower levels of government are generally responsible to higher levels of government. It must be clarified what debts and in what situations higher levels of government would take on what portion of debt responsibility for lower governments. This would prevent lower levels of government from making opportunistic decisions. Similarly, it must be clarified what portion of debt responsibility lower levels of government have when issuing municipal bonds through higher levels of government. This will keep higher levels of government from improperly using administrative powers to transfer debt responsibilities.

Clarification of borders between fiscal behavior and financial market behavior of local governments: It should be taken into account that local governments may very well try to obtain capital through banks. Since local governments have the power to interfere directly or indirectly in the affairs of local banking institutions or the local branches of banking institutions operating nationwide, a clear line must be drawn between the employment of different types of financial instruments, such as municipal bonds, and bank loans.[15] Whether in terms of underwriting loans, purchasing, transacting or repaying loans, governments must not be allowed to directly or indirectly use capital from lending organizations to repay municipal bonds. However, this does not preclude lending organizations from participating in the above-mentioned processes. Limitations on participation of lending organizations can be adjusted based on the direct or indirect interference of local governments, allowing for them to be tightened, relaxed or removed altogether.

Development and supervision of secondary market of municipal bonds: After a large-scale issuance of municipal bonds, it may be necessary to establish a market for municipal bonds in secondary markets, including national, regional and local over-the-counter markets.

Standardization of historical debts and linking them to new debts: As nearly all levels of government have some debt burden and a large portion of that is unrecoverable, the need by local governments to issue new debts to repay old debts is especially urgent. Before local democratic procedures are introduced, if there are no essential fiscal restrictions on local liabilities, such as setting an upper limit ratio of local GDP to fiscal revenue, laws must be put into place to strictly prohibit refinancing by issuing new municipal bonds. If this kind of restriction is put into place, prohibiting the refinancing would be unnecessary. In any case, there must be certain restrictions in place on new debts for a single project. The best option would be to put procedures in place for the approval of new debt financing of the same projects that require a certain portion of the previous debts to be paid off and revenue from these projects to have reached a certain level before new debts can be incurred.[16]

Concluding discussion

The above-mentioned issues are only one part of the problems with local government debt financing and bond issuance. There are no doubt many that have not been included. However, the key problem is that while we do support a standardized system that allows for local government liabilities as a channel for financing of local governments in China, it must be emphasized that municipal bonds alone cannot resolve the root of these problems. If this is not handled properly, it may result in a negative outcome. The most obvious example of this is China's stock market, where a few investors profited greatly and the vast majority of opportunistic investors lost out. The problem of low efficiency of state-owned enterprises was not resolved through the establishment of the stock market. From a wider historical perspective, it actually delayed the resolution of the root problem because of constant blood transfusions.

There are similar problems present in local government debt. Only a very small part of the problem of local government debt in China can be traced back to the public goods nature of some goods and services that local governments provide. Most problems of local government debt are connected to the lack of constitutional and fiscal rules constraining the central government and local governments, the absence of local democracy, the pressure of fiscal competition and economic performance in individual regions, the over-investment and excessive construction connected with it, the repercussions of fiscal reforms since 1994 that resulted in the centralization of fiscal revenue, and the haphazard changes in the terms of officials at higher levels of government. None of these problems can be resolved by simply issuing municipal bonds. Allowing issuance of municipal bonds is an opportunity that could bring these problems to the debate table and see resolution as the framework that manages municipal bonds is perfected. If issuing municipal bonds has ultimately only given local governments another vehicle to legally make money and higher levels of government more of an opportunity to push their responsibilities downward and gain more fiscal power, then not only will these problems go unresolved, the issue of local debts will most likely become increasingly serious and ultimately irreparable. As this chapter has tried to express, which of these two futures is chosen will fully depend on establishing a framework of rules and properly implementing those rules.

Notes

1 In this chapter, all levels of government below the national level are regarded as "local."

2 According to Breton (1996), the "competitive governments" paradigm refers to the fact that there is inter-, intra- and extra-governmental competition in federations such as the US and Canada, while according to Levitsky and Way (2013: p. 5), the "competitive authoritarianism" paradigm refers to regimes that "are civilian regimes in which formal democratic institutions are widely viewed as the primary means of gaining power, but in which fraud, civil liberties violations, and abuse of state and media resources so skew the playing field that the regime cannot be labeled democratic." Both paradigms stress the self-interest-driven competition of governments as a key feature that drives the political life in relevant countries. However, the competitive nature of a multi-layer government system doesn't only exist in real democracies or authoritarian quasi-democracies, but also in a formally unitary system such as the Chinese one. That is why it makes sense to extend the use of such paradigms to the Chinese system.

3 For the typical features of a "leviathan," see Hobbes (1651) and Brennan and Buchanan (1980).

4 In the following, the terms "urban investment bonds" and "local government bonds" refer to these two concrete types of bonds.

5 System-external revenue, or *zhidu wai shouru*, consists of illegal levies imposed by local governments upon the economy. They include "arbitrary fund raising, arbitrary fee charging, and arbitrary cost apportion" (called *san luan* in Chinese) by local governments.

6 These 36 local governments audited by the National Audit Office (2013) are governments of 15 provinces and those of their 15 respective capital cities, and governments of 3 municipalities under direct administration by the central government and those of their 3 districts. The narrowly defined debt balance of their vehicle companies and the debt balance of local government departments and institutions took 45.67 percent and 25.37 percent of their total debt balance at the end of 2012, respectively. In the audit report, all data refer only to the individual levels of local government and do not encompass the lower levels of local government. This applies in the following part of this chapter.

7 Local pension funds in many jurisdictions often run on almost empty or half-empty accounts. Funds are often diverted by local governments for other uses. They also do not pay in sufficient funds for employees from the public sector or local state-owned enterprises. This hidden debt is related to the amount that local governments have to inject into the pension funds to pay pensions as required by the law (Wang, 2013).

8 The People's Bank of China and China Banking Regulatory Commission on March 18, 2009, jointly released "Guiding Opinions on Further Strengthening the Adjustment of the Loan Structure to Push Forward a Stable and Relatively Rapid Development of the National Economy" to encourage local governments to establish local financing vehicle companies.

9 Already on June 10, 2010, the State Council issued a "Notice on Problems Related to the Strengthening of the Management of Local Government Financing Vehicle Companies" (Document No. guofa (2010) 19) and ordered debt financing of vehicle companies to be put in order and the management of these companies strengthened. The National Audit Office conducted a wide-scale survey of the debt of local financing vehicle companies, starting at the end of 2010 and released a report on "Audit Results on Local Government Debt in the Whole Country" (Report No. (2011) 35) on June 27, 2011. The report revealed the audit results on local governments' debt financing across China. Later on, various notices of the National Development and Reform Commission, People's Bank of China, China Banking Regulatory Commission, and Ministry

of Finance, Ministry of Land were issued, strengthening the control of loan disbursements and debt issuance, restriction of the qualification as vehicle companies, restrictions on using land transfer revenue as a pledge, prohibition of false capital registration and under-collateralization, etc.

10 The storm surrounding the default of Yunnan Province Roads Development Co., Ltd. ("Yunnan Roads") on its loans is a perfect example and marked the start of the vehicle company debt crisis. It is a vehicle company associated with the government of Yunnan Province. In April 2011, Yunnan Roads issued a letter to the bank lender saying that it would pay only the interest and not the principal. Yunnan Roads had nearly RMB 100 billion in loans from more than 10 banks including the China Construction Bank, the National Development Bank and ICBC (Shi, 2012). After the debt problem became known, the company retracted the letter on the advice of the provincial government, which then came out to discuss repayment of the loans in the company's place and avoided an all-out crisis. However, the scare of default sent unexpected shock waves through the urban investment bond market and new bonds were not issued for a period of time afterward.

11 Local party or government leaders are first nominated within the Party or the administration, examined by the organizational department of the Party secretariat at the local and the next higher level, and finally approved by the next higher level of the Party secretariat after the ceremonial or ritual "elections" through the local Party congress or local people's congress, respectively. The core principle is that the cadres are to be led by the Party according to the CCP's "Regulation on the Selection and Appointment of Party and Government Leaders" of July 23, 2002.

12 See Zhou (2007). Zhou's analysis shows that the close connections of the career of local government leaders to local economic performance constitute a strong positive incentive for these leaders to promote local economic development.

13 Some provinces, for instance, Guangdong Province, in 2012 started with the change of performance criteria for local leaders, to include other criteria such as the improvement of economic structure, the reduction of resource use per unit of GDP, environmental protection, autonomous innovations, coverage of public services for the migrant population, etc. However, economic performance is still a key criterion. Only in non-development zones where economic activities are in general forbidden is economic performance no longer a criterion in that province (Chen and Wu, 2012).

14 Here we can learn from the experience of the United States. In 1975, the United States established the Municipal Securities Rulemaking Board, which was responsible for creating rules that regulated broker–dealers and banks.

15 For example, the current practice of local banking institutions such as rural credit cooperatives requiring an endorsement from the local Party committee to put in or remove management from their positions provides a route for local government interference.

16 This suggestion is based on lessons from the improper operation of China's stock markets. Many of the listed companies on China's stock exchanges used allotments or extensions to collect a large amount of capital from small investors. Regulations limiting this type of practice only came into effect recently.

Bibliography

The original source of this chapter is: Feng, Xingyuan. Local Government Debt and Municipal Bonds in China: Problems and a Framework of Rules, in *The Copenhagen Journal of Asian Studies*, 31(2), 2013, pp. 23–53.

An, Y. and Wang, Z. Using Municipal Bonds to Drive the Construction of Urban Infrastructure. *China Investment*, 9, 2000, pp. 18–20.

Ba, S. and Yujing, X. From Urban Investment Bonds to Municipal Bonds: The Experience of Mature Markets. *Guandian Net*, November 24, 2009.

Brennan, G. and Buchanan, J.M. *The Power to Tax: Analytical Foundations of a Fiscal Constitution.* (Cambridge: Cambridge University Press), 1980.

Brennan, G. and Buchanan J.M. *The Reason of Rules: Constitutional Political Economy.* (Cambridge and New York: Cambridge University Press), 1985.

Breton, A. *Competitive Governments: An Economic Theory of Politics and Public Finance.* (New York: Cambridge University Press), 1996.

Cao, J. Withdraw the Hidden Debt Guarantees Is a Pressing Matter. *China Business News*, July 12, 2013.

Chen, H. and Wu, Z. Guangdong Said Good Bye to "GDPism" and Enforced Different Performance Criteria for Different Zones. *Enorth Net*, 16 November, 2012. Available at: http://news.enorth.com.cn/system/2012/11/06/010237423.shtml

China Industry Research Net. A Survey on the Development of the Market of Urban Investment Bonds, December 25, 2012. Available at: http://www.chinairn.com/news/20121225/524868.html

China Urban and Rural Finance Daily. The Amount of Policy Finance Bonds Issued This Year Will Exceed RMB 2 Trillion (in Chinese), December 24, 2012. Available at: http://www.how-buy.com/news/2012-12-24/1778051.html

Dong, Y. Local Financing Vehicle Companies Switched to Targeted Instruments Aiming at Fundraising With "Big Stomach." *China Business News*, August 23, 2012.

Fan, L. and Li, Q. *Analysis of Local Fiscal Practices in China.* (Beijing: Economic Sciences Press), 2001.

Feng, X. *Local Government Competition.* (Nanjing: Yilin Press), 2010.

Feng, X. and Li, X. 2005. Debts of Municipal Governments and Framework of Order for Municipal Bonds. *Management World*, 3, 2005, pp. 29–42.

Fisher, R.C. *State and Local Public Finance.* (Chicago: Richard D. Irwin, Inc.), 1996.

Gu, H. Local Government: How Big Is the Debt Risk? *Voice of Reform*, 5, 2000, pp. 31–33.

He, Y. and Man, Y. *Local Debt Scale in China and an Analysis of Its Risk.* Working Paper of Peking University-Lincoln Institute Urban Development and Land Policy Research Center, No. W093, October, 2011.

Herrmann-Pillath, C. *Die fiskalische und regionale Dimension des syste-mischen Wandels großer Länder: Regierungswettbewerb in China und Rußland.* Diskussionspapier, Fakultät für Wirtschaftswissenschaft der Universität Witten/Herdecke, Heft 42, September, 1999.

Herrmann-Pillath, C. and Feng, X. Competitive Governments, Fiscal Arrangements, and the Provision of Local Public Infrastructure in China: A Theory-driven Study of Gujiao Municipality. *China Information*, 18(3), 2004, pp. 373–428.

Hobbes, T. *Leviathan.* (London: Scolar Press), 1651/1969.

International Monetary Fund. *China: Explaining "Augmented" Government Debt and Deficit*, 2013. Available at: www.imf.org/external/np/sec/pr/2013/pdf/pr13192an

Jin, H., Qian, Y. and Weingast, B. Regional Decentralization and Fiscal Incentives: Federalism, Chinese Style. *Journal of Public Economics*, 89(9–10), 2005, pp. 1719–1742.

Levitsky, S. and Way, L-A. *Competitive Authoritarianism: Hybrid Regimes After the Cold War.* (Cambridge: Cambridge University Press), 2013.

Li, S. Examination of Problems in Local Government Debt. *Exploring Economic Issues*, 7, 2000, pp. 55–57.

Li, S., Li, S. and Zhang, W. Cross-regional Competition and Privatization in China. *MOST: Economic Policy in Transitional Economies*, 9(1), 1998, pp. 75–88.

Li, Y. Local Governments' Debt Ratios Are Too High: Be Cautious of the Outbreak of the High Tide of Bad Debt. *China News Service*, September 16, 2011.

Li, Y. Urban Investment Bonds Were Issued in an Immense Amount in 2012 and the Possibility of the Outbreak of a Crisis Is Increasing. *National Business Daily*, January 7, 2013.

Lu, X. *A Study on the Problems of Local Government Financing Vehicle Companies in China* (Dissertation). (Chengdu: Southwestern University of Finance and Economics), 2012.

National Audit Office. *Audit Results on Local Government Debt in the Whole Country.* Audit Report No. 35, 2011.

National Audit Office. *Audit Results on the Debt of Local Governments of 36 Local Jurisdictions.* Audit Report No. 24, 2013.

Netease Finance. *China Banking Regulatory Commission: The Balance of Loans of Local Government Financing Vehicle Companies Reaches RMB 9.2 Trillion* (in Chinese), January 29, 2013a. Available at: http://money.163.com/13/0129/17/8MDF79KV00253B0H. html

Netease Finance. *The Former Ministry of Railways Realized a Profit of RMB 196 Million While Held a Debt of RMB 2.79 Trillion* (in Chinese), April 27, 2013b. Available at: http://money.163.com/13/0427/16/8TFSS4QK002526O5.html

Nie, O. Local Financing Vehicle Companies Slam a Hard Brake on Debt Raising. *Business and Economy Weekly*, April 12, 2013.

Research Team of the Project on Problems with County and Township Level Government Finance in China. *Report on Problems with County and Township Level Government Finance in China.* (Beijing: Academy of Macroeconomic Research of National Development and Reform Commission), 2005.

Shen, Y. China's Population Expected to Reach 1.5 billion by 2030, Balanced Development Essential. *China Broadcast Net*, October 23, 2010.

Shi, J. A Year after Defaulting, "Yunnan Roads" Is Back in Business. *21st Century Business Herald*, November 22, 2012.

Shi, J. The New Policy of Classifying On- and Off-sheet Businesses Is Targeting the Financing Problems of Financing Vehicle Companies and the Real Estate Sector: The CBRC Announced Its Active Support for Investment in Key Projects in Railways, Roads and New Industries. *21st Century Business Herald*, January 29, 2013.

Standard Chartered. *Asia Leverage Uncovered*, July 1, 2013.

Sun, Q. Local Financing Vehicle Companies Got Implicitly Connected to Oversee Funds, With Microcredit Companies Acting as Intermediaries. *China Business News*, June 1, 2013.

Wang, M. About the Debt Size of Local Financing Vehicle Companies: The Difference between the Reports of the National Auditing Office and the China Banking Regulatory Commission. *China Business News*, May 30, 2013.

Wang, X. The Unification of Different Pension Systems Is Not Included in the Reform of the Income Redistribution System and the Ratio of Empty Accounts Is High. *Huaxia Times*, November 3, 2012.

Wei, J. Debt and Financial Risk in Local Government in China. *Commercial Weekly*, 5, 2004.

Xu, S. Municipal Bonds in the United States and Inspiration. *China Investment*, 7, 2001, pp. 38–41.

Xu, T. Trust Borrowing for Investment in Real Estate Is Boosting Up Only More Than One Month After the Rough Assessment of Local Government Debt through Auditing. *Securities Daily*, September 6, 2013.

Yang, Q. Moody: The Trend of the Increase in Local Government Debt Will Be Reversed with the Gradual Increase in Default Risks. *China Business News*, March 20, 2013.

Yang, Y. and Wu, L. SASAC Warns of Risks of Local Financing Vehicle Companies, With a Debt Size Amounting to RMB 13 Trillion by End 2013. *Economic Information Daily*, January 22, 2013.

Yu, B. and Wei, J. *A Study on Fiscal and Financial Risks in China*. (Beijing: China Development Press), 2012.

Zhang, T. The Net Increase of the Amount of Urban Investment Bonds May Reach RMB 1 Trillion. *China Securities Journal*, March 20, 2013.

Zhao, X. Rapid Increase of New Issuance of Local Enterprise Bonds with Rise of Medium and Small Scale Securities Dealers. *Shanghai Securities News*, January 4, 2010.

Zheng, C. The Real Risks of Local Government Debts in China: Risks Beyond the Default Risks. *Public Administration Review*, 4, 2012, pp. 52–76, 179–80.

Zhou, L. Incentive and Cooperation among Chinese Officials in an Increasingly Intense Game: Discussing Local Protectionism in China and the Reasons for Continued Re-construction. *Economic Research Journal*, 39(6), 2004, pp. 33–40.

Zhou, L. A Study on the Model of the Career-centered Economic Championship Contest of Local Government Officials in China. *Economic Research Journal*, 7, 2007, pp. 33–40.

8 Competitive governments, fiscal arrangements and the provision of local public infrastructure in China

A theory-driven study of Gujiao municipality

This chapter introduces an understanding of the complex changes and structures of the Chinese local fiscal system within the framework of the Competitive Governments (CG) paradigm. Summarizing our observations made in the context of a comparative case study, we note the fact that local governments control a local resource base in terms of income-yielding assets, as supposed by the regional property rights approach to Chinese political economy. Upper-level governments or the central government can interfere in this distribution of assets only on a case-by-case basis, but not disenfranchise the local governments completely. Status quo guarantees protect flows of income in terms of the implied distribution of income-yielding assets.

Further, these conditions are mostly independent of the specific policies that define formal institutions. Therefore, the effect of particular formal institutions defined and imposed by central government fiat depends on the competitive dynamics that results from strategies chosen by different level governments endowed with certain rights and resources. Hence, government competition is the larger game in which fiscal policies are embedded. As a result we note that the reforms of 1994 did not reach their objective as defined in the formal institutions promulgated by the central government. This is true for both the relative position of the central government as well as the actual institutions; there is a continuity of the standard fiscal bargaining model, now applied on a more rule-based tax system, yet without a stable assignment of single taxes. Hard fiscal budget constraints and a principle of subsidiarity are main regulatory features of this model; there is a continuing role of status quo claims that govern the bargaining process. Intergovernmental relations strongly rely on project-based exchange of resources; as a result of tightening budgets, a clear budgetary dualism has been emerging, with the regular budget mostly covering current expenses and salaries, and non-budgetary income covering investment. The latter includes indirect public debt via bank credits; one of the most important sources of infrastructure finance is the monetization and capitalization of local public land, which implies a further expansion of the regional property rights regime; the local provision of public services approximates principles of fiscal equivalence and follows different degrees of public ownership of goods; there is an increasing share of project-based public investment; there is a diversity of models of local public finance which reflects local economic conditions and provincial culture of economic policy.

Whereas different regional environments and initial conditions are a force of institutional divergence, interregional learning is a force of convergence. The three cities Gujiao, Tongxiang, and Zhangjiagang are almost ideal typical reflections of the provincial "economic styles." For example, this is highlighted in the very different budgetary policy. Tongxiang has the most de- or unregulated system, with a very high share of extra-budgetary funds and project finance with private involvement even in the education sector. Zhangjiagang has very entrepreneurial project finance, yet a major role for the regular budget, which reflects the collective economy philosophy of the Sunan model of economic development. Gujiao, though showing a similar importance of extra-budgetary funds, currently takes fast steps toward a unified budget management system. At the same time, in the area of project finance the three cities increasingly converge on approaches that maximize efficiency and profitability.

Role of the public sector

The role of the public sector has long been identified as an important determinant of the peculiarly Chinese way to the market economy. Major political economy and institutional approaches are the "entrepreneurial state" (ES) paradigm, the "market creating federalism" (MCF) or "market-preserving federalism" paradigm, and the "new institutional economics" (NIE) paradigm. These and related approaches predominantly concentrate on understanding the impact of government action on the emerging institutions and practice of the Chinese market sector.

For example, some contributions highlight the interaction between competition among local governments and competition from non-state sectors in the Chinese transition. It has become almost a commonplace that the administrative and fiscal decentralization in the 1980s led to the formation of local political interests and to a certain degree of regional and local autonomy with hard budget constraints for local governments. Zhang (1998) shows that this gave rise to territorial competition, and that the resulting fiscal pressure led to privatization. Jin et al. (2005) show that hard budget constraints, financial incentives and the competition from non-state-owned enterprises led to privatization of locally supervised state-owned enterprises. As we see, this part of the literature mostly does not deal with the role of government in providing public goods and services.

For an exception, Cai et al. (2004) model the competition between two regions from a game theoretical perspective, and argue that under certain conditions inter-jurisdictional competition will erode the capacity of central government to channel sub-national competition in welfare-enhancing directions and that under certain conditions, regional governments compete to attract capital less by investing in infrastructure than by protectionist measures such as sheltering firms from central tax collectors, bankruptcy courts or regulators. However, this static model contradicts the empirical observation of the pervasive establishment of economic development zones across China in the 1990s and the unabated drive to upgrade local infrastructure. A more convincing picture might be that both infrastructure investment and protectionist measures matter in inter-jurisdictional competition.

Hence, what this political economy research mostly leaves out of the picture is the role of the public sector properly indicated, i.e., the government as provider of "non-market-provided goods and services." This role is in focus when developmental issues are scrutinized, especially with relation to the interregional redistribution of resources, infrastructure or education. But in this context, there is less interest in the more theoretical issues of determining the systemic nature of the Chinese economy. Apart from the MCF/MPF literature, this question is only tackled in political science approaches, with paradigms like "fragmented authoritarianism" and "regionalism" dominating the debates in the 1990s, yet without a deeper repercussion on economic analyses. One notable exception is the Chinese debate on "state capacity" which started out from the diagnosis of the fiscal decline of central government in China. But that diagnosis is based on a logically inconsistent presumption of a "benevolent government" at the central level and "malevolent governments" at regional and local levels, since being deeply enmeshed with the Chinese policy discourse and, hence, being normative in nature.

Another research strand relates to the fiscal system and fiscal arrangements in the technical and institutional sense. Although there are numerous contributions, it almost exclusively focuses on the relations between center and provinces, with a groundbreaking economic contribution made by Ma Jun in 1997. There has been much emphasis on revenue sharing, but less on expenditures and hence, public goods and services. Work on local government is mostly descriptive, starting with Christine P.W. Wong (2000) and followed by Roy Bahl (1999), both employing strictly the fiscal federalism framework. Bahl's work involves a brief description of the forms of financing of local public goods in Guangzhou City. There are also a number of contributions on the supply of single kinds of local infrastructure in China, especially publications of the World Bank and the Asian Development Bank.

Finally, there is the research tradition of case studies on local development. Here we find competing paradigms of the Chinese political economy, as epitomized in the four ideal-types of "developmental state," "clientilist state," "entrepreneurial state" and "predatory state." Much ink is spilled on the proper labeling of complex local realities, the result strongly depending on the case and region in question. However, this literature opens the way to consider a conceptual synthesis between the more or less macro-institutional analyses of the fiscal system and micro-institutional ones of local economies. Because of the much richer empirical texture, this literature includes detailed studies of the way how local governments utilize resources to promote the local economy.

The key observation here is that the different ideal-types of government behavior are the expression of a more general competitive structure that has emerged as a result of the reforms in the recent two decades. None is sufficient to describe a presumed "average" or "representative" kind of local government in China, because the underlying behavioral patterns are competitive strategies in differing institutional and economic environments, which undergo a continuous revision because of political learning on the part of the actors. These competitive strategies are an integral part of the entire institutional structure. They are dependent on the incentives for responsible political actors, who at the same time decide about the mobilization of resources and the way these are invested in the local community. As a result, different patterns of government action emerge at different places, which lead to different effects on local development, thereby giving rise to path-dependencies and individual variations that contribute to the astonishing diversity of the Chinese way to the market economy. They feed back on further institutional change via market reactions and vertical mechanisms of political control and cadre assessment. In sum, government in China is deeply involved in an evolutionary process of administrative change, where the central government may sometimes plays a pivotal role, yet being only one player amongst others.

To understand this complex interaction between incentives, environment and individual strategy, we propose the general paradigm of "competitive governments," which is not a substitute of the aforementioned approaches, but a generalization which includes those different ideal-typical variants as special cases. Furthermore, the concept includes both the role of governments as providers of goods and services as well as of organizations legitimized to intervene in the market process either directly or through the creation of institutions.

Theory of competitive governments: the fundamentals

By employing the "competitive government" (CG) paradigm, we wish to draw on a comparative case study to interpret the role of the local state in the provision of non-market-provided goods and services in the context of inter-, intra- and extra-governmental competition. The CG paradigm has first been systematically expounded by the Canadian economist Albert Breton (1996). The advantage of this paradigm is its capacity to synthesize all the aforementioned different academic fields into a unified conceptual framework. At the same time, it starts out from economic theory and emphasizes the special role of fiscal arrangements in the broad sense, adding a strong dose of political economy considerations.

Breton defines goods and services as consisting of various characteristics which can increase the utility or disutility of individuals. They are provided by the non-market and the market sector, but are not necessarily mutually exclusive. Government-provided goods and services are a part of non-market-provided goods and services since some other non-market organization (for example, chambers of commerce) or even private persons (for example, donations for education) compete for the provision. The major difference to the MCF or MPF paradigm is therefore that there is an explicit rejection of the market/government dichotomy in terms of the possible und mutually exclusive demarcation between private and public goods. That is, government is regarded as a producer of goods and services like any other enterprise, yet operating under a special institutional regime with sovereign rights and duties, in particular the right to tax. Which kind of activities governments finally realize depends on a competitive process which is in turn determined by the institutional framework of government activities and of the regulation of market/non-market sector relations. Governments provide goods and services because they are demanded by the citizens or some citizens (or by some governmental officials themselves). In this regard, the government-provided goods and services include "goods" and "bads," such as "good" or "bad" laws and policies, justice or injustice, tax exemption or overtaxing, etc.

Apart from this market/non-market competition, in the CG approach every government is always regarded as being compound, because of explicit formal design (federalist, decentralized, functionally differentiated) or as a result of the limits of hierarchical control and centralization. In compound governments, there is always competition for resources and for power, also in terms of controlling the de facto regulatory framework and the rights to set the rules.

To illustrate this general approach, in China there is intergovernmental competition in the provision of tax laws and regulations. The central government releases tax laws alone, and fee regulations together with the provincial governments and several designated larger cities (such as Shenzhen, a special economic zone). But local governments collect fees based on their own written or unwritten regulations without any legal procedures. There is also the pervasive phenomenon of intra-governmental competition in the provision of "taxation service" in China. When a local taxation bureau might exempt some enterprise from income tax according to the local preferential policy, other departments such as the environmental department may charge more fees than formally allowed so that the preferential policy tends to be neutralized. Furthermore, government is not necessarily a monopoly in providing some goods and services. For instance, the social stability of a location is not solely "provided" by the government, but "co-provided" by the enterprises, social groups, citizens and other actors in this location. This is the phenomenon of extra-governmental competition.

In the CG paradigm it is of paramount importance to understand how government evolves in a particular setting in space and time. This implies that there is a clear distinction between the formal (e.g., legal) institutions and the "real institutions" that emerge endogenously from the competitive processes. The vast majority of researchers into the Chinese fiscal system treat formal institutions as the primordial institutions, and the informal institutions actually governing the behavior of state actors as deviations.[1] From the viewpoint of the CG paradigm, this order needs to be reversed: formal institutions are only a part of the entire institutional regime which evolves endogenously in the competitive processes.[2] The latter consists of two levels minimally, namely, the institutions governing the behavior of the state actors and the institutional regime of the competitive processes, which may partly overlap and can be further analyzed into formal and informal institutions.

In more detail, compound government can be described in the horizontal, the vertical and the political market dimension of the competitive regime. Vertically, the degree of decentralization of decision making is a major aspect of this regime. This can occur in the functional and/or the regional dimension, which leads to particular patterns in the horizontal dimension (inter-departmental and interregional competition), with this being related to different levels of vertical organizations.[3] The political market is part of the regime where demand and supply of government services is determined, as well as the special way how both meet. There are two fundamentally different settings of the political market, one defined by the political system proper (e.g., elections) and the other defined by the indirect reactions of economic actors to the taxation regime and supply decisions of state actors (e.g., mobility of capital, "voting with the feet," seeking tax exemptions or subsidies). Interestingly, these very broad concepts fit well into Chinese ways to understand the structure of government, namely, in the terms of lines and blocks (*tiaotiao kuaikuai*), and in the dimension of centralization and decentralization. The political market dimension, of course, is closely related to the fundamental issue of the nature of the political system and therefore, not as salient as in the Chinese discourse.

Analysis of competitive governments now means two different things. First, it is necessary to analyze and describe a particular institutional regime in the different dimensions. Observed phenomena have to be explained as reflections of this regime in the decisions and actions of the state actors. Obviously, an additional behavioral theory would be needed to put this causal analysis on a firm footing. Second, the change of the regime needs to be described and explained, again as result of the actor's actions and interactions, including government and the economy as an integrated whole.

Finally, some fundamental methodological presumptions have to be introduced. The most divisive point seems to be the question whether a neoclassical or an evolutionary perspective is adopted. Whereas the neoclassical view emphasizes rational choice, perfect (or Baysian) information and allocative equilibria, the evolutionary approach puts much more stress on individual and collective learning, uncertainty and institutional change. This methodological choice has not only implications for causal analysis, but also for appreciative reasoning and normative conclusions. For example, a neoclassical analysis frequently reaches the result of "race to the bottom" competition, whereas the evolutionary view holds that politico-economic innovations will be generated that counterbalance and even reverses this trend. Or, neoclassical analysis treats politicians as rational maximizers of self-interest, and hence, lobbyism as harmful rent-seeking and waste of resources, whereas evolutionary views interpret the latter as costs of communicating and revealing social preferences, and approach political behavior as being guided by normative commitments and ideology, too. These conflicting views are directly related to the Chinese debate about government competition, which frequently emphasizes negative outcomes (like waste of resources for the "multiple construction" of technology parks, excessive tax reductions, etc.).

From here, the chapter proceeds with a presentation of a field study in the light of the CG paradigm. We cannot do this in a comprehensive way, because, for example, there is no space to develop behavioral assumptions and check these with Chinese reality. Our main emphasis is on using the empirical observations to analytically reconstruct the de facto institutional regime of Chinese local government and fiscal management below the provincial level. We start with first outlining the basic economic conditions of Gujiao City and the two reference cases. We then analyze the fiscal arrangements emerging endogenously as a result of the interaction between central policies and local competitive strategies. In the next step, we describe the learning process of the political actors which has given rise to a series of institutional innovations in the provision of public infrastructure. In conclusion, we claim that the observed phenomena can best be understood within the CG framework, both in relation to process and result.

Examples from three counties: Gujiao, Tongxiang, Zhangjiagang[4]

Gujiao City is located 50 km to the northwest of Taiyuan – the capital of Shanxi Province. Tongxiang City is located in the middle between Shanghai and Hangzhou – the capital of Zhejiang Province – , with the Shanghai–Hangzhou National Street (*guo dao*) No. 320 and Shanghai–Hangzhou Highway going across it. It is 131 km to the southwest of Shanghai, 65 km to the northeast of Hangzhou and 74 km to the south of Suzhou. Zhangjiagang is 150 km to the northwest of Shanghai and 250 km to the east of Nanjing, the capital of Jiangsu, with a highway leading to Suzhou and with a deep-water harbor at the Yangtze River. Both Tongxiang and Zhangjiagang are located in the Lower Yangtze Delta.

Gujiao, Tongxiang and Zhangjiagang City were established in 1988, 1993 and 1986, respectively. Initially, the area of Gujiao belonged to two counties. It became a coal mining district (*gong kuang qu*) of Taiyuan City in 1958. The forerunner of Tongxiang City is Tongxiang County, which was established in 1958, by merging two counties at that time. The forerunner of Zhangjiagang City is Shazhou County, which was in turn established in 1962 by merging some marginal rural communes of two other counties and a state farm. The population in Gujiao was 208,200 people in 2000, much smaller than Tongxiang and Zhangjiagang (655,700 and 834,700, respectively). Population density is lower than in both other cities. Since Taiyuan is a prefecture-level city and at the same time the provincial capital, it has some special fiscal privileges that are related with its capital services, but which leave Gujiao as a county-level city (*xian ji shi*) at the periphery. With a share of non-agricultural population below 130,000, Gujiao is qualified as a "small city." The municipal government resides in Gujiao town (*Gujiao zhen*), which governs 5 urban neighborhoods, 3 towns (*zhen*) and 12 rural townships (*xiang*) with 200 villages.

From the viewpoint of the registration of the population, Gujiao is the most urbanized place (see Table 8.1, on non-agricultural population). However, this

Table 8.1 Selected economic indicators of Gujiao, Tongxiang and Zhangjiagang, year 2000

	Gujiao	*Tongxiang*	*Zhangjiagang*
Population (10,000)	20.82	65.57	83.47
Population density km^2	134.04	901.93	1081.22
GDP per capita (RMB)	10,078	17,261	31,600
Average yearly growth rate of GDP 1991–2000 (%)	12.43	21.46	25.52
Fiscal capacity per capita (RMB)[1]	326	559	1,205
Share of primary, secondary and tertiary sector in production value	4.5: 70.9: 24.6	9.9: 59.2: 30.9	3.7: 59.1: 37.2
Relation between light and heavy industry	0.2: 99.8	84.4: 15.6	45.5: 54.5
Share of non-agricultural population in total population	56.9	17.51	39.32
Share of SOE employment in total employment (%)	7.20	3.46	12.02
Number of industrial enterprises with a production value more than RMB 5 million	41	196	391
Volume of exports (USD 10,000)[2]	0	24,437	91,892
Share of exports in GDP (%)	0	17.91	28.17
Investment ratio (%)	60.50	n.a.	54.97
Ratio between investment in fixed assets and GDP (%)[3]	7.68	25.31	20.14
Share of foreign direct investment in total investment into fixed assets (%)[3]	0	0.18	9.362

Source: *Gujiao Economic Statistical Materials*, 1991–2001; *Zhangjiagang Statistical Yearbook*, 1990–2000; *Tongxiang Statistical Yearbook* 2001; *Yearbook of Zhangjiagang* 1990–2000; *Yearbook of Tongxiang* 2000. Authors' own calculations.

Annotations: 1: Local revenues without central government share (75% of VAT and consumption tax). 2: Exports of Foreign Trade Managing Units at the location. 3: The investment ratio includes inventories and is not available for Tongxiang. For Gujiao, investment in fixed assets does not include enterprises that are assigned to superordinate administrations (in particular, mining). If these were included, the share would rise to 14.02%.

is a misleading indicator, as it has to be taken as a reflection of the development model, with the Gujiao economy primarily relying on the state- and collective-run mining, coking and iron and steel industry. The majority of workers in these industries are registered as urban. Some other industries exist without playing a significant role, with products such as cement, bricks, agricultural and coal mining machines, slates and rubber products.

In contrast to Gujiao, there is no heavy industry in Tongxiang while Zhangjiagang lies in between. The main industries in Tongxiang are chemical and textile industry, being especially based on the so-called rural industry and its private sector, dominated by workers with a rural registration. The products in Tongxiang are diversified: paper products, textile products (silk and wool products, clothes), chemical fiber, fiberglass, cigarettes, leather shoes, composite feedstuff, fertilizers, pesticides, oil paint, cement, bricks, semi-manufactured copper products, fanners, electrical wires, lamps, etc. While a great number of small factories prevail in Tongxiang, a significant number of larger factories exists in Zhangjiagang. The main industries in Zhangjiagang are metallurgy, automobile, machinery, electricity, textile industry, light industry, and chemical and timbering industry with more than 3,000 kinds of products.

Comparing structural data on industry, employment and population in Table 8.1, we can make an intriguing observation, namely, that SOE employment in Zhangjiagang is even higher than in Gujiao, and that the number of large enterprises in Gujiao is the smallest of the three cities. Partly, this is a statistical artifact because some of the large resource extraction companies in Gujiao are assigned to the provincial or prefecture level, with a corresponding impact on employment data. On the other hand, when taken together with the employment shares, this shows that Gujiao has a large number of small industrial and mining companies with collective ownership. This can be related to the structure of industry: since in Gujiao heavy industry is absolutely dominant, this implies that it is mainly organized in small- and medium-scale enterprises with a suboptimal scale. Hence, in the other cities, precisely in the consumer and so-called light industries a stronger growth of enterprise size has already taken place, with the presumed effects on productivity and economies of scale.

In the field project, the three cities were selected because they represent well-known differences in developmental approaches and state-economy patterns. Shanxi Province is the case of state-led development with a large state sector based on the availability of natural resources and energy production, which is undergoing transformation. Zhejiang is the case of a private sector economy with laissez-faire government, and the Southern Jiangsu Region where Zhangjiagang is located is the homeland of the collective TVE-based development model (township and village enterprises). There is a clear awareness of these policy models in the narratives of local representatives, including a possible critical reflection in favor of the development model in Zhejiang in comparative terms. Zhangjiagang is one of the "economic miracle" places in China, having achieved a three times higher per capita GDP (Gross Domestic Product) than Gujiao, though Gujiao is still the most industrialized city of the three. However, this reflects an underdevelopment of services and hence, the long shadow of the Maoist planned economy in energy- and resource-intensive Shanxi Province. These differences in level of development and economic structure directly translate into a vast differential of fiscal capacity, with Gujiao showing the lowest fiscal revenue per capita of the three (Table 8.1). Another expression of these structural differences is the spread between the investment quotas, which in Gujiao is the lowest even if provincial- and prefecture-level enterprises were included that are not assigned to Gujiao City but are located there. These obvious differences in performance proved to be powerful triggers of policy change during the project implementation.

The different development models can be traced back to the different subcultures, factor endowments, role of local leadership and politico-economic and legal environments. Both Tongxiang and Zhangjiagang are nurtured by a merchant culture. But there are some differences between them. The subculture in Tongxiang is a mix between the Wenzhou subculture (*ouyue wenhua*) and the Southern Jiangsu subculture. The Wenzhou subculture values individual autonomy, the rejection of any dependence on government and the self-organization of economic activities, and shows strong reliance on social networks. On the other hand, the Southern Jiangsu subculture values collective action, especially that of the local community, and respects the authority of superordinate government officials. Having been influenced by the Southern Jiangsu subculture, people in Tongxiang value trust with traders from outside in social interactions, which is a distinct difference from the behavior of people in Wenzhou in the 1980s. In contrast, people in Gujiao are tough and thrifty. They are not as open-minded as those in coastal regions. This is a mirror of topography, as Gujiao lacks water and is surrounded by mountains. This behavioral pattern has been intensified by the strong bureaucratic control by the state of coal mining. Somewhat similar to the people in Zhangjiagang, people show respect and obedience to the authority in the hierarchy and tend to accept their life as given to them.

Summarizing and simplifying, people in Gujiao are less entrepreneurial than those in Tongxiang and Zhangjiagang, people in Tongxiang are more entrepreneurial in market processes than in political processes, whereas those in Zhangjiagang are very entrepreneurial in both market and political processes. This generalized differentiation does not mean that all people in one region act in that same manner as described above. It serves as a general "lock-in" factor for institutional change, whereas some individual actors in this region, with a learning process taking place, might be more entrepreneurial than others, which might lead to a breakthrough of a "lock-in" situation. In fact, among the governments in these three cities, the government in Zhangjiagang utilizes the political market most efficiently. It maintains a representative office in Beijing through which the Party chief and mayor of Zhangjiagang have direct connections to top politicians in China. In the 1980s, the central government decided to establish a free trade zone in each costal province. By lobbying at the provincial and central government, Zhangjiagang managed to get approval to establish such a free trade zone within its territory. On the other hand, the political entrepreneurship of the new Party chief and mayor in Gujiao cannot be undervalued. In 2000, the very year of taking their post, after the retirement of the old leadership (see below), the local GDP data were corrected downward by 33.07 percent, presumably now overshooting in the other direction to shelter fiscal resources. The correction itself was the result from lobbying of the Gujiao government at the provincial level and Taiyuan government where the good personal relations of the new Party chief could be "pulled." One direct impact of such a move is the release of the heavy burden of remittance of fiscal revenues to the upper-level governments, which is generally positively correlated with the economic growth in a city.

Apart from the cultural and political factors, the initial conditions for take-off in local economic development were different in three cities. As we have already mentioned, heavy industry in Gujiao is dominated by state-owned enterprises. The larger ones are affiliated to Taiyuan and the provincial government, while only the smaller ones belong to the Gujiao government. Some other smaller enterprises are collectively owned and affiliated to the city, towns and townships, or villages. Although the coal is "black gold," the central price control has always worked in favor of coal-importing provinces and regions. Few surpluses remained with the local government and citizens of Gujiao. State policies and weak demand hindered the emergence of private enterprise.

In Tongxiang and Zhangjiagang, the development before the Dengist reforms was similar: there existed only local state or collective enterprises from the 1960s to late 1970s. Since the Chinese government introduced a "dual-track" system reform in the 1980s, in which a market track was to be built up without touching the existing "plan" track, that is, the state enterprise sector, both Tongxiang and Zhangjiagang identified some market niches and set up new rural collective enterprises, the collective township and village enterprises, to boost their economy. With market competition getting fiercer in the late 1980s, Tongxiang started with the first enterprise reform, with Zhangjiagang following only in 1997 by transforming some state and collective enterprises into shareholding cooperatives, which embody both shareholding and cooperative elements. The reform was not successful since the state and collective shares still remained in the enterprises. This triggered the second enterprise reform in the beginning of the 1990s in Tongxiang and in 1999 in Zhangjiagang. The goal of this second wave was to privatize the local state and collective enterprises. As we see, the re-orientation in Tongxiang was much quicker than in Zhangjiagang. Enterprise reform in Gujiao began in the end of the 1990s, with the government closing down environmentally unqualified small collective-owned coal mines in accordance with the state industrial policy. However, real progress in the privatization of the 15 city-owned enterprises in Gujiao was only made after the change of the Party chief and mayor of the city in 2000.

The different speed of privatization can be explained by the different degree of ideological resistance to or acceptance of privatization by the aforementioned diverging subcultures, the different perception of the central policy, and learning processes. Tongxiang learnt in the beginning of the 1980s from the Southern Jiangsu region to develop more rural collective enterprises and turned to learn from Wenzhou in the beginning of the 1990s to develop the private sector since problems had accumulated in the collective enterprises similar to the state-owned enterprises, such as bad debts, low efficiency, lack of responsibility, explicit or implicit financial and administrative burdens and political risks. Zhangjiagang achieved outstanding growth in the 1980s and implemented large investment projects, including one of building up a new city center under the leadership of the then Party chief Qin Zhenhua, who implemented a policy in the manner of a developmental state. Capital and funds were concentrated on some larger projects, with strong social control and clear-cut developmental goals. Although the local leadership recognized the negative effects of the collective ownership, the local political cycle hindered the re-orientation of the local development policy in favor of privatization since the same leadership in Zhangjiagang had already acknowledged the great achievement of the Southern Jiangsu Model and felt publicly committed to this strategy.

In sum, as compared to the other two cases, Gujiao is a typical case of an aging economy in China which at the same time suffers from structural distortions, especially in the size distribution of enterprises, and a related employment problem. The government cannot rely on a strong economic base for extracting fiscal resources. Closeness to Taiyuan implies strong competitive pressure on the peripheral location. With the increasing perception of competitive disadvantages, the local government in Gujiao seemed to experience a strong pressure to change, which was first released in some attempts to deflate the statistical data on economic growth in 2000, as mentioned above.

Several months before starting the project, Gujiao City received some nationwide public attention because of a leadership scandal which triggered the aforementioned leadership change. During the *san jiang* ("Three Emphases") campaign of 2000, local leaders attempted to avoid public humiliation by a cadre assessment vote, which should have been secret. In fact they supervised the process and even falsified votes. An internal report by a journalist on this drew attention from President Jiang Zemin. Further investigation showed that the grassroots level of Gujiao was in a state of leadership vacuum, especially with the villages hollowing out by absence of cadres living in the city. It was discovered that economic data for 1999 had been faked, too. In September 2000, a new leadership was installed who immediately faced the task to regain public confidence and acclaim by the upper leaders. Most of the government action that is reported in this chapter goes back to these events and is therefore driven partly by the effort to regain legitimacy.

The 1994 fiscal reforms and their impact on local government in Gujiao

As we have seen, Gujiao has a low fiscal capacity. In comparative terms with Shanxi Province, however, Gujiao is in the middle field though showing a leading position in per capita income because of relatively low population density. We will now analyze under which institutional regime this relative fiscal position of Gujiao is determined, and how government competition leads to certain outcomes.

In recent analyses of the Chinese fiscal system much emphasis was laid on the 1994 reforms and the consequences for interregional redistribution and the relative position of the central government. Most observers diagnosed that the reforms at least partially failed to achieve their goals in both respects. Our analysis confirms this point, however, it stresses the aforementioned distinction between formal institutions and the actual institutional regime, with the latter being the primordial level of our analysis. Whereas the diagnosis of failure basically rests upon the view of the government as a formal, centralized and bureaucratic structure, we interpret the failure as a reflection of the actual institutional structure of the system, which is only partially grasped in the formal measures of the 1994 reforms. In other words, the 1994 reforms did not define a new game between the different levels of government, but were a central government move in a game that was not fundamentally changed. This game is the focus of the CG approach. As a consequence, the diagnosis of failure has to be revised in part, because the question comes to the fore, whether and how collective learning induces endogenous institutional changes that enhance the viability of the entire system.

Basic features of the 1994 reforms

The conventional approach would be first to describe the relation between the province and the central government and then to turn to the sub-provincial fiscal relations directly affecting Gujiao. However, from the CG perspective both levels should not be separated too sharply. One of the major aspects of fiscal institutions in recent years is how the reforms on the provincial level actually translate into the lower level, and how processes are triggered on the local level that feed back on higher levels, eventually changing the structure of the entire system. This is determined by six factors.

1 In the three case studies, there are two different approaches to governing the local level. One is prevailing in Jiangsu and Shanxi, where upper-level governments only determine the fiscal institutional regime on the next lower level, so that beyond that there is no unified system. In Jiangsu this implies that there is a great variety of fiscal models on the level of cities and counties, which are in turn created by the prefectural-level governments to which these bodies belong. In contrast, Zhejiang Province implemented a system where the province directly determines the fiscal relations on the county level, passing by the prefectural level and ruling out the possibility that the prefecture-level governments control the revenues of the subordinate government. These arrangements show that in spite of the high degree of formal centralization of the system, there is a kind of fountain with a ladder of basins, where authority flows from the top, yet it is held up by lower levels to be distributed from there in their own right. As we shall see below, this means that even though the higher-level governments are more powerful in designing competitive strategies, there is no simple and direct way to disenfranchise lower-level governments.

2 The most obvious symptom of this, albeit skewed, power balance was the fact that the introduction of reforms in 1994 was linked with a status quo

guarantee. This guarantee is mainly given in terms of the absolute revenue position, not necessarily in institutional terms: an implicit principle of "institutional fungibility" means that quantitative outcomes might be achieved with different institutional arrangements. There is a direct link between revenue centralization and vertical redistribution. All the upper-level governments normally argue that there is a necessity of horizontal fiscal equalization within the respective jurisdictions. Upper-level governments can change this remittance part arbitrarily since it is neither determined ex ante by consent of the lower-level governments nor by central government regulations. Lower-level governments often adopt similar behavior patterns in institutionalizing their fiscal relations with the next level of government, following the precedent set by their respective upper-level governments. The paradoxical result is that the new formal institutions promulgated by the central government in 1994 can actually serve as a tool for other purposes than originally intended, because similar regulations may produce different adaptations on different levels of the system. As had been stressed by the "fragmented authoritarianism" literature earlier, this observation demonstrates a fundamental lack of integration on the systems level, such that the multiplication of similar structures on different levels actually implies relatively high degrees of autonomy, with the organizational echo effect on lower levels resulting from a competitive strategy to provide formal legitimacy to otherwise autonomous action.

3 Possibly the main feature of the 1994 reforms is the attempt at imposing clear vertical budget constraints. That means, there is an implicit rule of subsidiarity in the system, with higher-level governments not redistributing funds across lower-level governments beyond the directly subordinate level. Regional imbalances, therefore, are primarily addressed within the reach of the responsible jurisdiction. This jurisdiction may receive some funds from a higher-level jurisdiction, but without taking the intra-jurisdictional disparities into consideration. This means that a poor county in a rich prefecture will not get the next upper-level support, whereas a poor county in a poor prefecture may indirectly participate in the next upper-level support for the prefecture. This arrangement also seems to acknowledge the partial autonomy of lower-level governments and, at the same time, imposes peculiar limits to national redistribution schemes.

4 However, this strict rule of subsidiarity is weakened by the fact that the fiscal reforms introduced clear regulations on revenue sharing, but no corresponding division of government tasks. In many fields, similar tasks are simply split between the different levels of government. This implies, of course, that there is much leeway to adapt the fiscal situation on the expenditure side, which directly affects the local governments because they can be relieved from certain tasks and responsibilities by shifting them to other levels. From the CG perspective this means that there is more room for a variety of formal competitive strategies on the expenditure than the revenue side.

5 Given the fundamental asymmetry of power between upper- and lower-level governments, with the former extracting lower-level local fiscal revenues, local governments have to find a way to compensate their revenue loss. They often turn to collect new fees even without approval by the central and provincial government or raise the fee rates without notice to the superordinate levels of government. To some extent this is tolerated by the upper-level governments who do not need to make up for the deficit. For example, the national family planning policy may be utilized as an instrument for local governments to collect fees and fines. In rural areas, families are requested to pay high amount of fines in exchange for having more children. Lower-level governments often complain that they lack funds for covering the growing expenditures for new tasks imposed upon them by upper-level governments, with a view of protecting the status quo of lower-level governments. Here, it is evident that vertical government competition can also take place on the level of institutions and regulations. The upper-level governments may claim the exclusive right to set the rules, yet the serious problems to control autonomous local-level revenue sources demonstrate that in the game such counter-strategies enjoy partial legitimacy.

6 Finally, the fiscal reforms only affected the tax system, which in the Chinese system implies that the role of the local government as owner of assets was not changed. This is very important, because the dualism between tax administration and fiscal administration was further strengthened by the reforms. Before 1994, the central government relied on the provincial governments' remittance of revenues. Taxes were collected by local taxation bureaus under the administration of the provincial taxation bureaus. The introduction of a national tax administration as distinguished from the local was not accompanied by a corresponding step toward an integrated national fiscal administration. This means that important public income sources resulting from asset utilization were not included in the reforms. This is a clear indicator for the partial autonomy of local-level governments.

These observations make sense in the context of the competitive governments approach. The basic point is that in China compound government is rooted in the implicit system of regional property rights that is clearly recognizable in the empirical patterns and which emerged as de facto institutional regime out of state ownership of land, resources and a large part of the corporate sector. Regional property rights imply that local governments enjoy formal or informal rights to control resources and to define the goals how these resources might be utilized. It is most obvious in the resulting structure and dynamics of vertical government competition. The central government as the exclusive formal representative of sovereign power could theoretically centralize all revenue. However, this would violate the implicit framework of regional property rights, which is the actual institutional setting. Remarkably, this is not simply resulting in a dualism between center and regions, but into a layered system where each level has autonomous rights. Thus, we observe a spillover of fiscal strategies from one level to another, and an interlocking bargaining process across levels.

Status quo guarantees mean that only increases of revenue can be the object of sharing. Furthermore, increases outside of the budget remain unaffected. On the other hand, hard budget constraints imply a basic protection of upper-level government assets and claims to revenue. Meanwhile, this distribution of property rights does not fully affect the distribution of tasks among the compound governments, so that here we find a major loophole where upper-level governments can control the actual situation of lower-level governments. However, as we shall see, this results in a kind of market process in infrastructure project design, if the positive interests in a certain deal are not exclusively with one side.

We will now have a closer look at the details of the fiscal arrangements that were introduced in 1994. We summarize the current situation of the fiscal system in the three cities in Table 8.2. The 1994 reforms have been frequently analyzed in the literature, so that we focus on the specific institutional adaptations on the local level. Evidently, the situation is very complex, with a large variety, yet also clear aspects of convergence. We show how the implementation of the national reforms triggered the aforementioned echo effect with complex strategic responses that finally hollowed out the formal rules. As a result, new steps were taken that even further reduced the unity of the system. The entire process is one of endogenous change in a CG structure.

Endogenous changes of the local fiscal system

The crucial step in the 1994 reforms was the transformation of the existing multiple turnover and product taxes into a much more simple system dominated by a general value added tax (VAT). The VAT at the same time served as the major vehicle of the recentralization of government revenue, with the more long-term goal to serve also as a source for interregional redistribution. The importance of this step is evident from the fact that this also meant that the administration of VAT would be handed over to the National Tax Administration (NTA), independent of a possible refunding in vertical redistribution. There was a clear rule on revenue sharing, with 75 percent of the VAT going to the center and 25 percent left to the regions.

The reasons for this central government measure have been extensively discussed in the literature, which agrees on the interpretation as a strategic move to centralize revenue and to increase central control over expenditures. From the CG perspective, this takes place in the context of vertical intergovernmental competition, given the structure of regional property rights. Hence, the many problems that have emerged in implementing the policies are interpreted as a result of the interaction between strategies on different levels of the Chinese

Table 8.2 Overview of the fiscal system in Gujiao, Tongxiang and Zhangjiagang after 1994

	Gujiao	*Tongxiang*	*Zhangjiagang*
1. Fiscal and tax administration			
1.1 Superordinate fiscal administration	Government Taiyuan, prefecture-level city	Provincial Government Zhejiang, by-passing Jiaxing, prefecture-level city	Government Suzhou, prefecture-level city
1.2 Fiscal bureau	Municipality	Municipality	Municipality
1.3 Local tax bureau (LTB)	Sub-unit of the prefecture level	Unit of the municipality	Unit of the municipality, with salaries being paid by the prefecture-level LTB
1.4 State tax bureau (STB)	Sub-unit of the prefecture level	Sub-unit of the prefecture level	Sub-unit of the prefecture level
2. Revenue assignment[1]			
2.1 General arrangements	1. Large steps of change in 1994 and 2002; 2. General package for revenue assignment since 2002: • province takes 35% of the total of the 25% of the VAT, and the business, enterprise and personal income taxes, resource tax and land use tax; • municipality: 65% of the total; prefecture level takes 35% of the increase of the tax rebate and municipality 65%; • prefecture level also reduces some subsidies for annual settlement of fiscal accounts.	1. Large step of change in 1994; 2. Change in the income tax assignment according to the central decision in 2002; 3. General package for revenue assignment since 1994: • as first round (FR), all local budgetary revenues are assigned to the municipality; • as second round (SR): a. municipality: baseline amount of local budgetary revenue 1993; 80% of the increase in the local budgetary revenue;	1. Large steps of change in 1994 and 2001; 2. Change in the income tax assignment according to the central decision in 2002; 3. General package arrangement since 2001: a. as the first round (FR), province gets the 2000 baseline amount of total remittance to it and 20% of the overall increase in the local revenues (but by deducting agricultural tax and special product tax for agriculture and forestry); municipality gets the 2000 baseline local revenue and 80% of the overall increase in the local revenue;

(*Continued*)

Table 8.2 (Continued)

	Gujiao	*Tongxiang*	*Zhangjiagang*
		b. province: 20% of the increase in the local budgetary revenue.	b. as the second round (SR), the prefecture level requests 0.6% of local budgetary revenue of the municipality.
2.2 VAT	1. Until 2002: • center: 75%; • municipality: 25%; 2. Since 2002: • center: 75%; • province: 8.75%; • municipality: 16.25%.	• center: 75%; • municipality: 25% (FR)	1. Until 2001: • center: 75%; • province: 12.5%; • prefecture: 4%; • municipality: 8.5%. 2. Since 2001: • center: 75%; • no separate VAT sharing below provincial level, VAT sharing is included in the package arrangement as above mentioned.
2.3 Excise	Center: 100%	Center: 100%	Center: 100%
2.4 Enterprise and personal income tax	1. Until 2002: • municipality: 100%; 2. Since 2002: • status quo protection for municipality: 2001 baseline amount; • center: 50% in 2002, 60% in 2003; • province: 17.5% in 2002, 14% in 2003; • municipality: 32.5% in 2002, 26% percent in 2003	Until 2002: • municipality: 100%; 2. Since 2002: • status quo protection for municipality: 2001 baseline amount; • center: 50% in 2002, 60% in 2003; • municipality: 50% in 2002, 40% in 2003 (FR).	1. Until 2002: • province: 20%; • municipality: 80%; 2. Since 2002: • status quo protection for municipality: 2001 baseline amount; • center: 50% in 2002, 60% in 2003; • municipality: 50% in 2002, 40% in 2003 (FR).

2.5 Urban land utilizing tax (*chengzhen tudi shiyong shui*)[4]	1. Until 2002: • province: 50%; • municipality: 50%; 2. Since 2002: • province: 35%; • municipality: 65%.	Municipality: 100% (FR).	Until 2001: • shared between province and municipality, percentages unknown; Since 2001: • municipality: 100% (FR).
2.6 Revenue from using the state-owned land use right against payment	1. Until 2002: • province: 20%; • prefecture level: 20%; • municipality: 60%; 2. Since 2002: • prefecture level: 20%; • municipality: 80%.	Municipality: 100% (FR).	Municipality: 100% (FR).
2.7 Revenue from using the use right for newly added construction land (in the category of funds)	Center: 30%; Province: 14%; Prefecture level: 7%; Municipality: 49%.	Center: 30%; Municipality: 70% (FR).	Center: 30%; Municipality: 70% (FR).
2.8 Cropping land conversion tax (*gengdi zhanyong shui*)	Province: 40%; Prefecture level: 5%; Municipality: 55%.	Municipality: 100% (FR).	Municipality: 100% (FR).
2.9 Tax for resource use collected locally (not including ocean petrol tax)[2]	1. Until 2002: • municipality: 100%; 2. Since 2002: • province: 35%; • municipality: 65%.	Municipality: 100% (FR).	Until 2001: • shared between province and municipality, percentages unknown; Since 2001: • municipality: 100% (FR).

(*Continued*)

Table 8.2 (Continued)

	Gujiao	*Tongxiang*	*Zhangjiagang*
2.10 Turnover tax collected from local enterprises (excluding banks and insurance companies)	1. Until 2002: • muncipality: 100%; 2. Since 2002: • province: 35%; • municipality: 65%.	Municipality: 100% (FR).	Municipality: 100% (FR).
2.11 Profits remitted from the city-level enterprises, subsidies to loss making state-owned enterprises[3], regulatory tax on fixed investments, city maintenance and construction tax, and locally collected building tax, vehicle and vessel tax, stamp tax, slaughter tax, agricultural tax, special local product tax for agriculture and forestry, contract tax, inheritance tax, tax on land value increase, waste disposal fee, water resource fee, and other tax and fees	Municipality: 100%; (city maintenance and construction tax includes that collected from the Xishan Mining Bureau within the territory of the municipality which is affiliated to the prefecture-level government).	Municipality: 100% (FR); (city maintenance and construction tax includes that collected from the enterprises which is affiliated to the central and provincial government).	Until 2001: stamp tax, tax on land value increase, waste disposal fee and water resource fee are shared between province and municipality; others belong to municipality.
3. Tax rebate by the center[4]	1. The baseline amount of tax rebate to the municipality from the center's sum of the excise and 75% of the VAT is equal to the 1993 net remittance to the center; 2. Increase in the tax rebate until 2002: municipality: 100%; 3. Increase since 2002: a. prefecture level: 35% b. municipality: 65%	1. The baseline amount of tax rebate to the municipality from the center's sum of the excise and 75% of the VAT is equal to the 1993 net remittance to the center; 2. Increase in the tax rebate: • province: 20%; • municipality: 80%.	1. Until 2001: • the baseline amount of tax rebate to the municipality from the center's sum of the excise and 75% of the VAT is equal to the 1993 net remittance to the center; • increase in the tax rebate: a. province: 16.67%; b. municipality: 83.33%

			2. Since 2001: • 2000 tax rebate from the center's sum of the excise and 75% of the VAT as the baseline amount of tax rebate to the municipality; • increase in the tax rebate: a. province: 20%; b. municipality: 80%.
4. Remittance to the center	1. Until 2002: • 1993 baseline amount of remittance will be fixed as old system dependent remittance; • the growth rate of remittance is 6%, 5% and 3.5% in 1994, 1995 and 1996–2001, respectively; 2. Since 2002: • annual fixed remittance equal to the 2001 baseline amount.	1. Since 1994: • 1993 baseline amount of remittance will be fixed as old system dependent remittance; • 1994: the growth rate of the remittance: 5.5%; 2. Since 1995: • fixed amount remittance at the 1994 level with the abolishment of the growth rate arrangement.	1. Since 1994: • 1993 baseline amount of remittance to the center will be fixed as old system dependent remittance; 2. Since 2001: • annual fixed remittance equal to 2000 baseline amount of remittance to the center and province.
5. Arrangement for pre-existing special purpose subsidies given by upper levels of government or remittance to them	1. 1994: annual general fixed subsidies (*ding'e buzhu*) by the prefecture level to the municipality are calculated by adding all kinds of the special purpose subsidies, net subsidies for changing the administration level of enterprises and undertakings and for policy changes in 1993.	• Special purpose subsidies given by the center and province will be given to municipality as it was done;	1. Since 1994: • special purpose subsidies by the upper levels of government will be given to municipality and remittance to the upper levels are made as it was done;.

(*Continued*)

Table 8.2 (Continued)

	Gujiao	*Tongxiang*	*Zhangjiagang*
	2. 1995–2001: • fixed subsidies abolished; 3. Since 2002: • annual fixed subsidies (*ding'e buzhu*) to the municipality are calculated by adding all kinds of the special purpose subsidies, net subsidies for transferring the administration level of enterprises and undertakings and for policy changes in 2001.	• annual general fixed subsidies given by the provincial level to the municipality or remittance to the province are calculated by adding all kinds of the net subsidies for changing the administration level of enterprises and undertakings and for policy changes in 1993, and reducing the remittance of the 20% of the amount of the VAT tax rebate for exports being borne by the municipality, etc.	2. Since 2001: • one part of special purpose subsidies by the province will be given to municipality and all special purpose remittances to the province are made as they were done; • another part of provincial special purpose subsidies will phase out in three years; • special purpose subsidies of other levels of government and remittances will remain
6. Other subsidies and remittances	New special purpose subsidies, subsidies or remittance for changing the administration of enterprises and undertakings and those for policy changes, etc.	New special purpose subsidies, subsidies or remittance for changing the administration of enterprises and undertakings and those for policy changes, etc.	New special purpose subsidies, subsidies or remittance for changing the administration of enterprises and undertakings and those for policy changes, etc.
7. Premiums and incentives granted by upper levels of government	No	1. Since 1995: • premium: a. 300,000 yuan for municipalities reaching a local budgetary revenue of 100 million yuan;	1. Until 2001: • No. 2. Since 2001: • 10% of the annual increase in the total remittance to the province will be given back to the municipality as "local development fund";

	b. 200,000 yuan for each incremental increase of the local budgetary revenue by 30 million yuan. 2. Since 1997: subsidies for technological improvement: 11% of the increase in the total remittance to the province (the grant is linked to the revenues size and increase of the municipality).	• 200,000 yuan premium for each incremental increase in local budgetary revenue of the municipality by 40 million yuan.

Source: Fiscal bureaus of Gujiao, Tongxiang and Zhangjiagang; Department of Finance of Shanxi, Zhejiang and Jiangsu Province.

[1] Revenues which are regarded as not being generated from the city are not part of local total budgetary revenues and thus not included in this table. For example, VAT and excise collected by customs offices, and customs duty are revenues of the center. They are not included in the local total budgetary revenues of a city and thus not included in the table.

[2] Resource tax is set as a shared tax in the 1994 fiscal reform.

[3] Subsidies to loss making state-owned enterprises are treated as negative revenues in the fiscal table of balance in China.

[4] For the calculation of the tax rebate, one calculates first the base year 1994 the baseline amount of tax rebate 1994: $R = C + 75\%V - S$, whereas R denotes the calculated baseline amount of tax rebate 1994, C the excise, V the VAT, and S the old system dependent transfer by the center 1993. The formula for tax rebate is: $R_n = R_{n-1}(1 + 0.3r_n)$, whereas R_n denotes the center's tax rebate in the year n since 1994, R_{n-1} that in the year $n - 1$, and rn the growth rate of the sum of the excise and 75% of the VAT in the whole of China in the year n.

compound governments. In fact, the seemingly clear VAT rule was made ineffective and diffuses because of two factors.

- As has already been thoroughly analyzed in the literature, right from the beginning the new regulation was accompanied by a status quo guarantee for the provinces which meant that the central government would only get a 70 percentage share of the increase of VAT revenue above the 1993 threshold value, such that the 75 percent total share was only a long-term goal to be attained. This was implemented formally via a refunding scheme, whilst in the first step the VAT entirely flows through the NTA. The problem here is that this kind of tax refunding continues to coexist with other vertical schemes of budgetary appropriations and transfers, which basically follow the old "responsibility system." These are an additional means to protect status quo claims of the two parties. As a result, the entire system still shows a strong resemblance to the old bargaining system. In that context, it should be emphasized that the new system of interregional redistribution introduced in 1995 is still of minor quantitative importance, so that its rule-guided approach (based on fiscal and economic indicators) only marginally changes the institutional nature of the fiscal system.
- A point less observed in the literature, yet very important in our case study, is the fact that the 75/25 rule does not determine which regional and local level receives the 25 percent share. This is very important because in the old system the turnover taxes were assigned to the jurisdictions to which the enterprises belonged administratively (ownership principle). The centralization of the VAT therefore did by no means only affect the relation between center and provinces, but also directly the relative position of local governments because they were stripped off this revenue without the certainty to become the target of refunding, i.e., it is uncertain that the reforms could be accompanied by an intraregional redistribution of revenue. As a consequence, the reform triggered a new bargaining process about the division of the 25 percent share among the different levels of provincial, prefectural and municipal governments.

The complexities of this system imply that the primary distribution of fiscal resources as indicated by the formal institutions is of no relevance for the actual final distribution. For example, Shanxi Province is a receiver of interregional redistribution funds: of a 2000 national total of RMB 8.5 billion the province got 321 million, whereas Zhejiang and Jiangsu did not receive any support. However, in the final state Shanxi is a net payer in the system with an average amount of about 17 percent of its total revenue in recent years (Table 8.3). This observation should be put into perspective: for a rich province like Zhejiang, the 1994 reforms actually resulted in an improvement of its position, because the former progressive system of tax transfers to the central government was abolished (which took the entire revenue of the province as a base, with an experimental stage in 1992/1993). Table 8.3 shows that Shanxi Province,

Table 8.3 Total revenue per capita, transfers and quota in Shanxi, Zhejiang and Jiangsu, 1999–2000 (RMB 100 million)

Year	*Shanxi*			*Zhejiang*			*Jiangsu*		
	A	*B*	*C*	*A*	*B*	*C*	*A*	*B*	*C*
1991	188.96	55,437	9.97	258.84	2.677	24.27	209.38	54.12	37.77
1992	194.59	57,117	9.85	276.16	3.036	25.65	220.38	67.57	44.36
1993	240.39	72,421	10.00	386.34	3.621	21.73	317.63	72.21	32.63
1994	319.47	147,296	15.14	482.33	5.517	26.35	417.93	106.2	36.2
1995	420.50	251,754	19.46	568.70	7.128	28.68	495.44	121.21	34.62
1996	482.91	321,005	21.38	663.05	7.809	26.77	601.94	142.24	33.23
1997	523.13	366,487	22.30	770.01	9.308	27.33	692.91	169.84	34.29
1998	574.27	279,041	15.32	903.56	8.9714	22.33	791.21	195.9	34.47
1999	566.70	232,497	12.81	1,068.62	10.826	22.68	885.62	215.56	33.74
2000	599.02	296,020	15.22	1,462.76	22.53	34.22	1,108.34	272.75	33.59

Source: Authors' calculations based on data from the *Statistical Yearbooks* of Shanxi, Zhejiang and Jiangsu, and complementary data from the Ministry of Finance and Shanxi Government.
A: Regular revenue per capita
B: Net transfers to central government
C: Net transfers to total revenue, %

though enjoying a lower net transfer quota to the center, still suffered from a rapidly increasing quota whereas the other two provinces did not experience any substantial change, but rather normal fluctuations of the quota around a base value.

For Shanxi this trend implies an increasing budgetary pressure. This was also felt in Gujiao. As we have seen, for assessing the situation on the local level it is important to understand the sharing schemes related to VAT and other taxes. As a rule, the national tax sharing system implies that minor taxes linked with local economic activities should belong to the local level. This includes, for example, the slaughter tax, the land use tax or the services tax (without financial enterprises). However, the local assignment rule was also applied on the VAT, therefore reproducing the rule of the traditional system of turnover taxes. For Gujiao, this is a mixed blessing, because most of the larger mining enterprises, though being located in the city, are assigned to the province and prefecture-level city Taiyuan. As we shall see in the next section, the resulting imbalance between tax flows and local resource utilization causes further adaptations in the local fiscal regime which finally transcend the tax system proper.

Since the intraregional distribution of the VAT was not determined by the 1994 reforms, this is also a major instrument of regional fiscal policies. Since 1994, there is no stable rule applying to this area. In all the provinces we observed, the upper-level governments' adjustment of the existing fiscal systems was legitimized by the objective of "regional equalization." This is interesting, because the central government policy actually triggered an intensification of lower-level government competition, in which the higher-level governments theoretically could impose any policies on the local level. Yet, in the given system of regional property rights, this would not be a perfectly legitimate act, such that the justification in terms of equity and overarching social goals needs to be provided.

For several years, Gujiao received the entire share of 25 percent of the VAT generated by the enterprises assigned to the city. However, this was complementary to a provincial participation with the local revenue resulting from land use (50 percent:50 percent), which is a typical example for the fungibility of institutional arrangements that we mentioned above. In 2002, the rule was changed, with the province now getting 8.75 percent of total VAT revenue, and Gujiao getting 16.25 percent, so that the prefecture-level government no longer participates in the plan. In Zhangjiagang, with the 1994 reform, the provincial government in Jiangsu and the prefecture-level government in Suzhou took away 12.5 percent and 4 percent of the total VAT, respectively, leaving 8.5 percent to the Zhangjiagang government. The province also participated in the sharing of revenues of minor importance, such as the stamp tax, the city and town land using tax (*chengzhen tudi shiyong shui*), the resource tax, the land appreciation tax, the emission fee and the water resource fee. It also took 0.05 percent of the central government's tax rebate to Zhangjiagang. In 2001, the provincial government adjusted the intra-provincial fiscal administration system. It set the 2000 total remittance to the province as a new threshold, so that this fixed amount should be transferred to the province since 2001 and the increase is then to be divided among the province and Zhangjiagang at 20 percent:80 percent. The prefecture-level city Suzhou requests 0.6 percent of the total local budgetary revenues of Zhangjiagang. In Zhejiang, since the prefecture-level city Jiaxing is excluded from participating in the sharing of the local revenues of Tongxiang, the system is much simpler: the increase in the total revenues of Tongxiang as compared with the 1993 baseline revenues will be shared, the province takes 20 percent and Tongxiang 80 percent.

Hence, we observe a process of incremental intrusion of upper-level governments into the resource bases of the local level, which is very complex because it is taking place within the existing structure of distributed regional property rights. In this process, central government policy directives are continuously re-interpreted or adapted in terms of lower-level competitive strategies, such that competitive strategies of lower levels become an implicit part of the central implementation process. A conspicuous example is the product tax on tobacco, for long an important source of local revenue, which therefore provided a major incentive to set up small-scale tobacco companies across China. This tax was transformed into a special consumption tax and centralized with the 1994 reforms, yet to protect the status quo it was completely refunded to Shanxi. Eventually, the tax was transformed into a VAT and a consumption tax, with the latter being entirely transferred to the center, and the former shared according to the 75/25 rule, yet preserving the 1993 status quo as a baseline. The assignment of the VAT follows the traditional rule of jurisdictional assignment of companies. In the other cases, we find even case-specific arrangements, so that the original central regulation seems to be without any substantial meaning.

We note that government competition is the framework for institutional evolution, and not vice versa: institutions evolve endogenously. In fact, the central government still interferes with continuing changes of formal rules, thereby undermining its very stability. Before 2002, enterprise and personal income taxes were fully local taxes of the Gujiao government, while the governments in both Zhangjiagang and Tongxiang took 80 percent and the provincial government in Jiangsu and Zhejiang 20 percent, respectively. The enterprise and personal income taxes are actually divided between the different levels of government since 2002, directly or indirectly, which is a major break of the formerly intended tax systematics. For Gujiao, only 50 and 60 percent of the total enterprise and income tax remain in the local coffers in 2002 and 2003, respectively, but the province takes 35 percent of the total of the VAT, business, enterprise and personal income taxes, resource tax and land use tax, a radical change of the local revenue sharing arrangements with a rather predatory nature. Taiyuan government also does not give up its share, by taking from the municipality 35 percent of the increase of the tax rebate 65 percent and deducting some subsidy to Gujiao for the annual account settlements. There is a guarantee of the status quo of all regional and local governments; that is, they are ensured to get a minimal amount of the 2001 local baseline income tax revenues. If the local part of income tax revenues after the first round of tax sharing is lower than the local baseline income tax revenues for 2001, the difference will be covered by the central government as baseline for the tax rebates.

If the local part of income tax revenues after the first round of tax sharing is higher than the 2001 local baseline income tax revenues, the local government should remit this difference to the central government in the second round as baseline figure for tax remittance. In Jiangsu, the overall 2001 tax sharing system remains stable since 2002, though the central government takes away 50 and 60 percent of enterprise and personal income taxes. The province still gets the 2000 baseline amount of remittances and its share in increases. Zhangjiagang, for example, now retains only 40 percent of business and personal income tax increases, Jiangsu province 10 percent and the central government 50 percent in 2002. The prefecture-level city Suzhou demands 0.6 percent of the local total budgetary revenues of Zhangjiagang. The overall fiscal system of Zhejiang is rather stable. With the central income revenue reform in 2002, the province leaves also the existing interprovincial income tax assignment rule unchanged and takes 10 percent of the total in 2002 and leaves the remaining 40 percent to the government of Tongxiang. Thus the 2002 reform is a déja vu of the 1994 reform, only affecting another kind of taxes: while guaranteeing the status quo of all regional and local governments, the actual part for the central government of both income tax and VAT will grow faster than that of the regional and local government. The formal reason for this 2002 reform is that the income taxes rose extraordinarily rapidly and that one part should be redistributed by the central government to poorer regions. However, the precise repetition of dysfunctional design of the reforms (distorting incentives for tax administration, reducing institutional stability, etc.) demonstrates the predominant role of competitive strategies in institutional change, as opposed to independent criteria of equity and legality.

In sum, the 1994 reforms actually produced a paradox. On the level of formal institutions, the reforms seem to amount to a transition from a bargaining system to a rule-based system. In fact, however, the bargaining system even increased in complexity because of endogenous institutional changes on the local level. Before 1994, the position of Gujiao was determined by a simple sharing rule based on the entire local fiscal revenue. After 1994, the rules have become complicated and non-transparent, especially after the reforms in 2001 and 2002, which interact with the former. This is the same case for Zhangjiagang, and less so in Tongxiang. In all the three cities, the rules governing the possible choices in competitive strategies include the general rule of status quo maintenance and baseline figure arrangements which continue with the old fiscal contracting approach. In this bargaining system, the new rule-based taxes turn out as the very object of bargaining that pinpoints the paradoxical nature of the policies.

Fiscal administration and budgetary dualism

An important question in the analysis of government competition is how and which of its rules determine its processes and structures. Since the 1994 reforms did not directly affect the intra-provincial system, there is an amazing continuity of systemic characteristics on the local level, which we have interpreted as an endogenous outcome of government competition. If we ask for the rules of the bargaining process, the most obvious candidate are the regulations for fiscal planning.

With increasing budgetary pressures and a low volume of possible redistribution, the need for planning became even more urgent than in the old system. This is done via quantitative tax quotas assigned by the upper-level tax administration to lower-level branches. These quotas are mirrored in sets of indicators for regular expenditure needs, so that finally a system of indicators can be deduced that allows estimating the needs to vertical redistribution. This system is applied across all levels of local governments and decouples the actual fiscal situation from the tax assignment rules governing primary distribution. It is mostly linked with an incentive system, that is, local governments are allowed to retain a larger share of any revenue increase above the planned level. In Zhejiang Province this approach is developed to considerable sophistication, because even provincial subsidies are coupled with increases of local revenue. Tongxiang, for example, transfers almost 50 percent of its revenue to upper-level governments, but receives special refunds linked to a further increase of its transfers, so that about 15 percent of the transfers flow back as special grants, e.g., in technology policy.

Obviously, precisely these rules are the medium by which bargaining prevails over rule-based administrative procedures, especially because, different from the revenue-sharing schemes, there is a clear link between revenues and expenditures. Therefore we note an interdependence between the enforcement of planning procedures and the continuation of certain forms of government competition, against which the planning procedures are partially directed. This further paradox inherits all solutions to the problem of regulating government competition which do not withdraw the rule-setter from the competitive process proper.

Table 8.9 (in the appendix) shows the development the budget of Gujiao City between 1988 and 2000. As we see, there is a clear breaking point of trends between 1993 and 1994. Growth rates of revenues, expenditures and transfers declined systematically. At the same time, the average growth of local expenditures surpassed the growth rate of revenues. Total expenditures including transfers, however, grew slower than local expenditures, since the absolute amount of transfers did grow under-proportionally. This has to be compared with the situation before 1994, when the transfers changed considerably between the years, because the share of project-related transfers was much larger. The overall impression is that the reforms indeed created a more reliable system, yet this does not work as the rules imply because the transfers do not follow the increase of revenue. Therefore, it is not possible to blame the reduction of transfers as the sole reason for the fiscal pressure. The other important reason is the growth of expenditures. However, we also have to note that in the most recent years a decline of available revenue occurred, with a turning point in 2000 when it is required that all taxes should be first collected and turned over to the fiscal accounts of the treasury before certain tax credits can be given by local governments to local enterprises.

The Budget Law of 1994 disallows local governments' debt financing and requests budget balance at all levels of governments. The basic budgeting principle is that government expenditure should remain within the limits of its own fiscal revenues, which is formally enforced by the principle of subsidiarity that we mentioned above.[5] The practical budgeting principle in the three cities is thus to guarantee first the costs for government-provided personnel and then those for construction and investment. In this way, the local governments have not enough incentives to reduce the number of personnel, in spite of strong pressures of downsizing. But facing ever-increasing tasks imposed by upper-level governments, and given the preference of bureaus to budget maximizing, the economic performance-based assessment of local officials, and the administrative reforms dictated by the central government, local governments actually upsize. The actual size is thus an outcome of these contradicting down- and upsizing trends. In 1993 and 2000, the ratio of the number of government-provided personnel to total population was 3 percent and 3.04 percent in Gujiao, 1.8 percent and 1.8 percent in Tongxiang, and 2.5 percent and 3.1 percent in Zhangjiagang, respectively.

The traditional budgeting method is the baseline expenditure-based budgeting, which has a strong status quo bias. Several years ago, the State Council was requested by some deputies in the National People's Congress to improve budgeting transparency. In response to this request, the central government decided to introduce the departmental budgeting method to each layer of government. Up to now, departmental budgeting is still experimental in some ministries and departments. Fewer local governments introduced it. The fiscal bureau in Gujiao had not yet started with departmental budgeting formally, but there has been a de facto one. This is obviously pushed by the budgetary problems which compel the local government to set priorities, even with attempts to introduce advanced planning procedures like zero-base budgeting. The fiscal bureau in Gujiao started with introducing zero-base budgeting in 1995, while Zhangjiagang did in 1997 and Tongxiang did not yet.

In Tongxiang departmental budgeting is not enforced. Zhangjiagang started with it in 1999. Up to now, there is no single city in China, in which a budget based on zero-base and departmental budgeting is submitted to the local parliament. A major reason for this is that departmental budgeting would imply comprehensive budgeting, which would include extra-budgetary funds. In all the three observed cities, the fiscal bureau attempted to put all extra-budgetary funds onto a consolidated account in accordance with a central regulation. In 2002 Gujiao has introduced the principle of comprehensive fiscal budgeting (*zonghe yusuan*), which means that the regular budget and the extra-budgetary funds are planned and implemented in one unified budget. This is a fiscal innovation imposed by the central government, yet adopted with very different speed on the local level. In Tongxiang, the government already started with the comprehensive fiscal budgeting in 1998 upon the request of the central government. In Zhangjiagang, the government started with it in 2001. But a significant part of extra-budgetary funds, not to mention the external funds (*zhidu wai*), remains dispersed in open or secret accounts or "small treasuries" of various governmental departments and units of public undertakings. Even officials at local level can only estimate the real size of the extra-budgetary funds. The local governments are also scared to reveal the real size and tend to underreport the figure since the upper-level government would otherwise take a share in it.

The difficulties in introducing advanced and rule-based budgeting procedures reflect the fact that this would interfere with strategic choices as well as with the informal system of regional property rights underlying Chinese government competition. The main expression of this is the budgetary dualism between budgetary and extra-budgetary funds and the institutional separation between tax administration and fiscal administration. Whilst the tax administration is the place where the results of intergovernmental bargaining are implemented, the fiscal administration reflects the partially autonomous position of different government units as players in government competition. In fiscal administration, the Chinese government reveals its compound structure.

Because of the dualism between tax and fiscal system, centralization policies and competitive strategies in both realms differ, such that measures and countermeasures can take place in different contexts. This is already obvious in the administrative structure. The tax administration is generally more centralized. Before the reforms, in Gujiao, Tongxiang and Zhangjiagang there was only a taxation bureau, respectively, which collected revenues for local, regional and central government under the direct leadership of the provincial tax bureau. The central government relied on the remittance of its part of revenues by the provinces. After the 1994 fiscal reform, the taxation bureaus of the three cities were split into national and local taxation bureaus, respectively. All the national taxation bureaus are responsible for collecting central and shared taxes. The local tax bureaus are administered by the provincial-level local taxation bureaus (*difang shuiwu ju*) at the top. The National Administration of Taxation in Beijing gives the local taxation bureaus only taxation-related technical and legal guidance. For instance, since the end of 2001 the local tax bureau in Gujiao is not a part of municipal administration but a branch of the prefecture-level administration. The salaries of the tax officials are covered by the prefecture-level government, which is the most reliable indicator of centralization even though the money is collected indirectly from the county-level government (which is also normally the case). Although the local tax bureau in Zhangjiagang is a part of municipal administration, the salaries of its tax officials are covered by the prefecture-level government. By comparison, only the salaries of tax officials of the local taxation bureau in Tongxiang are covered by the municipal budget and it is at the same time a part of the municipal government.

Since the local taxation bureau of Gujiao is no longer subject to the administration of the Gujiao government, it seems that the local revenue mobilization and fiscal policy (for instance, tax exemptions) will be hindered to some extent. In fact, the director of the fiscal bureau in Gujiao complains about this institutional change. But the reality shows that tax officials are still closely connected to the decision makers of the city. The Party chief and the mayor hold one monthly work meeting on economic development and tax revenues with the key officials in the government, involving the directors from the national and local taxation bureau in Gujiao. This is connected to the existing administrative assistance and cooperation mechanism in China. Furthermore, tax officials are still members of the local social network. As another example, the local tax bureaus in the three cities have also been implementing local governments' tax credit policy. Before 2000, a large amount of tax credit was given to local enterprises before these taxes are first collected and turned over to the treasury. They show here again a dual loyalty, that is, loyalty to the upper-level tax administration ("lines") and the local governments ("blocks").

In contrast with the local and national taxation bureaus, the fiscal bureaus in the three cities belong to the municipal administration. But they are required to comply with the upper-level laws and regulations on fiscal administration, though none is implemented fully. The fiscal bureau is the management unit of the entire local government activity in the economy. In Gujiao, however, this does not include the administration of land and resources, for which a special unit is responsible, the Bureau of Land and Resource Administration established in 2002 by merging the Bureau of Land and Bureau of Coal, following closely the national administrative reform in which the "State Administration of Land Resource" was renamed as "Ministry of Land and Resources." In Tongxiang and Zhangjiagang, the land is administered by their Bureau of Land, respectively.

The fiscal bureaus in the three cities plan the budget and control its implementation, manage government assets and supervise all non-budgetary financial flows. This would include the extra-budgetary funds and the related revenue, which therefore remains outside the reach of the tax administration. Like budgetary funds, extra-budgetary funds should be administered according to national laws and regulations, central guidelines and principles of budgetary planning. As has been stressed repeatedly in the pertinent literature, extra-budgetary funds are the most important expression of local fiscal autonomy, and therefore play a pivotal role in Chinese government competition. Its formal recognition and basic legitimacy is also a reflection of the limits of centralization for the central government competitive strategies.

The importance of extra-budgetary funds is vastly different across Chinese cities. Looking first at the regular budget and comparing the three cases, we note a remarkable similarity of structure (Table 8.10, in the appendix). Gujiao is the city with the largest retained share of local revenue, which matches its low fiscal capacity. If only the retained revenue is taken into consideration, in all three cities the industrial and commercial taxes are the dominant source of financing the budget, with some minor variations across the different kinds of taxes. However, this masks the pronounced differences between the three cities regarding extra-budgetary funds.

Tongxiang is radically different from Gujiao and Zhangjiagang, as is evident from Table 8.4. The data are estimates, and it has to be noted that there is no clear and open statistics on these funds, which frequently continue to be held on separate accounts of certain government organizations, as mentioned above.

Table 8.4 Extra-budgetary funds in year 2000 in Gujiao, Tongxiang and Zhangjiagang (RMB 10,000)

Type of Revenue	*Gujiao*	*Tongxiang*	*Zhangjiagang*
1. Regular local revenues (RMB 10,000)	6,796	36,668	100,605
2. Extra-budgetary revenues (RMB 10,000)	3,495	73,336	40,242
3. Total (RMB 10,000)	10,291	110,004	140,847
4. (2./1.) (%)	51.43	200	40
Per capita revenue (RMB)	494	1,678	1,687

Source: *Gujiao Economic Statistical Materials*, 2001; *Zhangjiagang Statistical Yearbook* 2000; *Tongxiang Statistical Yearbook* 2001. Extra-budgetary revenues are estimated by local cadres. Authors' own calculation based on these statistical and estimated data.

The figure in Tongxiang shows that a large part of public goods and services are financed from fees and user charges. Furthermore, in Tongxiang only the balances of revenues and expenditures are booked via the fiscal account, which implies that the entire volume is not accessible to systematic statistics. This overlaps with the so-called funds (*jijin*) that are simultaneously held by local governments. The difference is that funds income is clearly earmarked to be expended via the fund. In all three cities, and especially in Zhangjiagang, there is a larger number of funds, which, however, do not amount to a substantial fiscal weight in quantitative terms.

There is a clear trend to finally implement the central government's policy of larger transparency and clear regulation, yet frequently with new complications. This means that funds are increasingly abolished and mostly transformed into extra-budgetary funds, as for example, in Gujiao, where the social security funds have been transformed into extra-budgetary funds already in 1996 – which, however, does not mean that they are managed as extra-budgetary funds, since they are not yet included in the respective statistics. The regional and local practices of administration of budgetary and extra-budgetary funds are much diversified. The relevant reforms have been dictated by the central government. But none was implemented fully. The cities show different degrees of adherence to central directives, with Zhangjiagang being especially stubborn in preserving the funds, in spite of its minor size of only 3 percent of the entire budget.

The distinction between the regular budget and the extra-budgetary funds is very important. Local budgets always distinguish between current expenditures and investment. The typical Chinese local government has to use more than two thirds of the regular budget for personnel costs, such that one Chinese expression for current expenditures is *chifan caizheng* (budget only for eating). This is the main reason why budgetary problems very quickly translate into problems of paying wages of local government employees, as happened in Gujiao and Shanxi in general with the teachers' salaries in several counties and townships. To secure the salaries in rural townships and towns, the salary administration had to be centralized on the county level whereby the funds are required to come from the township level via the fiscal transfer and settlement, and the payments are made by the education bureau of the city. The "eating up" of the budget by employees is a fact in all three cities, with Tongxiang even using the entire regular budget for this purpose, Gujiao about 80 percent and Zhangjiagang roughly 65 percent.

Of course, this implies that the funds for investment have to come from other sources. These are mostly extra-budgetary funds and system-external revenues (*zhidu wai shouru*), that is, illegally raised funds or illegally collected fees. Hence, we diagnose a de facto institutional regime with a dualism between budget and extra-budget reflecting the division between salaries and investment, if leaving the system-external funds aside since that amount is non-transparent and unavailable but can be regarded anyway as an extended part of extra-budget. If we look at the structure of expenditures (Table 8.5), we learn that this is a very substantial distinction in quantitative terms. Such a

Table 8.5 Share of current expenditures and investment in total local budgetary expenditures in Gujiao, Tongxiang and Zhangjiagang (%)

	Current Expenditure	*Investment (productive and non-productive)*	*Other*	*Total*
Gujiao	56.1	13.5	30.4	100.0
Tongxiang	51.6	25.5	23.0	100.0
Zhangjiagang	37.6	39.2	23.2	100.0

Sources: Authors' own calculations based on data in *Gujiao Economic Statistical Materials*, 2001; *Zhangjiagang Statistical Yearbook*, 2000; *Tongxiang Statistical Yearbook* 2001. Excluding funds and extra-budgetary funds.

dualism will also necessarily lead to crowding out of some taxes by collecting some extra-budgetary and system-external funds since some of these funds themselves are parts of tax bases.

In the next section, we explain the effects of this dualism on the local provision of services and infrastructure. Budgetary dualism is also a dualism of two different kinds of revenue. As we have seen, the local budget is mostly financed out of taxes, for which the 1994 reforms drew a new institutional framework. Extra-budgetary funds are mostly fed by variable surtaxes, fees and other payments. Furthermore, the redistributive schemes are only relevant for the budget and not for the extra-budget and system-external revenue and expenditure. As a result, there are at least two important reasons for developing extra-budgetary funds and system-external revenue: first, only these funds can be a source of local investment, and second, these funds remain outside the control of upper-level governments. What we note, however, is that this is by no means a deviant behavior but seems to be an inherent feature of the Chinese fiscal system now for decades.

Budgetary dualism implies that the basic institutional structure of regional property rights will be reproduced by the process of local public investment. This is because the respective rights in the capital created are assigned to the level of government on which the funds were invested, implying that the revenue rights – actually a return on capital – will also accrue to this level. In this regard, we should not only consider the vertical intergovernmental relations but also the horizontal ones. The difficulties in controlling funds also stem from the fact that there is also competition for resources between different departments of the same local government unit. This includes access to upper-level support. Therefore, the local public investment process in China is embedded into a complex bargaining system where all participants face serious informational asymmetries regarding the actual fiscal capacity of the others, and where they try to exchange resources in a way that mutual interests are respected. As a consequence, government competition gradually transforms the system of local public investment into a "quasi-market," on which there is a tendency for efficient institutional solutions to emerge. This is the most important expression of social learning on the part of the local political actors.

Financing local infrastructure and public services

There is a deep gap between local taxes and local tasks and government capacity. Let us look at one example (Table 8.6). There is a local urban construction tax in the regular budget. When compared to the local urban construction expenditures the result is an under-financing of about 40–50 percent with Zhangjiagang achieving a much higher share, which reflects the low importance of extra-budgetary funds. In Gujiao, this means that a large share of urban investment projects has to be covered either via other budgetary revenue or via additional income.

This is a typical situation which leads to two significant trends. First, apart from the general use of extra-budgetary funds there is a trend to project-related financing schemes. Second, there is an increasing differentiation of government activities according to the principle of fiscal equivalence. Both trends go back on the same reason, namely, that the budgetary dualism implies that investment is increasingly treated as an economic activity possibly yielding income to cover the initial outlays. However, generating income depends on the nature of the services, which can be priced according to different criteria, either with political objectives in mind or with including economic costs of pricing. In the former case, it depends on political decisions whether an investment will be priced according to full-cost principles or not, which mainly affects social policies. In the latter case, it depends on technical considerations and transaction costs, whether and to which extent pricing policies can be implemented.

The different solutions to these problems that can actually be observed in Gujiao, Tongxiang and Zhangjiagang show a remarkable fit with certain assumptions of economic theory about the general rules to finance local public goods.

Table 8.6 Urban construction tax and expenditure in Gujiao, Tongxiang and Zhangjiagang (RMB million)

Year	*Tongxiang*		*Zhangjiagang*		*Gujiao*	
	A	*B*	*A*	*B*	*A*	*B*
1995	1,090	1,040	3,009	6,358	222	452
1996	1,267	1,032	3,960	6,300	332	703
1997	1,846	1,176	5,027	6,408	391	911
1998	2,149	1,227	5,172	7,189	n.a.	933
1999	2,256	2,097	5,518	8,162	215	812
2000	2,671	5,123	8,410	11,897	405	711

Source: *Gujiao Economic Statistical Materials*, 1996–2001; *Statistical Yearbooks of Tongxiang*, 1996–2001; *Statistical Yearbooks of Zhangjiagang*, 1995–2000; data of Ministry of Finance.
A = Urban construction tax revenue B = Expenditures for urban construction

Of course, there is also a strong impact of special characteristics of the Chinese fiscal system. Both observations can be synthesized in the hypothesis that government competition actually leads to the discovery of efficiency-enhancing fiscal and administrative procedures. Gujiao is a case in point, because up to the political turnaround of 2000 the local leadership tried to avoid adaptations to the increasing economic pressures. The new leadership designed new competitive strategies and started a learning process. Learning causes a diffusion of entrepreneurial models of government activity. This is pushed by the budgetary dualism maintained after the 1994 reforms and has been made even more pronounced by the effects of hard budget constraints. The most conspicuous example is the rapid spread of funding schemes based on the utilization of public land, which are frequently linked with the creation of special management units that operate outside the formal budget. These are independent from the fiscal model that is realized, as the convergence of practice in the three cases demonstrates, the wide differences in formal fiscal structure notwithstanding.

Subsequently, we classify different models of local public goods provision in Gujiao in contrast to these two other cities according to these general considerations. We will differentiate some ideal-types such as public and private provision, and public and private production of local public goods as well. This implies that there is a spectrum of alternatives between public and private provision, and one between public and private production. The existing different models can be viewed as outcomes from institutional learning and competition between jurisdictions. We start with the Chinese systemic peculiarities.

Impact of the bargaining system

As we have noted above, a major problem for Gujiao is the different assignment of larger companies located in Gujiao to upper-level administrations which results in an actual loss of tax revenue. At the same time, these companies are a burden for local infrastructure. Therefore, the allocation of benefits and costs is a major object of bargaining strategies between different levels of government. At the same time, this is also affected by horizontal government competition, because the relative position of localities as well as of departments is also strongly influenced by these assignments.

One outcome of these bargaining processes is the project-related participation of higher-level administrations in infrastructure provision. In Gujiao, this is especially the case in water and electricity supply. Major projects have been realized by the higher-level mining bureau of the Xishan mining area. For example, since the bureau had to build a water treatment plant for its companies anyway, this project was enlarged to include wastewater treatment for the municipality, too. Because of the interaction between horizontal and vertical government competition, such projects are not merely bargained between two parties, but there is a broader competitive setting.

In electricity, there are competing public providers on the local, provincial and national level. Although these operate in a homogenous national regulatory framework (especially on prices), there is much leeway for making profits because administered prices more than completely cover costs. Power plants will make more profits if they get larger quotas of network access for their generated electricity. To be successful in building up a power plant, a city government, first of all, should get approval by the provincial planning commission and thus be more entrepreneurial in rent-seeking in the political market, competing against other localities and projects. Jinye Group, a private company in Gujiao, is applying for building a new power plant related to mining activities. At the same time the mining bureau is also applying for building a new power plant. In Tongxiang, there is no power station, which means that it is a sole price taker in electricity consumption. In contrast to Gujiao and Tongxiang, there are several power stations in Zhangjiagang, which means that the city has good connections to the planning commission of the province Jiangsu and could attract projects and get them approved. The water treatment plants in Tongxiang and Zhangjiagang are all municipal ones. The two cases of electricity and water in three cities differ in terms of the application of the fiscal equivalence principle. Electricity rates cover costs including return on investment, whereas water rates only cover current expenses. In reality, given the asymmetrical information between the suppliers and the users, water rates approved by the price bureau in the three cities might well include some profits since both the local administration and the users have no sufficient information on the costs of production.

Reverse build, operate, transfer

An interesting approach can be found in many areas where, as in the case of water and electricity, pricing is possible in principle. Given the already high burden of personnel costs, running public services may turn out to be a problem. To avoid this, local governments may fund basic investment and auction off management to private entrepreneurs. This is akin to a reverse BOT (Build, Operate, Transfer) procedure, with the government being the first investor. In Gujiao, fiscal pressure is highest as both the absolute amount of budgetary and that of extra-budgetary funds are limited, which led to institutional learning, imitations and innovations by the new entrepreneurial leaders. For example, Gujiao City invested in public parks, but transferred management to a private company, which pays a rent for the right to the municipal budget. The same was done with the public toilets. The private company has to follow certain regulations on minimum standards of maintenance of the park. The municipal government has much discretion to emphasize social considerations here, because it may choose between different regimes of open access, partial- or full-cost pricing via the contracts with the private suppliers.

In both Tongxiang and Zhangjiagang, the aforementioned services are still produced and delivered by the municipal service units, which seem to be connected to less fiscal pressure in comparison with the case in Gujiao. As far as we observed, the Party secretaries and governments in all three cities, sometimes also the upper-level Party organs and governments, organize annual visits to other better-developed cities in China. Leaders and officials from these three cities also join information programs for visiting abroad. They also join work meetings organized by upper-level governments. What happened with the reverse BOT in Gujiao is connected obviously to the perception of the local leaders of the fiscal pressure and the institutional competition that serves as a discovering procedure for them to identify better institutions.

Privatizing public services

The latter example in Gujiao shows that in many fields it may become attractive to privatize public services by means of hiring out. For example, this is increasingly done in the area of city cleaning and road maintenance. Gujiao even introduced an open competitive auction for private as well as government employees in street cleaning. That is, the task was offered against a fee to internal as well as external applicants. Municipal employees who refused to take part in the procedure were laid off.

This approach of *tui xiang shichang* ("pushing into the market)" should be regarded as a major structural change in local government in China because it amounts to a hollowing out of neighborhoods. This, of course, reflects the declining role of mobilization and voluntary services in local public services. In street cleaning, Gujiao developed the model that services are commercialized, yet control is done mainly via the neighborhoods, and also to a small extent via the local government, which means a double relief for the local budget because supervision of standards is on a voluntary basis. In contrast, these services are still provided by municipal service units in Tongxiang and Zhangjiagang.

Enterprising government

The reverse procedure of privatization is the entrepreneurial action of local government. This is mostly linked with financing infrastructure via bank credits. This notable fact is of far-reaching significance for assessing the entire Chinese fiscal system because formally local governments are forbidden to run deficits and public debts, get loans and grant loan guarantees. What the governments in the three cities do is to form local public construction companies or project-specific companies. These corporatized entities are eligible for borrowing and guarantees.

In fact, there are different ways in how credit is used to finance public services. One simply is supplier's credit occurring when procurement is with delayed payment or funds advanced by a hired construction team being paid back after the construction. This is often done in the context of informal agreements about public–private cooperation in local projects. The supplier's credit and funds advanced by construction teams play an important role in the three cities because the suppliers and construction teams do not fear default since the government

Table 8.7 Source of funds for road investment outside city area, Gujiao 1996–2000 (RMB 10,000)

Source	*Amount*
1. Subventions by Shanxi Province and Taiyuan City	995
2. Regular municipal budget, Gujiao	990
3. Outside funds raised by companies, mining enterprises and rural population (jizi)	646
4. Labor services by farmers and other groups	1,103
5. Funds internally raised or allocated by the Transport Bureau, Gujiao (zichou)	2,928
6. Bank credit	15,000

Source: Gujiao Transport Bureau

grants normally implicit guarantees to cover the debts occurring in infrastructure projects. Especially in Gujiao, the government views it as one of the most important intermediate sources of funding. In a tunnel construction project of 2000 at the Gujiao road where a small toll station is also built up, the total investment was 46 million yuan, 21 million yuan out of which were funds advanced by the construction company, 20 million yuan were loans and only 5 million yuan were fiscal rotational funds (*caizheng zhouzhuanjin*), which are quasi-loans provided by the fiscal system. In general, more significant is direct bank credit which plays an important role in projects which have a semi-commercial nature. The typical example is again the construction of roads, especially on the regional level. Here, tolls can be used to fund investment that is first financed via credit. As is shown in Table 8.7, in Gujiao bank credit is by far the most important source of road investment.

One surprise is that the loans for such projects in all three cities come mostly from the prefecture-level state-owned commercial banks, which reflects a bad credit standing of local enterprise and a low level of trust between local banks on the one hand, and local enterprises and government on the other hand. One explanation is that the local governments helped local state and collective-owned enterprises to evade debt service so that both the government and enterprises lost credibility.

The governments in all three cities collect various kinds of extra-budgetary funds for vehicle and road uses or road construction. Together with the regular municipal budget, the funds raised play an important role in Gujiao. In contrast, the extra-budgetary funds play the most essential role in road construction in Tongxiang whereas the budgetary funds and other financial sources play a minor role. In Zhangjiagang, the budgetary funds, with extra-budgetary funds in addition, are the most important sources in financing of road construction whereas other financial sources only play a minor role.

Credit finance is also a dominant way to fund economic development zones, and technology and industrial parks. In this area we observe a large diversity across our three cases. Gujiao is much more conservative in using the instrument of local public investment and development corporations to manage infrastructure projects within a newly established technology development park and to access banks. Its earlier attempts at launching industrial parks riding on the national wave of 1993/1994 resulted in failure, the main reason being that the coal price was too low so that the investment climate was not favorable for investors to come from outside. With the new mayor coming to power, the government in Gujiao revitalized its plan and established such a technology park in 2002. An administrative committee is in charge of the administration of this zone and will be also responsible for infrastructure investment, which is authorized by the government Gujiao to deal solely with land and infrastructure projects whereby the different departments must give full necessary administrative supports. This, of course, is a risky venture because local government in this case is a de facto, but not de jure guarantor of such an undertaking. In Tongxiang, infrastructure projects within its economic development zone are managed by a development company, which has a second face as an administration committee. This is also the case for the economic development zone, the local tax-free zone and the different technology parks in Zhangjiagang. This is the core activities of the "entrepreneurial state." Of course, the extent of those activities is mainly determined by the opportunities perceived on the market.

The development of such zones and parks in the three cities is even more complicated by the different ways of their approval. The new technology park of Gujiao will be, but has still not been approved by the government Taiyuan, though it has been running for more than one year with the acquiescence of the government Taiyuan. The Tongxiang economic development zone was established upon approval of the provincial government, while some township-level economic development zones were established without any approval, serve as functionally extended parts of the Tongxiang economic development zone and grant the same benefits to the investors. The tax-free zone in Zhangjiagang was established upon the approval of the central government, while the Yanjiang (Riverside) Economic Development Zone was established without any approval, very similar with the case in Tongxiang, and serves as a functionally extended part of the free trade zone and grants the same benefits to the investors. The Zhangjiagang Economic Development Zone was established upon the approval of the government in Suzhou. Some industrial parks were approved by the local government or the provincial government. The different levels of approval correspond with different degrees of flexibility of formal tax and fiscal policies. But in reality, the benefits that the investors gain are dependent of their bargaining power.

Cashing in on public land

By far the most important way to fund public investment in all three cities is the use of public land. In Tongxiang, revenue related to land use is estimated to be as large as the regular budget. Without going into the regulatory details here, this is also a systemic feature because there are still no private property rights on land, such that either in the urban areas the local government is the owner or the rural communities otherwise. Land use is closely regulated on the national level, in particular with regard to the preservation of agricultural land. All land use is centrally registered and controlled in the three cities. Yet, there are ways to adapt to the local needs for commercial uses, as in the trade of land use quotas between Southern and Northern Jiangsu which preserves the total quota for the province where the Northern part sells quota to the Southern part informally while opening ways for industrial expansion in the South.

In Gujiao, control is implemented via the central registration of land use, and a simultaneous use of satellite data and a network of informal informants in the rural areas. This control enables local governments to squeeze substantial revenues out of land use fees and taxes, which are then divided between the budget and the extra-budget, depending on their character. In all three cities centralization of land management is the major vehicle to reap the benefits of the increasing economic importance of land. Basically, Gujiao government partakes in every land deal several times:

- There is a fee on the conversion of land use, which also applies if only re-registering is done, probably also as a result of ex-post controls.
- There is a tax on land use for non-agricultural uses as well as a tax on value gains. Assessment is made by a public list of reference values.
- Industrial and commercial land (*jingyingxing tudi*) use rights can be traded. The primary market is directly controlled by the government, since collective land first has to, mostly even is forced, to be sold to the city government which then sells the rights. Since 2002, the obligatory organization of this market is an auction. On the secondary market, every transaction is linked with taxes and fees benefiting the local coffers.

It is a similar case for the governments in Tongxiang and Zhangjiagang. However, the difference in Tongxiang is that the government started already in 1999 with auctioning off land use rights while those in Gujiao and Zhangjiagang have done it only since 2002, following the new central regulation. The current model of mobilizing land revenue for infrastructure investment is the "revolving land development" (*tudi gundong kaifa*). This means that the diverse possible revenues from land use that is related to an investment are directly included in the funding scheme of that project. For example, as a result from the bargaining between local government and commercial investors, building a new road may be accompanied by sales of land use rights at a lower price to the latter ones. Another approach is to sell government-owned premises to build new ones, which has the attractive side effect that tax sharing with upper-level administrations can be avoided. The office building of the government in Gujiao came into being in this way, which is now the best and highest mansion in the city center. In Zhangjiagang the aforementioned models are systematically linked with credit finance.

Public–private cooperation

Coming back to the more narrow forms of public services, a major approach is a sort of public–private partnership. The most current practice is that government acts as a leading agency that requests and motivates contributions by different groups in society. This need not be based on altruistic action. For example, a typical constellation is that the pecuniary external effects of public investment on private assets are monetized. This happens when an infrastructure project causes a rise in the value of real estate in three cities. Owners are then asked to contribute to the project, apart from the tax on value gains. Other related cases are the investment in roads by resident firms in Gujiao.

Regular budget

Finally we consider the case of regular budgetary finance. This is the necessary way when no income can be generated from the public activity. In the three cities, one of the most important areas is education. In Shanxi Province, one result of the tightening budgets was the increasing difficulty in meeting expenditure goals in education. Disparities across townships and towns increased the difficulties and triggered a partial centralization of school administration on the local level. This compares with the other two cities: Zhangjiagang relies on rich local resources to maintain a public school system, though it collects a great number of different fees and tuitions. It adapted in one middle school a model of state-controlled and private-run schooling, in which the majority of the shares are controlled by the local government and the rest by private investors. Also a part of profits flow out of the school-run collective enterprises comes to the budget of the corresponding schools. In contrast, Tongxiang follows its private sector approach and supports a partial privatization of the education system and introduced also new private schools beside the existing public schools. The partial privatization took the form of an incremental private capital injection. Some new dormitories, teaching building or laboratories are built with the private capital.

Because of the less advantageous economic situation, Gujiao cannot rely on increasing tuition fees. Schools are therefore funded mainly via the budget (Table 8.8). Among the budgetary funds, there are some small amount appropriations by the central government, including funds from the rural dangerous school building renovation fund, compulsory education fund and national debt-to-loan funds (*guozhai zhuan dai zijin*). However, the share of one third of own funding shows that the government is no longer able to support the system independently. Apart from tuition fees which are differentiated across the basic education and more market-oriented additional training, these are public contributions, school-related companies and private projects linked to funding equipment against user fees in Gujiao. In the school infrastructure projects, the funds advanced by the construction team play again a significant role in the financing scheme.

Table 8.8 Funding of education in Gujiao

Type of Funding	*1997*	*1998*	*1999*	*2000*
Total educational expenditures (RMB 10,000)	2,341.7	2,428.3	2,721.7	–
Total public expenditures per pupil (RMB)	620.4	679.7	721.2	–
Public expenditures for education excluding salaries for teachers and expenditures for pupils per pupil (RMB) (*gong yong jing fei*)	65.5	60.3	60.5	713.86
Funding via regular budget (RMB 10,000)	1,521.5	1,726.2	1,863.2	2,268
– of which: urban educational surtax (RMB 10,000)	69	153	53	89
– of which: rural educational surtax (RMB 10,000)	157	59.1	24	0
Own funds (RMB 10,000)	820.2	702.1	858.5	–
Share of own funds in total educational expenditures	35.03	28.91	31.54	–

Source: Education Bureau of Gujiao.

Institutional innovations and the political market

As we have seen, Gujiao has introduced many institutional innovations in public finance recently. Obviously, this reflects the strong competitive pressure on the new leadership after the 2000 scandals. This refers theoretically to the so-called Salmon mechanism, which is a kind of benchmarking. The new leadership had to sell its policies to the public as well as to upper leaders. The public did not only include the local population (who were reaffirmed in the right to evaluate the leader's performance), but also newspapers, which systematically pursued follow-up investigations in 2001.

This kind of political market process is very similar in the three locations and reflects the unified institutional framework of the political system. The Party chief is appointed according to nomenclature rules. The mayor is also pre-selected by the Party organ and recommended to the representatives of local parliaments (people's congresses) for election. In this way, the Party chief and mayor are not directly responsible to the citizens but to the superordinate governments and Party organs. Their entrepreneurial spirit is focused on the creating of performances (*yeji*) for a better career, which will be again evaluated by upper-level governments and Party organs. However, as far as public opinion indirectly influences the outcome of policies implemented by the local leaders, this can set powerful incentives for their behavior. Therefore, in the field of public investment projects there is an increasing impact not only of governmental competition in the narrow sense, but also of the political market. Demand revelation mechanisms in the political market are: (1) elections; (2) regular meetings with people's congress, Party, administration, political consultative conference, and some democratic parties; (3) own study and visit; (4) suggestions and recommendations written by members of people's congresses, and political consultative conferences, government officials, letters by citizens and visits of citizens; (5) the annual government work report to be read before the parliament; (6) public events and informal meetings with local business and other elites.

As a result of these institutional givens, although the supply of local public goods is still decided arbitrarily by local leaders, there is an increasing relevance of the fiscal equivalence principle, which means that the relation between government and citizens is more and more based on rules of exchange. This opens many ways for horizontal government competition. So far, the most important channel is investment, as is most obvious in the differential success of development parks and related projects.

Concluding discussion

To conclude, the comparative study of Gujiao shows that recent analyses of the Chinese fiscal system and government may fall into the trap of applying a misplaced theoretical lens: if some Weberian ideal type of rational-bureaucratic government is referred to, many practices of local government in China appear as outright deviant behaviors. This begs the question why deviance is tolerated at all. We argue that our recurrent diagnosis of government failure, loss of control and fiscal mismanagement simply reflect our misplaced theoretical stance. In fact, if the CG approach is taken as a framework, many observations can be interpreted as revealing the ubiquity of government competition in China. There are patterns emerging out of an endogenous process in which the central government and its formal institutions are only a part of the game. As we have seen, these self-organizing patterns show their own trends of an increasing rationalization and efficiency in terms of competitive behavior and outcomes. This is another important part of the Chinese transition, which is left out of sight, if transition is only viewed as a process of marketization and privatization.

As compared to theoretical alternatives in the literature, the main advantage of the CG approach is to be less value-laden than, for example, the concept of "predatory government." Government behavior is explained as an adaptation to resource constraints, institutional givens and strategic choices resulting from a dynamic learning process. This may result in "entrepreneurial" or "predatory" regimes, but these can also change almost overnight, as we observe in our study of Gujiao. The CG approach is also richer in grasping the complex interactions and fuzzy boundaries between market and state, whereas the "federalist" explanations implicitly argue normatively and presuppose a clear-cut boundary between both realms. The CG approach is more easily to integrate with political and administrative science approaches that, for example, emphasize the intergovernmental relations and bargaining processes. However, here we could only begin with a very rudimentary exposition of the CG paradigm. The main deficit lies in the thin description of actors and interest groups. The CG paradigm has a close relation with Public Choice approaches of explaining government behavior, which means that the micro-foundation needs to be made more explicit.

Appendix

Table 8.9 Budgetary revenues, expenditures and transfers of Gujiao (RMB 10,000)

Year					*of which*						*of which*						
	A	*B*	*C*	*D*	*E*	*F*	*G*	*H*	*I*	*J*	*K*	*L*	*M*	*N*	*O*	*P*	*Q (percent)*
	A=D–M–N	*B=C+E*		*D=E+F+G+H+I*												*P=C+I+M–F–G*	*Q=P/B* 100 percent*
1988	1,768	1,995		3,035	1,995		790	250		3,035	1,557		1,267		211	477	23.91
1989	2,975	3,064		4,427	3,064		1,152	211		4,427	2,168		1,452		807	300	9.79
1990	3,719	3,726		5,259	3,726		726	807		5,259	2,643		1,540		1,076	814	21.85
1991	4,039	4,452		6,460	4,452		932	1,076		6,460	3,110	2,421			929	1,489	33.45
1992	3,619	4,047		5,948	4,047		972	929		5,948	3,148		2,329		471	1,357	33.53
1993	4,683	4,663		6,340	4,663	350	516	445	366	6,340	3,662	1,657	334	318	370	1,125	24.13
Total of 1988–1993	20,803	21,947		31,469	21,947					31,469	16,288					5,562	25.34
Yearly average rate of growth, 1993	21.51	18.51			18.51					15.87	18.65						18.72

1994	5,773	6,808	2,048	7,646	4,760	1,590	548	370	378	7,646	4,694	1,863	10	392	687	1,783	26.19
1995	7,546	8,887	2,984	9,654	5,903	1,807	930	687	327	9,654	6,133	1,956	152	462	951	2,355	26.50
1996	9,475	10,426	3,678	11,791	6,748	1,932	1,193	951	967	11,791	7,345	2,024	292	777	1,353	2,869	27.52
1997	9,952	11,336	4,118	12,047	7,218	2,002	1,316	1,238	273	12,047	8,177	2,095		608	1,167	2,895	25.54
1998	9,842	12,419	4,476	12,010	7,943	2,054	1,117	1,167	–271	12,010	9,027	2,168		49	766	3,473	27.97
1999	7,983	10,138	3,727	10,227	6,411	1,951	1,457	766	–358	10,227	7,722	2,244			261	2,563	25.28
2000	8,987	10,929	4,133	11,310	6,796	2,015	1,253	244	1,002	11,310	8,698	2,323			289	3,188	29.17
Total of 1994–2000	59,558	70,943	25,164	74,685	45,779					74,685	51,796					19,126	26.96
Yearly average rate of growth, 1995–2000 (percent)	7.66	8.21	12.41	6.74	6.11					6.74	10.83					10.17	

Sources: Authors' own calculation based on data provided by the fiscal bureau of Tongxiang, Zhangjiagang and Gujiao City, and the Ministry of Finance.
A = usable local budgetary revenues; B = regular local revenues, total; C = of which; central revenues;
D = local revenues, total; E = local regular budgetary revenue; F = fixed subsidies; G = project-related subsidies;
H = balance from previous year; I = others; J = total local expenditure; K = total regular budgetary expenditure;
L = systemic transfers to central government; M = project-related transfers to central government;
N = other expenditures; O = balance brought forward to next year; P = net transfer to central government;
Q = proportion of net transfers to total local budgetary revenues

Table 8.10 Regular budgetary revenue in Gujiao, Tongxiang and Zhangjiagang in year 2000

		Gujiao			*Tongxiang*			*Zhangjiagang*		
		A	*B*	*C*	*A*	*B*	*C*	*A*	*B*	*C*
1	Total local budgetary revenue	11,010	100.00	–	84,988	100.00	–	203,429	100.00	–
2	Central government revenue	4,133	37.54	–	41,900	49.30	–	102,824	50.55	–
2.1	75 percent of VAT	4,131	37.52	–	41,031	48.28	–	101,601	49.94	–
2.2	Consumption tax	2	0.02	–	869	1.02	–	1,223	0.60	–
3	Local government revenue	6,877	62.46	100.00	45,088	53.05	100.00	100,605	49.45	100.00
3.1	Industry and trade tax	5,751	52.23	83.63	38,068	44.79	84.43	85,497	42.03	84.98
3.1.1	25% of VAT	1,377	12.51	20.02	13,677	16.09	30.33	33,867	16.65	33.66
3.1.2	Turnover tax	908	8.25	13.20	7,359	8.66	16.32	14,681	7.22	14.59
3.1.3	Corporate income tax	526	4.78	7.65	8,400	9.88	18.63	16,179	7.95	16.08
3.1.4	Personal income tax	852	7.74	12.39	3,364	3.96	7.46	7,011	3.45	6.97
3.1.5	Tax on resource use	400	3.63	5.82						
3.1.6	Regulatory tax on fixed investment	166	1.51	2.41				98	0.05	0.10
3.1.7	Urban construction tax	405	3.68	5.89	2,671	3.14	5.92	8,410	4.13	8.36
3.1.8	Estate tax	930	8.45	13.52	1,800	2.12	3.99	3,173	1.56	3.15
3.1.9	Stamp tax	16	0.15	0.23	797	0.94	1.77	1,246	0.61	1.24
3.1.10	Land utilization tax	158	1.44	2.30				257	0.13	0.26
3.1.11	Tax on land value increase		0.00	0.00				40	0.02	0.04

3.1.12	Vehicle and boat tax	7	0.06	0.10				387	0.19	0.38
3.1.13	Slaughter tax	6	0.05	0.09				148	0.07	0.15
3.2	Agricultural tax	65	0.59	0.95	2,514	2.96	5.58	8,052	3.96	8.00
3.3	Others	1,061	9.64	15.43	4,506	5.30	9.99	7,056	3.47	7.01
3.3.1	Administrative fees	354	3.22	5.15					0.00	0.00
3.3.2	Special income	279	2.53	4.06	1,659	1.95	3.68	3,645	1.79	3.62
3.3.3	Fines	293	2.66	4.26	2,847	3.35	6.31	3,375	1.66	3.35
3.3.4	Other income	135	1.23	1.96				36	0.02	0.04

Source: Authors' own calculations based on the *Gujiao Economic Statistical Materials*, 2001, *Zhangjiagang Statistical Yearbook*, 2000, and *Tongxiang Statistical Yearbook* 2001. Some data were collected from the Fiscal Bureaus of Tongxiang, Zhangjiagang and Gujiao City.

A: Total volume in RMB 1,000 B: Share of total regular budgetary revenue C: Share of local budgetary revenue.

Notes

1 For example, Wang Shaoguang, "China's 1994 Fiscal Reform: An Initial Assessment," *Asian Survey*, September 1997. Available at: http://www.cuhk.edu.hk/gpa/wang_files/94REFORM.doc

2 The distinction between formal and informal institutions had been introduced into economics with the seminal study by Douglass C. North, *Institutions, Institutional Change and Economic Performance* (Cambridge: Cambridge University Press, 1990). In the analysis of government, this has been applied systematically in the context of constitutional economics by Stefan Voigt, *Explaining Constitutional Change – A Positive Economics Approach* (Cheltenham: Edward Elgar, 1999).

3 Interestingly, these very broad concepts fit well into the Chinese way of understanding the structure of government, namely, in terms of lines and blocks (*tiaotiao kuaikuai*), and according to centralization and decentralization. The importance of these distinctions has been emphasized by almost all descriptions of the Chinese system of government. The *locus classicus* is Franz Schurmann, *Ideology and Organization in Communist China* (Berkeley and Los Angeles: University of California Press, 1966).

4 The focus in this section is Gujiao. We refer to the other cases to highlight special features of the Gujiao case and to extrapolate some general properties of the Chinese fiscal system on the local level. In order of appearance: Gujiao in Shanxi Province, Taiyuan City (Prefecture level), capital of Shanxi; Tongxiang in Zhejiang Province, Jiaxing City (Prefecture level) and Zhangjiagang in Jiangsu Province, Suzhou City (Prefecture level).

5 Budgeting Department, Ministry of Finance, ed. *Zhongguo guodu qi caizheng zhuanyi zhifu* (The fiscal transfer in the transit period of China), 1999.

Bibliography

The original source of this chapter is: Herrmann-Pillath, Carsten and Xingyuan Feng. Competitive Governments, Fiscal Arrangements, and the Provision of Local Public Infrastructure in China. A Theory-driven Study of Gujiao Municipality, in *China Information*, 18, 2004: 373–428 (Supplementary Paper).

Asian Development Bank. *Making Cities Work: Urban Policy and Infrastructure in the 21st Century*, 1999. Proceedings of the Urban Policy Workshop in the People's Republic of China. Available at: http://www.adb.org/Documents/Conference/Making_Cities_Work/default.asp

Bahl, R.W. *Fiscal Policy in China: Taxation and Intergovernmental Fiscal Relations*. (South San Francisco: The 1990 Institute), 1999.

Breton, A. *Competitive Governments: An Economic Theory of Politics and Public Finance*. (Cambridge: Cambridge University Press), 1996.

Budgeting Department, Ministry of Finance, ed. *Zhongguo guodu qi caizheng zhuanyi zhifu*. (Beijing: China Finance and Economy Publishing House), 1999.

Cai, H. and Treisman, D. *State Corroding Federalism: Interjurisdictional Competition and the Weakening of Central Authority*, 2002. Available at: http://www.polisci.ucla.edu/faculty/treisman/pages/state.pdf

Department of Statistical Evaluations, Ministry of Finance, ed. *2001 nian yusuan danwei juesuan baobiao bianzhi shouce*. (Beijing: China Finance and Economy Publishing House), 2001.

Jin, H., Qian, Y. and Weingast, B. Regional Decentralization and Fiscal Incentives: Federalism, Chinese Style. *Journal of Public Economics*, September 2005, 89(9–10), pp. 1719–1742.

Ma, S. and Hongxia, Y. Zhuanyi zhifu yu difang jingji shoujian. *Jingji yanjiu*, 33, 2003, pp. 26–33.

Wong, C.P.W., ed. *Financing Local Government in the People's Republic of China*. (Hong Kong: Oxford University Press), 1997.

Wong, C.P.W. Central-Local Relations Revisited. The 1994 Tax-Sharing Reforms and Public Expenditure Management in China. *China Perspectives*, 31, 2000, pp. 52–63.

World Bank. *China National Development and Sub-National Finance. A Review of Provincial Expenditures.* Report No. 22951-CHA. (Washington, DC: World Bank), 2002a.

World Bank. *World Development Report 2002*, 2002b. Available at: http://econ.worldbank.org/wdr/WDR2002/text-2394/

Zhang, L. Chinese Central-Provincial Fiscal Relationships, Budgetary Decline and the Impact of the 1994 Fiscal Reform: An Evaluation. *The China Quarterly*, 157, 1999, pp. 115–141.

9 Features, problems and reform of the county fiscal administrative system in China

As is known to all, there exist huge problems in China's county fiscal administration system. While a large number of documents to date focus on analyzing fiscal difficulties facing counties[1] (Jia et al., 2002; Tao et al., 2003), interpreting relevant government policies (e.g., the rural tax and fee reform) and consequences (He et al., 2000), and studying problems and countermeasures concerning specific operations of the county fiscal administration system (Zhou, 2000; Wu et al., 2003), there is less overall research on the system and its operation from the perspective of a multi-tier fiscal system. Further, less empirical analyses have been done on functions and powers, fiscal powers and expenditure responsibilities,[2] although a sound normative framework depends on this type of research. The county fiscal administration system is in direct connection with a series of issues, including higher-level administration of county and township finance, county-level administration of township finance, respective fiscal administration systems of counties and townships, fiscal revenue and expenditure of counties and townships, transfer payment from higher levels to the township, allocation of functions and powers, expenditure responsibilities and revenues powers across levels of government. Starting from an analysis of a multi-tier fiscal system and intergovernmental relations, this chapter discusses problems existing in the county fiscal administration system. Because of space limits, township finance will be regarded as a part of county finance in general and not be treated independently in this chapter. First, the chapter examines the status, features, problems and causes of higher-level administration of the county fiscal system, and dissects the allocation and operation of functions and powers, expenditure responsibilities and right to revenue across levels of government; then, from normative perspectives, it puts forward some thoughts for resolving the problems existing in the county fiscal administration system.

Features, problems and causes of the county fiscal system in China

The higher-level administration system of county finance in China mainly involves a hierarchy of administration, distribution of revenue, division of functions and powers regarding expenditure responsibilities, and the fiscal transfer payment system. The tax sharing system, either central-provincial or provincial/prefectural-county, emerges in the form of decentralization on the premise of a centralized administrative system.

As a whole, China is a unitary state that pursues the fiscal administration system of "supervising the lower level." There are two levels of government that administer county finance – the provincial level and the prefectural/municipal level. The model in which the provincial-level government directly administers county finance is called the system of "province supervising county" (or "province directly supervising county"), and the model in which the prefectural/municipal-level government administers county finance is called the system of "city supervising county."

In sum, the basic features of China's county fiscal administration system include the following points: (1) The allocation of budgetary revenue is carried out by means of the administration instead of legislation; (2) Higher-level and county governments are playing games in terms of revenue assignment. While higher levels dominate the allocation of budgetary revenue, counties take strategic countermeasures by taking advantage of the autonomy they have to a certain extent to pursue other revenues (extra-budgetary revenue, land transfer income, etc.), or by highlighting fiscal difficulty to acquire general or special transfers from higher levels and to create favorable conditions for next-round bargaining of revenue assignment; (3) Following the beaten path, division of expenditure responsibilities at all levels is unclear, making higher levels arbitrary in changing and shifting expenditure responsibilities; (4) The design of the current tax sharing system for administration of county finance does not effectively consider, and thus fails to meet, the preferences and requirements of county governments and residents.

The fiscal administration system reform featuring "province supervising county" and "county strengthening and power expansion"

The 1994 reform of tax sharing fiscal administration system, implemented in light of the Decision of the State Council on Implementing the Tax Sharing Administration System (No. 85 [1993], promulgated by the State Council, hereinafter referred to as "Decision") defined central–provincial fiscal relations. Without specific provisions on sub-provincial fiscal administration systems, the Decision provided in general terms that provinces should formulate systems for fiscal administration of cities and counties within their jurisdictions in accordance with the Decision.[3] In response to it, provinces have carried out reform of sub-provincial fiscal administration systems since 1994. At the outset of reform and opening-up, most provinces adopted the principle of "supervising the lower level" and established a vertical fiscal administration system, following the hierarchy from "province supervising city" to "city supervising county," except that Zhejiang Province stuck to the old system of "province supervising county." Thus in specific operations after 1994, which level administered county finance differentiated two major county fiscal administration systems: one was direct provincial oversight of county finance, called the "province supervising county" system; the other was municipal oversight of county finance, called the "city supervising county" system. With the promulgation of the No. 1 Document by the central government in 2009, many counties and cities pushed forward the fiscal system reform of "province directly supervising county (city)" and the similar pilot reform of "county strengthening and power expansion" (Hu et al., 2006).

The "province supervising county" system involves direct provincial allocation to counties of fiscal revenue and expenditure and budgetary funds, direct arrangement of year-end settlement, and direct linkage between county finance and provincial finance, which is similar to the municipal–provincial fiscal linkage. The "city supervising county" system, in contrast, requires putting counties (cities) within the same economic district under the administration, including fiscal administration, of a central city which is therefore turned into a first-class local authority under direct provincial leadership. The fiscal system of "province supervising county" has remained in effect since the founding of new China until the implementation of the tax sharing system in 1994; since then, this model was replaced with the system of "province supervising city, city supervising county," with the exception of Zhejiang Province, which stuck to the old "province supervising county" model.

The fiscal administration system of "province supervising city, city supervising county" was gradually put into place at each level from 1994, with a view to breaking administrative barriers and urban–rural disconnection, making central cities economic engines to drive the development of surrounding counties. Accordingly, the merit of the "city supervising county" system was that some economically strong prefectural cities at a higher level of administration could drive the economic growth of surrounding counties to a certain degree by, for example, providing transfer payments that may exceed the share of fiscal revenue to be turned over by surrounding counties. Nonetheless, the "city supervising county" model added a tier to the intergovernmental fiscal hierarchy. The more levels, the more institutional constraints county and township governments suffered. In many areas, the proceeding of "city supervising county" system was not in smooth waters: (1) Administrative efficiency fell off due to increased government levels; (2) The "city supervising county" system allowed most prefectural cities to share county fiscal revenue and centralize a portion of county fiscal resources (i.e., "city exploiting county"); (3) A number of prefectural cities did not provide reciprocal fiscal and administrative supports; indeed, the administrative intervention or non-action of prefectural governments became an obstacle to continuous county development and fair competition between counties and cities ("city coercing county"); the experiences of county-level cities under the jurisdiction of Suzhou City was a case;[4] (4) A number of prefectural governments tended to "decentralize duties and responsibilities while centralizing control over revenue," leading to fluctuation of service of lowest-level governments; (5) Cities with a smaller scale of economy and less strength could hardly drive the development of surrounding counties[5] (Chen et al., 2009).

Strong points of "province supervising county" fiscal administration system included: (1) weakening of prefectural/municipal-level fiscal functions and avoidance of reduction in administrative efficiency by removing the intermediate link of municipality; (2) convenience for provinces to observe the fiscal conditions of various counties and thereby increase supports to those in fiscal straits and speed up provincial transfer payment;[6] and (3) provision of room for county economic growth by avoiding "the big coercing the small," a situation likely to take place in city vs. county competition (Lin et al., 2006). Examples include the "province supervising county" fiscal administration system implemented in Zhejiang, which covered direct provincial allocation of fiscal revenue and expenditure, earmarked transfers and budgetary funds, and directed arrangement of year-end settlement to 63 counties (including county-level cities) and cities (excluding municipalities with independent planning status); while the county/city finance was directly linked with provincial finance, they had no settlement relations under the system (Lin, 2006). The weakness of the "province supervising county" system involved aggravation of information asymmetries caused by limited government manpower and difficulty putting into action provincial administration of county finance; in provinces with an expansive territory and a large number of counties and cities, it was hard for the governments to conduct effective supervision of counties' fiscal behavior.

Comparison of respective strengths and weaknesses of the two fiscal systems, "city supervising county" and "province supervising county," brought about "province supervising county" or "county strengthening and power expansion" reformation, carried out by the central government in recent years. While most counties across China applauded the reform, some counties in the practice of the "city supervising county" system held the opposite view, for they acquired from the prefectural/municipal level fiscal and administrative supports at an amount larger than the compliance cost they had to pay (including the portion of fiscal revenue to be turned over). In an investigation conducted by one of the authors, some poor counties under the jurisdiction of Nanning City, Guangxi Province, acquired substantial transfer payments from the city each year; Liyang City of Jiangsu Province, with a quite booming economy, still received considerable fiscal support from prefectural Changzhou City due to old revolutionary base areas under its jurisdiction. Either in the poor county of Nanning City or in the booming Liyang City, some officials were opposed to carrying out the fiscal system reform of "province supervising county."

Anhui and Hubei Provinces launched the fiscal pilot reform of "province supervising county" in 2002. Up to June 2007, 18 provinces across China adopted the "province supervising county" administration system, with the fiscal system as a component;[7] added by four municipalities directly under the central government, which were already in practice (due to the absence of prefectural/municipal level in their administrative hierarchy), a total of 22 provinces, municipalities and autonomous regions put into effect the "province supervising county" system.

In the center's 2009 Document No.1, the fiscal system of "province directly supervising county" was promoted with suggestions to incorporate major producers of grain, oil plants, cotton and live pigs into the reform, make steady progress in the pilot reform of "county strengthening and power expansion," encourage qualified provinces to take the lead in streamlining government, and accomplish these goals in accordance with the law. So far, an increasing number of provinces have implemented the pilot reform of the "province supervising county" fiscal administration system.

Over the past few years, China has implemented the aforementioned trial reform of "county strengthening and power expansion" (Jiang, 2009), mainly involving delegation of fiscal powers to the lower level, that is, provinces directly administer county finance under the two-level fiscal system while prefectural/municipal-level leadership of administration over counties remained. In essence, it was a form of the preceding "province supervising county" model, supplemented with a certain degree of decentralization in economy, investment and administration (Zhang, 2008). In 2007, for example, Sichuan Province chose Anyue County (under the jurisdiction of prefectural city Ziyang) as a pilot to implement the reform of "county strengthening and power expansion," which included the contents of the "province supervising county" fiscal system. The pilot reform was also carried out in provinces which were already practicing the "province supervising county" system.[8] By direct administration of a unified tax sharing system, effective in Anyue County and Ziyang City, Sichuan provincial government aimed at securing its interests and realizing incremental regulation. As of January 1, 2007, Ziyang City no longer participated in sharing of Anyue's fiscal revenue, while the central and provincial governments continued doing so under the fiscal system.[9]

The system of "county strengthening and power expansion" had the following advantages in specific operations: (1) It helped to streamline government, simplify administrative procedures, as well as reduce or even eliminate prefectural control and intervention, and centralization of county fiscal resources; (2) It promoted autonomy in power-expanded counties; (3) It highlighted the importance of economic districts in promoting regional economic integration, instead of the consolidating or even coercing effect of prefectural cities as an administrative division. On the other hand, the system had a series of problems:[10] (1) Supports from prefectural cities to power-expanded counties were reduced. While prefectural cities centralized a portion of county fiscal resources, they also provided financial support to some backward counties under their jurisdictions. With "county strengthening and power expansion," prefectural cities reduced financial support to power-expanded counties. The issue of matching funds is an example: while provincial subsidies were delivered for approved projects, the required matching funds from prefectural cities were not available, and provincial governments had no relevant policies of direct subsidization leaving backward counties (cities) in a funding bottleneck; (2) Land, finance, industry and commerce, taxation and other vertical administrative departments under direct provincial control were self-contained and reluctant to shift powers down to counties. With a decisive impact on local economic growth, these departments had their own respective vertical administrative systems, making the power-expanding policy impotent before the centralized structure; (3) The reality that power-expanded counties were unlikely to separate totally from prefectural cities to which they belonged (e.g., personnel administration of county governments may remain under the control of prefectural governments) drove prefectural–county contradictions when county governments had to deal with two bosses – the provincial government and the prefectural government – at the same time; (4) With "county strengthening and power expansion," provincial governments had to deal with a great number of counties, making it necessary to enhance supervision and administration by, for example, establishing "regional administrative offices" at the prefectural level as government agencies dispatched by provinces. Besides, the expansion of county powers stopped at the level of government and left local democracy unchanged, weakening the counterbalance to local governments.

Both the "province supervising county" model or the "city supervising county" model and the reform of "county strengthening and power expansion" involved two deep-seated structural problems: (1) With the old thinking of "supervising the lower level," reformations of the vertical government system were unlikely to eradicate problems related to the vertical fiscal and administration systems, wherein the most serious problem was information asymmetry between higher and lower levels. To address the problem, a sound democratic system at grass-roots level needed to be established. (2) While all reforms proceeded within the administrative framework, division of functions and powers and allocation of revenues and expenditures ought to have been determined by NPC legislation. The Budget Law of China stipulates that the State Council shall promulgate separate regulations on allocation of revenue and expenditure. The Regulation for Enforcement of Budget Law promulgated by the State Council further stipulates that the State Council shall issue separate regulations on the intergovernmental tax sharing system; both only need to be submitted to the NPC for the record. In light of international practice, the adjustment of central–local fiscal relations, as part of intergovernmental redistribution of powers, should be determined by legislation rather than administration. Both of the administration-oriented regulations need to be rectified, for they violate basic legal principles and the spirit of law and are inconsistent with procedures of democratic finance. The existence of deep-seated structural problems makes it hard for local governments to achieve good governance.

Allocation of revenues

In China, county-level governments have very limited fiscal powers, especially with regard to levying taxes: (1) Governments at provincial and lower levels have no authority to formulate tax laws; fee collection events are decided by the center, provinces or major municipalities, and are finally controlled by the center. County-level governments have no power to collect fees in the locality for own needs without the approval of higher levels. (2) While rigid restrictions are imposed on county government borrowing, they still manage to borrow by using subordinate enterprises or projects. As stipulated in the 2004 Budget Law, local budgets across levels shall be prepared under the principle of "making ends meet," list no deficits and prohibit local government debt issuance, except as otherwise provided by laws or State Council regulations. Restrictions, however, do not include enterprise borrowing or borrowing for projects, and fail to prevent provision of invisible guarantees by local governments for enterprise or project loans. (3) Higher-level governments are in the driver's seat in administration of county tax sharing systems and allocation of county revenue, but such dominant control is affected by the bargaining power and countermeasures of county governments. In their administration of county fiscal systems, provincial or municipal governments take the following procedures in allocating revenues:

1 Under the tax-sharing administration system, the central government cuts off a large share of revenues (the center's regular revenue and the central portion of shared revenue) from the province (including counties). The provincial government then cuts off a share of revenues from municipalities and counties under its jurisdiction (the provincial government's regular revenue and the provincial portion of shared revenues with municipalities and counties).
2 Many central cities practicing the "city supervising county" fiscal system or the system of "county strengthening and power expansion" cut off a share of revenues from counties and cities under their jurisdictions, usually in the name of "centralizing a portion of revenue."
3 Governments from central to prefectural levels keep control over lower-level governments through redistribution and centralization of revenue, and transfer payment of disposable revenue.

In the process of revenue allocation, governments at different levels pay attention to maintaining their respective vested interests. The higher level tends to centralize revenue from the lower level with a view to increasing future revenue, thus forming a multi-tier model of revenue allocation featuring "the below following the behavior of the above" and "supervising the lower level." The centralization of county/city fiscal resources by higher-level governments is not infinite but restricted by local bargaining power, and the strength of rent-seeking and countermeasures like "leaving wealth with the people."

The 1993 State Council Decision ruled that provinces have decision-making power on sub-provincial-level fiscal administration systems, so the county fiscal systems effective after 1994 showed systematic diversity. While all provinces called their fiscal systems below the provincial level part of the "tax sharing system," a standard sub-provincial tax sharing system does not exist: practices of the "fiscal contracting system" and the "base method" remain effective in many places, and "tax sharing" is achieved by applying the bases of actual county and township revenues before 1994, with a focus on revenue allocation. Common practices, as seen in various regions, include maintaining the original hierarchy for sharing except for the types being transferred to higher or lower levels, and adjusting the allocation of business taxes in a few places. Thus, 75 percent of the value added tax (VAT) is allocated to the center and the remaining 25 percent is left to cities and counties for sharing in most areas. It is shared by provinces, cities and counties in a small number of areas. In most areas, the types to be allocated from the central to local level and newly collected tax items are shared by provinces, cities and counties.[11] As stated above, some localities implement the fiscal administration system of "city supervising county," under which prefectural governments participate in sharing of county revenues; some other localities implement the "province supervising county" system, under which prefectural governments do not participate in sharing of county revenues.

The 1994 fiscal reform brought a significant increase in the ratio of fiscal revenue to GDP (Gross Domestic Product) and a high degree of centralization of revenue toward the central government. According to statistics, the ratio of fiscal revenue to GDP in 1993 was 12.3 percent, rising to 20.8 percent in 2007. The central revenue made up only 22 percent of fiscal revenue in 1993, but rose to 54.1 percent in 2007. Table 9.1 shows the revenue assignment breakdown at all levels of government in 2006, including general budget revenue, fund revenue and extra-budgetary revenue. In the same year, the central government accounted for 52.8 percent of total general budget revenue, while county-level and township-level governments accounted for 13.6 percent and 6.2 percent, respectively; and the center accounted for 43.2 percent of the aggregation of general budget revenue, fund revenue and extra-budgetary revenue, while counties and townships shared 16.4 percent and 4.9 percent, respectively. In addition, debt revenue played an important role in supporting the "payroll finance" and "construction finance" of local governments, including counties and townships. As estimated by the Research Institute of Fiscal Science, Ministry of Finance, the overall balance of local government debt would exceed 4,000 billion yuan by the end of 2008 (Han et al., 2008).

Taking the case of Anyue County, Sichuan Province, we may analyze China's county tax sharing fiscal system. Table 9.2 reflects provincial and low-level government administration of Anyue's fiscal sharing system. The county is under the jurisdiction of prefectural city Ziyang. With a total population of 1.54 million and an agricultural population of 1.4 million in 2006, Anyue is populous, and a major county of hill-type agriculture. In 2005, it produced a GDP of 6.33 billion yuan, despite general budget revenue of only 88.05 million yuan.

Table 9.1 Revenue assignments breakdown at all levels of government, year 2006

Type of revenue	*Amount (100 million)*						*Percentage (%)*				
	National total	*Central*	*Provincial*	*Prefecture*	*County*	*Township*	*Central*	*Provincial*	*Prefecture*	*County*	*Township*
Total general budget revenue	3,876	2,045.7	467.4	598.6	535.9	228.4	52.8	12.1	15.4	13.8	5.9
Fund revenue	725.3	170.7	215.8	192.5	142.4	3.9	23.5	29.8	26.5	19.6	0.5
Extra-budgetary revenue	640.8	46.7	195.1	195.6	181.3	22.1	7.3	30.4	30.5	28.3	3.4
Total	5 242.1	2 263.1	878.3	986.7	859.6	254.4	43.2	16.8	18.8	16.4	4.9

Source: *China Finance Yearbook* 2007 and other data provided by the Ministry of Finance.

Table 9.2 Breakdown of tax revenues shared by higher-level governments and Anyue County, year 2003–2006

Types of Revenue		*Coverage and Percentage of Sharing by Province, municipality, county and township (percent)*
1. Taxes and fees	VAT	Central; 75, provincial; 8.75, county; 16.25
	Consumption tax	Central; 100
	Business tax	
	Business tax for banking and insurance industries	Provincial; 100
	General business tax	Provincial; 35, county; 65
	Enterprise income tax	County enterprise. central, 60, county; 40
	Personal income tax	Central; 60, provincial; 14, county; 26
	Resource tax	Provincial; 35, county; 65
	Urban maintenance and construction tax	County; 100
	House property tax	Provincial; 35, county; 65
	Stamp tax	Provincial; 35, county; 65
	Urban land use tax	Provincial; 35, provincial; 65
	Land value increment tax	County; 100
	Vehicle and vessel usage Plate Tax	County; 100
	Slaughter tax	Cancelled
	Agricultural specialty tax	Cancelled
	Deed tax	Provincial; 35, county; 65
Other revenues	Operating income of state-owned assets	County; 100
	Subsidy for state-owned enterprise losses	–
	Administrative charge	County; 100
	Fine and confiscatory revenue	County; 100
	Special revenue	Sewage central; 30, provincial; 15, municipal; 15, county; 40%, education surtax county; 100
	Others	County; 100
2. Tax increment refund	VAT refund	–
	Consumption tax refund	–
	Enterprise income tax refund	–
	Personal income tax refund	–
3. Portion of revenue in excess of base		County; 100
4. Other sharing		–

Source: Feng Xingyuan, "Research Report on County and Township Fiscal Problems of Anyue County, Sichuan Province. Sub-report for Research on County and Township Fiscal Problems," Joint Project by NDRC and Australian Government, October 28, 2006.

From 2003 to 2006, the allocation of Anyue's revenue to the central, provincial, municipal and county governments was as follows:

- VAT: 75 percent went to the center and 25 percent to the local; for the local portion, 8.75 percent went to the province and 16.25 percent kept by the county (allocated based on the administrative division to which it belongs).
- Consumption tax: 100 percent was allocated to the center. Business tax (excluding business tax for banking and insurance industries): 35 percent taken as tax base for provincial-level allocation of revenue; 65 percent kept by the county.
- Vehicle purchase tax: all acquired by the center. Local enterprise income tax: 60 percent went to the center; the remaining 40 percent went to the province in the form of provincial enterprise income tax, or was kept by the county in the form of county enterprise income tax.
- Personal income tax: the center shared 60 percent, the province, 14 percent, and the county, 26 percent.
- Business tax: railway business tax and business tax for central banking and insurance industries was allocated to the center; business tax for local banking and insurance industries was allocated to the province; for general business tax, 35 percent went to the province and 65 percent to the city.
- Resource tax: offshore oil resource taxes all belonged to the center; for others, the province shared 35 percent, and the county shared 65 percent.
- House property tax, urban land use tax, stamp tax and deed tax: 35 percent went to the province and 65 percent was kept by the county.
- Urban maintenance and construction tax, land value increment tax, vehicle and vessel usage plate tax and farmland occupation tax: 100 percent was allocated to the county.

It can be seen from the table that the central and Sichuan provincial governments acquired a large part of Anyue County's revenue while Ziyang City only shared 15 percent of sewage charges.

The general budget revenue of Anyue County in 2005 only amounted to 88.04 million yuan, compared with the total local general budget revenue of 164.36 million yuan (Table 9.3); the gap between the two was the portion shared by central, provincial and prefectural levels, making up 46.4 percent of total local general budget revenue. Besides, central and provincial subsidies (including all sorts of tax refunds) came to 598.96 million yuan, 6.8 times local general budget revenue. County-level fund revenue was 19.9 million yuan, 22.6 percent of local general budget revenue. The extra-budgetary revenue was large, totaling 74.42 million yuan, 84.5 percent of local general budget revenue. The fiscal dependence rate of Anyue County can be computed by using the formula as in the following text (after Table 9.2).

Table 9.3 Anyue County final accounts of general budget revenue in fiscal year 2005 (RMB 10,000)

Item	*Amount*	*Item*	*Amount*
I. Total local general budget revenue	164,360	3. Administrative fee	20,330
(i) Local general budget revenue	88,040	4. Fine and confiscatory revenue	5,930
1. Total fiscal revenues	52,910	5. Special revenue	2,720
wherein: VAT	8,370	6. Others	260
business tax	19,030	(ii) Central revenue	49,910
enterprise income tax	1,540	VAT	38,610
personal income tax	5,660	consumption tax	210
resource tax	370	others	11,090
urban maintenance and construction tax	7,680	(iii) Provincial revenue	26,270
house property tax	2,140	(iv) Prefectural revenue	140
stamp tax	230	II. Central and provincial subsidies	598,960
urban land use tax	270	1. Refund of consumption tax and VAT	22,460
slaughter tax		2. Income tax base refund	1,240
agriculture tax		3. Special subsidies	129,820
agricultural specialty tax		4. General purpose transfer payment	153,870
land value increment tax	2,530	5. Transfer payment subsidy for salary adjustment	90,450
vehicle and vessel usage plate tax	920		
farmland occupation tax	730	6. Transfer payment subsidy for rural tax and fee reform	84,690
deed tax	3,440	wherein: transfer payment subsidy for primary and secondary school teachers salaries	27,660
2. Operating income of state-owned assets	5,890		

(*Continued*)

Table 9.3 (Continued)

Item	*Amount*	*Item*	*Amount*
7. Transfer payment subsidy for cancellation of agricultural specialty tax and reduction in agriculture tax rate	65,050	III. County fund revenue	19,900
		wherein: paid land use revenue	18,790
8. Transfer payment subsidy for alleviation of county and township fiscal difficulties	8,600	IV. County extra-budgetary revenue	74,420
		wherein: administrative fee	74,420
9. Subsidy for further issuance of national debt	34,780	V. County disposable financial resources	781,320
10. Settlement subsidy	5,780		
11. Subsidies for agriculture tax deduction or exemption caused by disasters, subsidy for enterprise and public institution budget			

Source: Feng Xingyuan. "Research Report on Fiscal Problems of Anyue County, Sichuan Province. Sub-report for Research on County and Township Fiscal Problems." Joint Project by NDRC and Australian Government, October 28, 2006.

Note: Provincial subsidies include subsidies and refunds from the central and provincial governments.

The formula of fiscal dependence rate can be defined as: fiscal dependence rate = (central, provincial and municipal subsidies – refunds of consumption tax and VAT – income tax base refund) / total county disposable financial resources * 100 percent. The fiscal dependence rate of Anyue County in 2005 is computed as 73.6 percent. Accordingly, the county's fiscal self-sufficiency rate under the current tax sharing fiscal administration system can be defined as: fiscal self – sufficiency rate = 100 percent – fiscal dependence.

By computation, the fiscal self-sufficiency rate of Anyue County in 2005 was 26.4 percent. It is noteworthy that the revenue list and computation did not include debt revenue and social security funds. Outstanding debts of the county and its townships came to 1.44 billion yuan by the end of 2005, 16.4 times the local general budget revenue. In addition, village-level debts amounted to 89.59 million yuan, or on average, 100,000 yuan per village. The total amount of village-level debts was 1.02 times the county-level general budget revenue.

Anyue's agriculture tax revenue in 2003 reached 51.91 million yuan, or 47.5 percent of the local general budget revenue of the same year. With the rural tax and fee reform, the agriculture tax revenue dropped to 26.68 million yuan in 2004, or 27.6 percent of the local general budget revenue of the same year. By 2005, the agriculture tax revenue fell to zero. It is thus clear that for Anyue, a county with a large agricultural population base, agriculture tax revenue was once the primary source of revenue. After the cancellation of agriculture tax, however, the business tax became the single primary source of revenue. A great quantity of expenditure was filled in by central and provincial transfers.

As of January 1, 2007, Sichuan Province made Anyue County a pilot for "county strengthening and power expansion," implementing the "province supervising county" fiscal administration system. As prescribed in Opinions on the Fiscal Administration System Reform in Power Expanding Pilot Counties issued by the Sichuan provincial government, a basic principle of reform was the safeguard of interest and increment regulation, that is, to properly regulate revenue increment of future years on the premise of maintaining vested interest of counties (cities).[12] Table 9.4 provides details of what higher-level governments did in fiscal administration of Anyue's tax-sharing system since the 2007 reform of "county strengthening and power expansion."

The administration-based revenue distribution system at provincial and below levels in China, including higher-level administration of the county tax sharing system, offered flexibility in provincial budgeting and contributed to intergovernmental equality in revenue within the province.[13] Cost had to be paid though: (1) Municipal and county governments sacrificed autonomy; a lot of backward cities and counties depended to a great degree on central and provincial transfers, with a weakened sense of responsibility. (2) Lack of a stable, formal system of distribution with general budgets led to reduced predictability of local revenue and shrinking budgetary organization and appropriation. (3) Lack of such a system generated counter incentives for revenue mobilization as local governments were driven to shift fiscal resources off-budget, or even hide them in extra-systemic revenues.[14]

Table 9.4 Higher-level administration of Anye County tax sharing fiscal system since year 2007

Type of Revenue	*Allocation of Fiscal Revenue to Sichuan Province, Ziyang City and Anyue County*
Tax revenue	Provincial–county allocation of tax revenue: for 8 types of taxes, including the 25% local portion of VAT, and business tax, the province and pilot counties share at a ratio of 35:65; minority county pilots do not currently share. Enterprise income tax is shared by the center and local government, the 40% local portion going to the province if paid by provincial enterprises, and to the county if paid by county enterprises. Then, 92.5% of export refunds are provided by the center; for the 7.5% local portion, the province and pilot counties shared at a ratio of 35:65, and minority county pilots follow the preceding rules to bear 100%.
	Municipal–county allocation of tax revenue: Pilot counties and cities do not participate in tax sharing. The center and the province participate in sharing of pilot county revenue, but cities do not.
Other revenue	Administrative fee, special revenue, governmental fund and other non-tax revenues of pilot counties should be paid to central, provincial, pilot county treasuries or special fiscal accounts, pursuant to relevant provisions. The municipality to which the pilot county belongs does not participate in sharing of county non-tax revenues.
	According to principles concerning the allocation of economic responsibilities and functions and powers, non-tax revenues and corresponding expenditures do not partake in base transfer.
Revenue base and refund	The province determines the revenue base and expenditure base and allocates them directly to pilot counties (cities). With 2006 as the base year, the province separates the share of tax refund, income tax base, export refund base, other base subsidy (to be turned over) and special base subsidy (including matching fund payment to pilot counties as arranged in 2007 municipal budget) that should belong to pilot counties from municipal finance, reduces (increases) the base of provincial subsidy to cities and pilot counties, and delivers payments to pilot counties according to relevant settlement approaches. In 2007, the province delivers the whole share of 2007 county real revenue increment that should go to the municipality if computed under the original system to the municipality as a subsidy by means of year-end settlement. From 2008 to 2010, the province delivers 50% of the share of that very year's county real revenue increment that should go to the municipality if computed under the original system to the municipality as a subsidy by means of year-end settlement, and includes it into the base.
Enterprise affiliation and revenue base	For municipal enterprises and public institutions located within pilot counties, the provincial fiscal department shall conduct procedures to transfer their relationship of administrative subordination, revenue base and expenditure base on consensus between the city and the county involved.

Source: Sichuan Province Opinions on the Fiscal Administration System Reform in Power-Expanding Pilot Counties, July 10, 2007.

Division of functions and powers and expenditure responsibilities

In the national administration of the provincial fiscal system, the central government overemphasized redistribution of revenues but neglected adjustment of functions and powers, leaving the latter, to a certain extent, undefined, ambiguous and highly decentralized.[15] Such problems similarly exist in the sub-provincial fiscal administration system.

The 1994 tax sharing system reform was designed to improve the ratio of fiscal revenue to GDP and fiscal centralization. As stipulated in the 1993 Decision of the State Council on the Tax Sharing Fiscal Administration System (No.85 [1993] issued by State Council), central and provincial governments negotiated a rational range of fiscal expenditure across levels based on the central–local assignment of functions and powers, and unified taxes into the categories of central tax, local tax and shared tax under the principle of "corresponding revenues to responsibilities." By naming their fiscal administration "tax sharing system," sub-provincial level governments across China all adhered to (at least nominally) the model of responsibility-based assignment of revenue.

The principle of corresponding revenue to responsibilities is in line with international practice in form, but differs greatly in terms of specific operations. Internationally, the principle of correspondence implies preconditions and mature practices. Implicit preconditions include division of functions between government and market and division of functions and powers at all levels of government. Mature practices involve determining needs and expenditures in light of government duties and responsibilities, wherefrom determining revenues and allocation. Reflected here is the principle of "expenditure determining revenue," which follows another "functions determining expenditures." The tax sharing system in China is absent the foregoing preconditions. Higher-level governments, in their administration of lower-level fiscal systems, focus on distribution favorable to themselves, for which they allow or wink at lower-level governments to dig for a large quantity of off-budget revenue. The more that is earned, the more that is typically spent, a reflection of "revenue determining expenditure," and a manifestation of "unlimited government," which is an obvious feature of government hierarchy in China. County and township division of functions and powers and expenditure responsibilities have the following characteristics:

1 The Constitution of China and the Local Government Organization Act set out local government functions and powers (authority); documents regarding the tax sharing system promulgated by administrative departments do not stipulate government functions and powers (authority).
2 Government hierarchy makes it impossible to realize rational assignment of functions and powers (authority) at all levels by legislation. Provisions on local government functions and powers (authority) touch upon extent of authority at each level, but, with a high degree of overlapping, do not made explicit which level of government bears responsibility for what functions.

3 Government functions and powers (authority), as provided by existing laws, require lower-level governments to carry out mandates, decisions and commissions made by higher levels, thus leaving room for higher-level governments to shift responsibilities onto lower-level governments and exacerbating the problems of fiscal administration and expenditure responsibilities at county and township levels.
4 Legislation does not stipulate government expenditure responsibilities. Some localities follow provisions provided in tax sharing system documents issued by administrative departments; others determine expenditure responsibilities by applying previous expenditure base. Provisions on expenditure responsibilities provided in tax sharing system documents envelop all local affairs to be addressed by local governments at the same level, virtually overlapping that of the higher level, which allow higher-level governments to shift their own-level expenditure responsibilities onto lower-level governments.

Specifically, Article 107 of the Constitution of China defines extent of authority of local governments, according to which, county and above level local governments administer economy, education, science, culture, health, sports undertakings, urban and rural construction, finance, civil affairs, public security, nationalities affairs, judicial administration, supervision, family planning and other administrative affairs, promulgate decisions and orders, appoint and dismiss, train, examine, reward and punish administrative staff within their respective administrative divisions. Township people's governments enforce resolutions passed by township-level people's congress and decisions and orders promulgated by higher-level government departments and manage administrative work within their respective administrative divisions.

The functions and powers, or authority, of provincial, prefectural/municipal, county/city and township governments are specified in Articles 60 and 61 of the Organic Law of Local People's Congresses and Local People's Governments of the People's Republic of China. Core contents are as follows:

1 To enforce resolutions of the same level people's congress (governments above the county level also enforce decisions of the standing committee of the same level people's congress), decisions and orders of higher-level government administrative departments, to promulgate decisions and orders. Governments above the county level can develop administrative measures.
2 Local governments above the county level shall lead the work of subordinate departments and lower-level people's governments, change or abolish improper orders and instructions of subordinate departments and improper decisions or orders of lower-level people's governments.
3 Local governments above the county shall appoint and dismiss, train, examine, reward and punish government administrative staff as prescribed by laws.

4 To implement national economic and social development plans and budgets, to administer all matters related to economy, education, science, culture, health, athletics, environmental and resource protection, urban and rural construction, finance, civil affairs, public security, minority affairs, judicial administration, supervision, family planning and other administrative affairs within their respective administrative regions.
5 To protect property owned by the whole people and collective property owned by the working people, protect citizens' lawful private property, maintain social orders, safeguard citizens' rights of the person, democratic rights and other rights, and protect the lawful rights and interests of economic organizations.
6 To protect the rights of ethnic minorities and respect their customs. Local governments above the county level shall provide aid for areas inhabited by ethnic minorities to practice regional autonomy pursuant to the constitution and law, and help them to develop politics, economy and culture.
7 To safeguard women's equality, equal pay for equal work, freedom of marriage and other rights endowed by the constitution and law.
8 Governments above the county level shall carry out other tasks mandated by higher-level administrative departments. Township-level governments shall engage in other issues mandated by higher-level governments.

The foregoing fourth point is rather ambiguous: while it states that local governments at each level assume similar functions within their own jurisdictions, they are not assigned functions and powers corresponding to the public goods and services they provide. The first and eighth points provide that lower-level governments shall carry out decisions and orders made by higher-level administrative departments and other tasks mandated by higher-level administrative departments or people's governments; this would, from the legal point of view, inevitably result in a low degree of autonomy at the lower levels, with their administrative responsibilities and expenditure responsibilities easily influenced by higher-level governments.

From the angles of democratic finance and fiscal federalism, public goods and services to be provided by governments across levels are determined democratically by public procedures within respective jurisdictions. That is, governments are accountable to citizens by providing public goods and services autonomously within the extent of authority defined by law. Here, government functions and powers shall be decentralized to the lowest possible level. In other words, the principle of subsidiarity shall be followed. According to the principles of fiscal federalism and subsidiarity, if public goods and services provided at the local level have externalities, or spillover effects, local governments should consider internalization by means of self-organizing protocol or higher-level government participation (e.g., transfer payment or co-provision) and takeover (turning them into their own functions and powers). Compared to the requirements of democratic finance and fiscal federalism, China's current fiscal administration system is still far behind.

It can be said that under the five-level government system in China, formal division of government functions and powers and expenditure responsibilities is absent. While the Constitution stipulates the extent to which the central government exercises authority over local governments in principle, it does not make a distinction between different levels. Except for the central government's exclusive authority over foreign affairs and national defense, the government's functions and powers at the local level are virtually a replica of the center's (Table 9.5).[16] The Budget Law ensures local budget autonomy, but in reality, budget autonomy is non-existent. Regarding the central–local division of expenditure, it does not make explicit how to assign expenditures among governments at sub-provincial levels. The common practice is the approach of "supervising the lower level," that is, a higher-level government exerts control over the expenditures of the government one level below within its jurisdiction. Provincial (under the "province supervising county" system) or prefectural (under the "city supervising county" system) governments determine expenditure assignments of county governments while county governments determine expenditure assignments of township governments. This way, division of functions and powers can be different in various provinces and prefectures (World Bank, 2002). Despite that, higher-level governments are not free to unilaterally determine expenditure responsibilities of the lower levels because in practice, it is county and township governments rather than higher-level governments that provide the vast majority of public goods and services. County and township governments, however, have to shoulder the heavy burden of spending as a result of lacking revenue autonomy and primary revenue. The downward shift of expenditure responsibilities by higher-level governments was a significant trend by 2003,[17] which then began to reverse after the central government substantially increased investment in agriculture, rural areas and farmers. Even so, county and township governments still need to shoulder the main burden of providing basic pubic services.

Because a great quantity of public goods and services that fall into the local category entail local provision, management, payment or payment on others' behalf, the local proportion of expenditure in form is neither low nor high. In 2006, the local general budget expenditure accounted for 73.1 percent of total general budget expenditure, in which the county and township portion made up 27.9 percent and 6.7 percent, respectively (Table 9.6);[18] if adding general budget expenditure, fund expenditure and extra-budgetary expenditure, the local portion constituted 75.6 percent of the total, of which counties and townships shared 27.2 percent and 5.6 percent, respectively (Table 9.7). Statistics showed that in 2010, local general budgetary revenue accounted for 48.9 percent of total general budgetary revenue, and local general budget expenditures covered 82.2 percent of total general budgetary expenditure. The international index for fiscal decentralization refers to the ratio of local fiscal

Table 9.5 Overview of government expenditure responsibilities across levels

Level	*Classification*		*Nature of Government*	*Primary Expenditure Responsibilities*
National	Central government		National	Central government operation, national security and foreign affairs, investment subsidy to enterprises directly under the center, national key construction, macro-control, higher education of universities directly under ministries, social security of key state-owned enterprises, cultural undertakings of the center
Provincial	Province (autonomous region)		Local	Provincial government operation, investment subsidy to provincial enterprises, major provincial infrastructure
	Municipality directly under the central government		Municipal and local	Municipal government operation, investment subsidy to municipal enterprises, urban construction
Prefectural	Prefecture-level city	Governing counties	Municipal and local	Municipal government operation, urban education, investment subsidy to municipal enterprises, urban construction, local infrastructure, unemployment and pension insurance and relief
		Not governing counties	City government	City government operation, urban education, investment subsidy to city enterprises, urban construction, unemployment and pension insurance and relief
County level	County		Local government	County government operation, education, medical care and public health, spending on rural support, county infrastructure and urban construction, family planning
	County-level city		Municipal and local	City government operation, education, medical care and public health, spending on rural support, urban construction and local construction, family planning, unemployment and pension insurance and relief
Township-level	Township		Rural government	Township government operation, rural education, family planning

Source: World Bank (2002), Yin Haibo (2002), Tian Fa, Zhou Chenying (2004).

Table 9.6 Intergovernmental assignment of general budget expenditure (part of), year 2006 (RMB 100 million)

Budget Accounts	*National*	*Central*	*Province*	*Prefect*	*County*	*Township*
Capital construction	439	148.4	101.7	109.8	71.1	8.1
Enterprise innovation fund	96.5	1.3	18.2	37.7	24.7	14.6
Agriculture, forestry, water conservation and meteorology	216.1	109.3	18	18.6	49.9	20.3
Industry, transportation and circulation departments	58.1	13.5	15	11.4	16.7	15.5
Recreation and sports and broadcasting	84.2	8.4	17	17.6	28.9	12.4
Education	478	29.5	71.5	81.8	242.8	52.5
Medical care and public health	132	2.4	26.9	36.2	605.3	5.9
Operating expense for other departments	146.2	11.1	42.4	37.4	47.3	7.9
Pension and social relief	90.8	0.6	7.4	21.6	50.7	10.5
Retirees of administrative institutions	133	10.9	25.1	24.9	58.1	14
Social security	212.4	24.1	76.4	68.3	41.4	2.3
Administrative expense	335.6	46.1	36.1	76.3	120.9	56.2
Public security organs	217.4	9.9	50.4	75.4	78.3	3.5
Urban maintenance	153.7	0	9.5	65.6	65.5	13.1
Total expenditure	4,042.30	1,089	709.9	845.9	1,127.70	269.7

Source: Calculated according to *China Finance Yearbook* 2007 and other data provided by the Ministry of Finance. Expenditure here refers to the expenditure of respective levels.

expenditure. Measured by ratio, China seems to have a high degree of fiscal decentralization, but it is problematic to measure the degree of fiscal decentralization by using a single expenditure ratio. Taking into consideration the distribution of revenues and expenditures, and the division of powers and responsibilities, our fiscal administration system is actually rather centralized. The ratio of local expenditure as an index of fiscal decentralization works on the premise of a centralized fiscal system in China, and this premise cannot be challenged or overthrown.

Table 9.7 Breakdown of government expenditure at all levels of government in year 2006 (RMB 100 million)

	National	Central	Province	Prefecture
Total general budget expenditure	4,042.3	1,089	709.9	845.9
Fund expenditure	699.3	170.7	175.1	192.8
Extra-budgetary expenditure	586.7	37.8	1,801.10	1,807.10
Total	5,328.3	1,297.5	10,652.10	12,194.10

Source: *China Finance Yearbook* 2007 and other data provided by the Ministry of Finance.

Note: Estimated data. Estimate proportions of provincial-, prefectural- and county-level extra-budgetary expenditures by applying proportions of extra-budgetary revenues, then compute amounts of extra-budgetary revenues at three levels and other summed data accordingly.

Transfer payment

Many types of transfer payment systems have been established in China since 1994. Common international practice classifies transfer payments into general purpose transfer payments and special transfer payments: the former includes tax refunds and transfer payments for fiscal equalization (general transfer payment subsidy) and the latter includes transfer payments for salary adjustment, transfer payment subsidies for rural tax and fee reform, transfer payment for minority areas, original system subsidy, special transfer payment subsidy, and so on.[19]

Central-to-local transfer payment

General Purpose Transfer Payment: Tax refund. The 1994 tax sharing fiscal system reform incorporated VAT and consumption tax into the category of central tax, and simultaneously set up the VAT refund accounting subject and the consumption tax fund accounting subject to ensure provincial revenue from the two types of tax at 1993's level. The refund amount of VAT/consumption tax at that time was equivalent to the refunded amount of the previous year plus 30 percent of the VAT/consumption tax of the same year. As in 2002, personal income tax and enterprise income tax[20] also fell into the category of shared tax. The two taxes then were shared by the central and provincial governments at a ratio of 50:50, but from 2003, the central share rose to 60 percent. Considering stability of provincial fiscal revenue, the central government set up corresponding income tax refund accounting subjects to ensure provincial revenue from income taxes would not fall lower than the 2001 level. In 2008, the refunds from VAT and consumption taxes amounted to 337.2 billion yuan, and the refund to the income tax base amounted to 91.019 billion yuan, totaling 428.219 billion yuan (Table 9.8).[21]

Transfer payment for fiscal equalization (general transfer payment subsidy): Transfer payment for fiscal equalization belongs to formula-based general transfer payment; here we call it general transfer payment subsidy. In order to reduce regional financial inequality, the central government initiated a formula-based payment mode – the fiscal equalization transfer payment in 1995 (called "transitional transfer payment" before 2001). The amount of this payment is decided by three factors – the relevant province's standard fiscal revenue, standard fiscal expenditure and standard fiscal gap in proportion to the national revenue–expenditure gap. The scale of this item is controlled by the central government flexibly, depending on each year's disposable fiscal resources, and incremental growth of fiscal resources in particular. Although growingly rapidly from 2.07 billion yuan in 1995 to 351.052 billion yuan in 2008, the formula-based general transfer made up only 15.3 percent, a rather low proportion of total central-to-local transfer payment.

The net amount of general purpose transfer payment from the center to the localities is equal to the foregoing tax refund plus the fiscal equalization transfer (general transfer payment subsidy) minus the revenue turned over by localities. The amount of turnover in 2008 was 93.993 billion yuan,[22] so the same year's net amount of general purpose transfer payment was computed to be 685.278 billion yuan.

Special transfer payment

According to international standard of classification, China's special transfer payment in 2008 came to 1,515.29 billion yuan (Table 9.8), constituting 66 percent of total central-to-local transfer payment.[23]

While the center's fiscal expenditure for the central level was 1,337.431 billion yuan in 2008, central-to-local transfer payments, including tax refunds, came to 2,294.561 billion yuan, 1.7 times the former, and 63.2 percent of total fiscal expenditure of the central government. The local-level revenue of the same year was 2,356.504 billion yuan, plus the central transfer payment of 2,294.561 billion yuan, local fiscal revenue came to 5,065.06 billion yuan. The central transfer payment shared 46.8 percent of funding for local fiscal expenditure, which was 4,905.272 billion yuan.

A large part of the foregoing central-to-provincial transfer payment goes to central and western regions as well as counties, townships and villages. In central and western areas, for example, 54.4 percent of local fiscal expenditures on average derive from the center's transfer payments. Hierarchic centralization of county and township general budget revenues by higher-level governments produces heavy dependence of county and township finances on higher-level transfer payments. Figure 9.1 shows the general budgetary gap of governments at all levels in 2006. On the whole, governments across sub-national levels depend on transfer payments, from the central government in particular, to fill in their revenue–expenditure gaps. This is reflected by the vertical gaps between revenue and expenditure of governments at the same level.

The high ratio of local expenditure can be largely attributed to the center's return en masse of centralized revenue to local governments by means of transfer

Table 9.8 Transfer payment from central to local governments in year 2008 (RMB 100 million)

Item of Transfer Payment	*Amount*
I. Central-to-local general purpose transfer payment	779.271
General transfer payment subsidy	351.052
Refund of VAT and consumption tax	337.2
Income tax base refund	91.019
II. Special transfer payment	1,515.29
Transfer payment for minority areas	27.579
Reward and compensation fund for county and township basic fiscal resources safeguard mechanism	43.818
Salary adjustment transfer payment	239.23
Transfer payment subsidy for rural tax and fee reform	76.254
Compulsory education transfer payment	26.936
Subsidy for rural compulsory education debt solution	15
Fiscal resources transfer payment for resource-exhausted cities	2.5
Quota subsidy (original system subsidy)	13.614
Subsidy for enterprise and public institution transformation	33.5
Fiscal resources subsidy for settlement	35.466
Transfer payment to administrations of industry and commerce in compensation for the fees they used to collect from sole proprietors and fair trade markets	4.7
Special transfer payment subsidy	996.693
Education	68.763
Science and technology	8.588
Social security and employment	239.931
Medical care and public health	78.002
Environmental protection	97.409
Rural water resources	151.313
Other special transfer payment	352.687
Total central-to-local transfer payment	2,294.561

Source: Xinhua News Agency, March 6, 2009.

payment, the majority of which is special transfer payment, rather than transfer payment for fiscal resources equalization (general transfer payment subsidies). Among the central-to-local transfers in 2007, transfer payment for fiscal equalization reached 250.5 billion yuan (Li, 2008), only 13.8 percent of the national total, but accounting for closing 81 percent of the local standard fiscal gap,

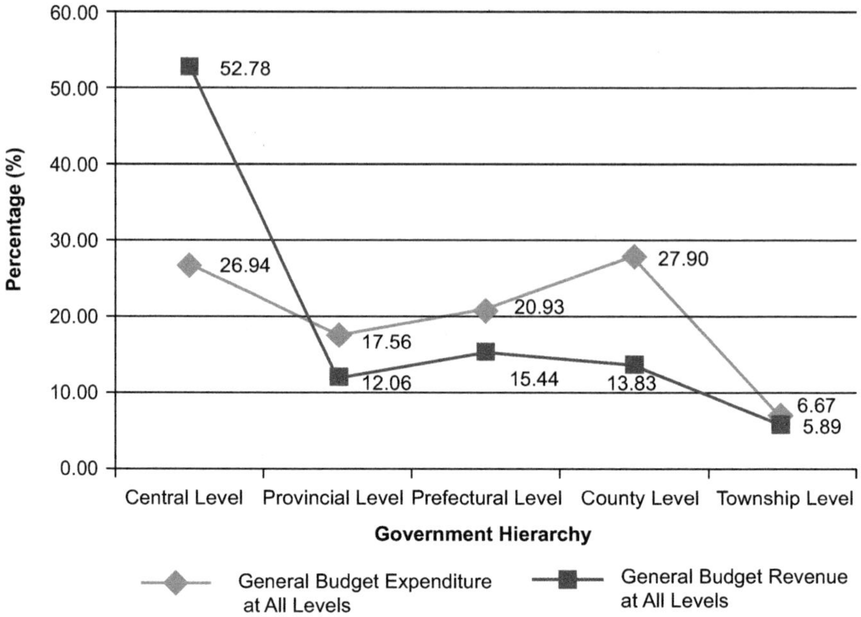

Figure 9.1 General budget gap of government at all levels in year 2006
Source: *China Finance Yearbook* 2007 and other data provided by the Ministry of Finance.

compared to 9.6 percent in 2000. This clearly shows that it played a crucial role in lower-level fiscal equalization in various provinces. Different from fiscal equalization transfers, special transfer payments are required to reflect the center's policy direction, directives and centralized control. In reality, it is often a means for government departments, or a number of officials, to control resources and reap financial benefits.

Transfer payment from provinces and prefectural cities to lower-level governments

It should be noted that besides central-to-local transfer payment, provinces and prefectural cities also provide transfer payment to a number of counties. Sources of funding involve central-to-local transfers and funds allocated by local governments themselves. Such transfer payments include general purpose transfers and special transfers (Table 9.9).

General purpose transfer payments include tax refunds, subsidies for system adjustment and general transfer payment subsidies. Special transfers include provincial and municipal matching funds for centrally financed county projects, funds for province- and municipal-financed county projects, and incentive

Table 9.9 Type of transfers from province to lower-level governments

Type	*Sub-Type*	*Example*
General purpose	Tax refund	Heilongjiang: in 2007, revenue base to be turned over and refund of consumption tax, VAT, enterprise income tax, personal income tax and business tax allocated directly to counties (determination and allocation of business tax base to be turned over excluding counties subordinate to Harbin municipality).
	Subsidy for system adjustment	Shanxi Province: starting in 2007, began to regulate provincial and low-level government fiscal systems, and implement the "province directly supervising county" model in 35 national-level key counties for poverty alleviation and development. New bases determined for pilots: taking 2006 as a base year this plan transferred upward or downward according to new regulations to ensure the vested interest of all levels. Municipalities determined the range of revenue, subsidies for system adjustment (or revenue to be turned over) and quota subsidies for fiscal resources according to united provincial rules. Schemes for implementing system adjustment and county and township bases are reported to provincial government for approval.
	General subsidy	Shaanxi Province: provided general transfer subsidies to poor cities and counties in 2008, totaling 12.16 billion yuan.
Special transfer	Matching funds for county and township projects provided by the center	Guizhou Province: in 2009, planned investment in 88 rural drinking water safety projects totaled 50.375 million yuan, including budgetary investment increases of 40.3 million yuan, provincial matching funds of 5,038,000 yuan, and prefecture matching funds of 5,037,000 yuan. Xiuning County of Anhui Province: in 2009, NRCMS-participating farmers each volunteered to pay 20 yuan per year, added to by national-, provincial- and county-level subsidies of 80 yuan for each farmer each year (central: 40 yuan, provincial: 30 yuan, county: 10 yuan), totaling 100 yuan per person per year.
	Provincial special subsidy	Anhui Province: in 2009, 2.5 billion yuan of special transfer payments were arranged for establishing SME credit guarantee funds and loan risk compensation.
		Jiangyan City of Jiangsu Province: in 2008, NRCMS funding criteria was set at 100 yuan/person, therein individuals paid 20 yuan/person, with provincial subsidies of 40 yuan/person, and city and township (district) matched funds of 40 yuan/person.

(*Continued*)

Table 9.9 (Continued)

Type	*Sub-Type*	*Example*
	Province incentive transfer to cities and counties	Hubei Province: in 2008, the province rewarded governments of municipalities, prefectures, cities directly under provincial jurisdiction, forest districts, counties (cities, districts – hereinafter referred to as cities and counties) for supporting industrial cluster development, 90% of incentive funds used to support key growth in industrial clusters, 10% for other growth in industrial cluster development.

Source: Documents from relevant provincial and municipal governments.

transfers such as "rewards in place of subsidy," "rewards for deficit reduction" and "rewards for step-up of fiscal revenue." Provincial transfer payments to lower levels are set at a single, uniform size. In many provinces, the announced scale of transfer payments actually included the central portion transferred downward via province, as shown in the Anhui case: in 2007, the Anhui provincial government arranged 56.27 billion yuan for transfer downward, which included 26.78 billion yuan of fiscal resources transfer payment. Only a few provinces have established the formula-based downward general transfer subsidy system; most provinces simply deliver central-to-city/county transfers to destinations (Wang, 2008) and provide, in a passive way, matching funds as required by the center. Shaanxi Province, for example, allocated 12.16 billion yuan as general transfer payment subsidies to cities and counties facing financial troubles in 2008.[24] In 2006, the Hubei provincial government paid to 102 counties (cities, districts) 34.3 billion yuan of fiscal resources transfers, accounting for 67 percent of county (city, district) general budget expenditure (Wang, 2007). Zhejiang Province arranged 600 million yuan of transfer payments for ecology and environmental protection.[25]

Poor counties have a high degree of dependence on central, provincial and prefectural transfer. An example is Anyue County of Sichuan Province which, as shown in Table 9.2, is highly dependent on central and provincial transfers. Transfer payment provided by provinces and prefectural cities to lower-level governments mainly serves the following purposes: (1) General purpose transfer payment: including tax refund and general transfer payment subsidy; the latter is designed to safeguard basic fiscal resources of counties facing fiscal difficulties and to achieve a certain extent of fiscal equality at provincial and municipal levels; (2) Special transfer payments: referring to special provincial and prefectural expenditure on counties and townships, including special transfer subsidies provided by provinces and prefectures themselves, matching funds for centrally financed county and township projects, and incentive transfer payment, by which it means some provinces and prefectural cities develop reward and punishment standards and provide transfer payment accordingly as an incentive by taking into consideration the growth of county fiscal revenue, excess over the required standard, financial balance, loan repayment to higher-level governments, control of the number of civil servants on the government payroll, and so forth. Some other provinces arranged transfer payment to exceptionally poor townships, such as Anhui Province.

County fiscal administration system: problems and causes

So far, there exist a lot of problems in county fiscal administration systems, the most overarching of which are summarized below:

- The existing county fiscal administration system protects vested interest by focusing on fiscal revenue regulation and avoiding crucial problems in fiscal and tax system reform, such as lack of clear definition in functions and powers, and expenditure responsibilities. The intergovernmental fiscal system is under an administrative framework rather than a legislative one, left with residues of the precious fiscal contracting system and base method.
- Original system subsidy, tax refund and some other practices make the system more complicated and less transparent.
- Under the current county fiscal administration system, intergovernmental division of functions and powers and expenditure responsibilities are ambiguous. Powers of higher-level governments, endowed by law to decide, change, reverse, transfer and adjust functions and powers of the lower levels drive indefinitiveness and instability, leaving higher levels with extensive room to shift expenditure responsibilities downward.
- Intergovernmental distribution of both fiscal resources and expenditure responsibilities lies under the control of the central and higher-level governments. While revenue allocation is centralized, responsibilities are shifted down tier by tier. Serious mismatches between revenue and expenditure assignments drives lower-level governments to adopt countermeasures (including extra-budgetary and extra-system levies) to combat this system.
- While the legislative power of taxation belongs solely to the central government, the legislative power of fee collection is under the firm control of the center, provinces and major cities. Local mobilization of revenue sources is not encouraged, nor are local governments empowered to adjust tax rates.
- A sound system of local taxation is not in place. Sub-provincial governments have neither a formal system of revenue distribution nor primary taxes, and can easily be deprived of original primary taxes by higher-level governments (e.g., by putting some taxes into the category of shared tax). Therefore, local revenue depends greatly on extra-budgetary funds, extra-systemic funds and debt financing.

- The current intergovernmental fiscal administration system is designed to safeguard vested interests of government across levels by consolidating incremental revenue. Despite the rapid growth of general transfer payment subsidies in recent years, its aggregate amount is limited and inadequate to safeguard basic fiscal resources for provision of nationally determined basic public services.
- The tax sharing reform has resulted in centralization of revenue allocation and decentralization of expenditure responsibility. The rural tax and fee reform realized tax reduction or exemption, abolition of "fees paid by farmers for overall township planning and village reserve," and reduction or cancellation of rural labor accumulation and volunteer work. The broadening fiscal gap makes poverty-stricken counties highly dependent on transfer payment.
- Relatedly, many county and township governments fall into debt, willingly or not, by undertaking their own functions and responsibilities or in implementing mandated services. Heavy debt burdens, including contingent liability, exacerbate the fiscal predicament of many counties and townships.
- The excessively high proportion of transfer payments to local disposable fiscal resources in poorer areas indicates a neglect of formal revenue allocation to increase local fiscal revenue. Besides this, general purpose transfer payment as compensation for fiscal resources has an excessively small share in transfer payments while special transfer payment has an excessively large one. The former is determined formulaically for computing basic fiscal gaps; the latter is subject to government discretion and lacks of transparency.

There are also some specific problems in the county fiscal administration system:

- The proportion of refunds of over-base VAT or consumption tax falls off year by year, showing intensified centralization of local finance.[26]
- The growing number of special funds controlled by government departments and poor transparency of management makes these departments' interest groups and targets of non-governmental interest groups for rent-seeking. This accounts for the large number of special fund projects of low efficiency.
- Intergovernmental responsibilities are ambiguous in terms of project management and division of labor. Which level of government bears responsibilities for a specific project is unclear and intrinsic to this system is a certain degree of arbitrariness – the higher levels have excessively broad discretionary authority. The center can require localities to pay for centrally financed projects and determine the size of local matching funds. Examples include grain risk fund, the food self-sufficiency project, comprehensive agricultural development, prison/re-education-through-labor, infrastructure loan interest subsidies and other projects, which all require local governments to provide matching funds, bringing a heavy burden to poverty-stricken counties.[27]
- The structure of fiscal expenditure is irrational; general budgets are virtually equal to "payroll finance." In most counties of China (especially in central and western regions), the vast majority of fiscal expenditure is administrative

expenditure, 80–90 percent used for guarantee of payroll payment and maintenance of public services and facilities (Guo et al., 2005).

- There is an overlarge number of statutory expenditure or higher-level mandated expenditure, combined with serious intervention. All sorts of intervention from central authorities bring obstacles for localities to arrange financial, human and material resources. Statutory and higher-level requirements relate to every aspect. For example, a lot of regulations and policies set requirements for spending on such key undertakings as agriculture, science and technology, education, public health, family planning and cultural propaganda, some requiring a growth rate higher than that of recurring revenue, others requiring a certain proportion to GDP. Such practices impair fiscal autonomy of local governments, create inflexible spending and rigid fiscal structure, and so add to local burden of expenditure.

Causes of above problems involve the following aspects:

- In China, government at all levels is still amidst a transition of functions from an unlimited government to a service-oriented one; in this course, governmental fiscal power is not effectively constrained, division of functions between government and market is not clearly defined, and the "serviceability" government at present lacks an orientation toward civil demands.
- Promotion of local government officials partly depends on individual performance achieved within their administrative divisions. Such performance is often linked with GDP growth rate, construction and project initiation, in other words, it is linked to fiscal input, thus representing a strong incentive for local governments as a whole to inflate fiscal revenue and expenditure.[28]
- The local fiscal system at each level is centralized with a division of power dominated by the higher levels. This allows higher-level governments to change allocation revenue, centralize receipts or arbitrarily adjust and shift responsibilities and expenditures down to lower levels.
- Government functions and powers and expenditure responsibilities at all levels are not clearly defined. For systemic reasons, a large part of local functions and expenditures are related to implementing higher-level policies and regulations, which creates favorable conditions for higher-level governments to adjust and shift down responsibilities and expenditures.
- Tax sharing is controlled by higher-level administrative departments (empowered inappropriately by the Budget Law passed by the legislature) rather than legislative procedures, thus creating favorable conditions for higher-level governments to adjust allocation and centralize local revenue.
- Established on the basis of old fiscal contracting systems and methods, the administration-dominated tax sharing system is not geared toward responsibility requirements and expenditure needs of government at county and other local levels, nor does it follow the established international practice that division of functions and responsibilities takes precedence over distribution of revenues. The result is a mismatch between revenue assignments and expenditure needs, with a broad fiscal gap arising at county and township levels.

- The rural tax and fee reform deprived counties and townships of revenues from agriculture tax and agricultural specialty tax; townships and villages lost fees paid by farmers for overall township planning and village reserve, and other income sources. The further broadening fiscal gap leads to a high degree of dependence of counties, townships and villages on transfer payment from central and other higher-level governments.

County fiscal administration: solving the problems

To solve current problems in the county fiscal administration system, it should truly clarify the functions and powers as well as fiscal responsibilities and powers at all levels and implement a real tax sharing system. The following suggestions may be feasible policy prescriptions.

Distribution of functions and competence

The competences of governments at all levels should be divided in the form of law. Five kinds of local government authority should be clearly distinguished, that is, existing competences for local governments, new established competences for local governments, competences entrusted by higher-level governments, competences shared by local governments and higher-level governments, and undefined competences. If undefined competences are related to the competences for local governments which are not defined in law, without special stipulations it will come under the governments of the lowest possible level. The basis of competence assignment is the principle of subsidiarity.

Division of expenditure responsibilities

Being consistent with four kinds of competences for local governments and the undefined competences, five kinds of expenditure responsibilities can be distinguished: assuming expenditure responsibility for existing competences for local governments, new established competences for local governments, authority entrusted by governments of higher levels, authority shared by local governments and governments of higher levels and undefined competences. If aforementioned existing competences for local governments are adjusted, the corresponding expenditure responsibility should be adjusted too.

Distribution of revenue powers

Being consistent with five kinds of authority and expenditure responsibility of local governments, in order to fulfill these competences and responsibility, local governments should clarify and obtain corresponding revenue powers. Governments at county and township levels could realize revenue rights through various means:

- Fulfilling functions and powers entrusted by higher-level governments and corresponding expenditure responsibilities, governments at county and township levels should get equivalent transfer payment from the higher levels.

- Besides, other revenue powers of governments at county and township levels are first realized through dividing the revenue between counties and higher-level governments; county revenue issue can be solved by flexible ways (the county can put the tax sharing system and other fiscal systems into practice in some townships) and then by transfer payment according to principle of subsidiarity.
- Currently, a large amount of functions and powers and expenditure responsibilities flock in county- and township-level governments. The problem that the central, provincial and some prefectural/municipal governments over-centralize revenue could be solved by canceling prefectural power in centralizing county revenue and by reducing central and provincial centralization over county revenue according to the "province supervising county" fiscal administration system. In fact, since the implementation of fiscal reform in 1994, the fiscal revenue brought by economic growth has contributed a lot to the sharp rise of central and provincial finance, so it is not necessary any more to centralize county revenue.
- To implement the tax sharing system in the real sense, the practice of distributing revenue according to enterprise subordinate relations should be broken, and revenue should be distributed in the light of dependent territory principle uniformly. Generally, through revenue redistribution, measures should be taken to cancel residues of the original base method and contracting system used as the transitional forms of 1994 fiscal reform, to simplify revenue distribution among governments, to promote fiscal transparency and institutionalize the revenue distribution at the level of law not administration. Definition of revenue allocation among governments should be done through legislation not administrative means. Budget Law should be adjusted correspondingly. The power that defines fiscal administration system among governments should be taken over by the legislative branch, but not shifted to the executive branch simply through legislative delegation.
- Through redistribution, governments at county level should obtain their major tax categories, such as redistributing the proportion of local share of VAT which can be higher than 25 percent, at the same time, cancelling tax revenue refund and original system subsidy, simplifying revenue distribution. Provincial governments do not centralize revenue from local share of VAT.
- Steps should be taken to build a relatively stable and independent local tax system, and endow provinces with legislative power to some local taxes, especially the legislative power for revenues from local resources.
- When setting the range of tax rate of some tax categories (such as business income tax), local governments could decide the actual ad valorem rate by themselves in the light of the actual requirement within the stipulated range, thus to some extent leading to rule-oriented tax competition.

Transfer payment

There are still many problems about intergovernmental transfer payment, and the following improvements are required:

- Transfer payment of higher-level governments should permit the existence of fiscal gap among areas and no absolutely equal fiscal resources. Key measures can be made to guarantee that all areas at least could reach the lower or lowest basic public service level in uniform requirements.
- Efforts should be made to increase the proportion of general transfer payment, to compute general transfer payment in accordance with the gap of various regions between the lowest basic standard expenditure requirements and standard fiscal resources. In this way, the lowest general transfer payment could be worked out and provided.
- As mentioned above, lower-level governments should be provided with corresponding transfer payment fund to compensate their expenditure if they are entrusted with authority and expenditure responsibility. Up to now, the ordinary practice is that higher-level governments only provide support from the level of policy, but provide no or less fund.
- Although local governments should undertake the part of shared authority and expenditure responsibility that comes under lower-level governments, governments of higher levels should provide corresponding special transfer payment subsidy or additional revenue power stipulated in legislation, if governments of higher levels expect governments of lower levels to assume more shared authority and expenditure responsibility in policy.
- In general, the local governments should be empowered to have primary tax, levy local tax and expand the local share of shared revenue. Correspondingly, transfer payment should be reduced to promote financial expenditure efficiency.
- Special funds types which are too many should be reduced and general transfer payment should be added to promote financial expenditure efficiency and transparency.
- With the increasing proportion of general transfer payment to special transfer payment, requirements on provision of matching funds by county and township governments should be cut off, because excessive requirements for matching fund will drive county and township governments to incur debt and cook the books.

Tax collection and administration

On the basis of redistributing revenue with strict following of the tax sharing system, tax collection and administration should annul the practice of separating domestic enterprise, foreign invested enterprise and foreign enterprise taxes. Except tariff, all the revenue will be administrated with the principle of dependent territory, be first handed into the national treasury and then transferred to local fiscal accounts so as to lower collection cost and the compliant costs of paying taxes.

In addition, China currently carries out the system of five-tier government, under which it is hard to distinguish authority, expenditure responsibilities and revenue powers, to prevent authority shuffle and ambiguity in responsibility among governments. Too many levels of government also lead to a heavy burden for taxpayers and lower governance efficiency due to the overlong decision-making chain and a high degree of information asymmetry. To better carry out the aforementioned county fiscal administration system reform, efforts are still needed in cutting off government hierarchy and conducting reform of administrative division. Specific suggestions are as follows:

1 Efforts should be made to constantly pursue fiscal administration system reform of "province supervising county" or "county strengthening and power expansion" and annul the system of "city supervising county." In principle, with the gradual building and improvement of a market economy system and gradual transformation of government functions, the advantages of the "province supervising county" or "county strengthening and power expansion" system become more prominent, such as reducing one administrative level, lowering fiscal withholding and cutting off administrative costs. Besides, this kind of reform could contribute to the administrative and fiscal systems reform at provincial, city and county levels. At present, "province supervising county" or "county strengthening and power expansion" reform encounter obstacles in some administrative fields, which exactly reflects the lag of government administrative system reform and the necessity of further strengthening "province supervising county" fiscal administration system reform and the whole "province supervising county" reform (including administrative, fiscal, economic, social and other fields).

   Some people believe some prefectural cities can continue to have "city supervising county" fiscal administration system, for these places provide part net transfer payment for the counties under their administration. In fact, it could achieve better results through increasing central and provincial general transfer payment based on standard form. Moreover, in the perspective of economic development, economic region and market will come into play. That prefectural governments play the role of administrative region through the system of "city supervising county" will easily restrain county development instead. In the short term, however, some municipal governments could keep the "city supervising county" fiscal administration system, which provide part net transfer payment for counties under their administration.

2 As the "province supervising county" fiscal administration system requires a province to administrate multitudinous cities and counties, considerations must be taken to reduce some provinces' jurisdiction area by division reform or reintroduce area administrative office in some places. If some provinces' jurisdiction area must be reduced, then it must be noted that some of our

provinces and counties follow the natural border line of ancient times and around these places subculture areas have taken shape. Artificial reduction of some provinces' jurisdiction area will cause destruction to our country's cultural tradition. Therefore, giving consideration to the cultural tradition factor, we only reduce the area of the prefectural city within its jurisdiction and of the provinces with too many cities and counties or a wide range of territory.

3 In the short term, townships can be managed in accordance with "county supervising township finance" or by retaining the township's status that "government of each level makes its own budget"; in the medium term, townships can be managed by adopting systems of village office or township government; in the long term, with functions transformation of government across levels, the system of village office can be taken into consideration. With the reform of rural taxes and administrative charges and comprehensive rural reform, many townships lose one revenue source, that is, tax and charges, and the function of township government shrinks dramatically.

   Under such circumstances, these townships could rely on the transitional method – "county supervising township finance" – to become accustomed to the new environment. In the medium term, in these areas township government and budget level should be annulled and village offices should be set in accordance with new legislation. In the long term, with the transformation of government functions, township governments will be all replaced by village offices. Regarding the more developed townships with dense population, they can share equal status with the county in reference to America's and Germany's practice of treating cities and townships equally (all are local self-governing bodies).

Finally, if China's fiscal administration system is to meet the demand of residents within the prefecture and provide them with public goods and services, local democracy is required to help the residents participate in the policy making, governance and supervision of local public affairs.

Concluding discussion

That China's counties and townships are in a fiscal predicament is an acknowledged fact. The problem is largely attributed to the current multi-tier fiscal system, the county and township fiscal administration system in particular. This chapter has analyzed the multi-tier fiscal system and structure and in that process thoroughly discussed the status, features, problems and causes of the county and township fiscal administration system. It has sorted out the distribution and operations of functions and powers, expenditure responsibilities and fiscal powers across levels of government, and from the angle of principles of fiscal federalism, put forward some thoughts for resolving these problems. The result is clear: the fiscal administration system of "supervising the lower level" and the functions and powers "mandated by higher levels" not only conflict with the internationally accepted principle of fiscal federalism, but are also free from the restriction of local democratic fiscal rules and procedures – both unfavorable to the efficient operation of the county and township fiscal administration system. This is why further reforms are necessary.

Part of the necessary reform is to clarify the functions and powers as well as fiscal responsibilities and powers at all levels, and implement a real tax sharing system. The competences of governments at all levels need to be divided in the form of law, with the basis of competence assignment being the principle of subsidiarity. From this follows the need for a corresponding expenditure responsibility. In order to fulfill these competences and responsibility, local governments have to clarify and obtain corresponding revenue powers. As a crucial framework for an efficient implementation of the aforementioned competencies, responsibility and powers, local democracy is required to help the residents participate in the policy making, governance and supervision of local public affairs.

Notes

1 Including townships under their jurisdiction.

2 The multi-level fiscal system viewpoint mainly focused on the central and provincial government incidentally took into account the municipal government's financial administration system, and neglected deep analysis of county and township fiscal issues in the multi-level fiscal framework. See, for instance, Song Li and Liu Shujie, *Deployment of Public Services Administrative and Financial Power in All Levels of Government* (Beijng: China Planning Press, 2005).

3 The "provincial power," despite a division of power under the centralized system, is conducive to local diversity of the fiscal administration system. The existence of "provincial power" makes some scholars regard China's fiscal system as "quasi-fiscal federalism" or "quasi-federalism." See B. Krug, Z. Zhu and H. Hendrischke, "China's Emerging Tax Regime: Devolution, Fiscal Federalism, or Tax Farming?" ERIM Report Series Reference No. ERS-2004–113-ORG [2004], and Y. Zheng, *De Facto Federalism in China: Reforms and Dynamics of Central–Local Relations.* Series on Contemporary China. Vol. 7. (Hackensack, NJ: World Scientific, 2007).

4 A county-level city under the jurisdiction of Suzhou City, Jiangsu Province, once sought the status of "deputy-prefectural level city" in order to combat prefectural Suzhou's restriction on its development. Wujin District of Jiangsu Changzhou City used to change from "county" to "county-level city"; Changzhou City, for convenience of control, got approval in 2002 to change Wujin to "district."

5 Calves pulling large carts.

6 For this point, see *Notice of Anhui Provincial People's Government Regarding the Implementation of "Province Directly Supervising County" Fiscal System Reform* (No. 8 [2004] issued by Anhui Provincial People's Government).

7 "Twenty-Two Regions Throughout China Have Carried out the System of 'Province Directly Supervising County,' " *China Economic Weekly*. June 14, 2007.

8 Zhejiang Province started the fourth-round pilot reform of "county strengthening and power expansion" in 2006, with Yiwu City as the only pilot for this trial: 131 administrative powers that used to belong to Jinhua City and 472 provincial powers for economic and social management were decentralized to Yiyu City in various forms; for a time, Yiwu was called by the media "the most powerful county in China." By the end of 2007, transfer of authority related to 603 events

was completed, with 572 events and powers in place. See " 'Province Directly Supervising County' Still in the Trial; Whether Prefectural Cities Relinquish Powers Is the Key," *China News Week*. August 7, 2008.

9 Sichuan Provincial People's Government, *Implementation Opinions of Pilot Development of Expanding Power and Strengthening Counties* (No. 58 [2007] issued by Sichuan government).

10 Partly refer to Zhang Zhanbin (2008).

11 Local Affairs Department of Ministry of Finance, ed. *The Tax Sharing Fiscal Administration System in China* (Beijing: China Financial and Economic Publishing House, 1998), p. 14.

12 Appendix to *Implementation Opinions on Pilot Development of Expanding Powers and Strengthening Counties* (issued by Sichuan Provincial People's Government), July 10, 2007.

13 Centre for Public Policy Studies, Shanghai University of Finance and Economics, p. 186.

14 Ibid., p. 186.

15 Ibid., p. 178.

16 Center for Public Policy Studies, Shanghai University of Finance and Economics. China Finance and Economy Development Report, 2007, pp. 178–179.

17 In 2001, China began to implement a fiscal system with county-level government as the investment subject so that the subject of united government and public investment in rural compulsory education upgraded from township to county. Expenditure responsibilities remained at county and township levels and were not turned over to higher levels.

18 Fiscal expenditure here does not include national repayments of debt principal, added sinking fund and balance of fiscal revenue and expenditure in 2004.

19 Transfer payment in China usually includes three types: fiscal resources transfer payments, tax refunds and original system subsidies, and special transfers. Among this final category, fiscal resource transfer payments include general purpose transfer payments, transfer payments for minority areas, transfer payments for salary adjustment, transfer payments for rural tax and fee reform, and fiscal resource transfer payments for year-end settlement. Such classification tends to confuse general purpose transfer payments belonging to fiscal resource transfer payments with non-general transfer payment, or even cause them to appear identical. This is why we follow the internationally accepted method of classification in this chapter. For the usual method of classification in China, refer to Center for Public Policy Studies, Shanghai University of Finance and Economics, ditto, pp. 213–214.

20 Income tax coming from the following enterprises shall belong to the central government and not be shared: railway transportation, national postal service, Industrial and Commercial Bank of China, Agricultural Bank of China, Bank of China, China Construction Bank, China Development Bank, Agricultural Development Bank of China, Export-Import Bank of China, offshore oil and gas companies, China National Petroleum Corporation, China National Petroleum and Chemical Corporation.

21 *Table: The Center's Expenditure for Tax Refund and Transfer Payment to Localities in 2008*. Xinhua News Agency, March 6, 2009. Available at: http://www.gov.cn/2009lh/content_1252791.htm

22 Ministry of Finance, *Report on Central and Local Budget Performance in 2008 and Central and Local Drafted Budget in 2009 (Summary)*, delivered on 2nd session of 11th National People's Congress, March 5, 2009.

23 Computed according to data from the Ministry of Finance *Report on Central and Local Budget Performance in 2007 and Central and Local Drafted Budget in 2008* and the *Report on Central and Local Budget Performance in 2008 and*

Central and Local Drafted Budget in 2009, the two figures should be 718.81 billion yuan and 996.693 billion yuan, separately. Here data in the Report is replaced by data in Xie Xuren, ed. *China's Financial Reform for Thirty Years* (Beijing: China Financial and Economic Publishing House, 2008) and the computing result is 689.8 billion yuan. See p. 91 of this book.

24 *Provincial Announcement to Cities and Counties on the Method of General Transfer Payment in 2008* (No. 86 [2008] issued by Shaanxi Provincial People's Government General Office), August 6, 2008.

25 Zhejiang Provincial Department of Finance, *Zhejiang Province's Overall Implementation of Ecological Finance Transfer Payment System*, issued on *Huangyan Financial Information Net.* June 3, 2008.

26 Budget Department of Ministry of Finance, ed. *Intergovernmental Fiscal Relations in China* (Beijing: China Financial and Economic Publishing House, 2003), p. 132 and other pages. According to 1993 tax sharing methods, the central-to-local refund amount is given by applying last year's refund base and growth rate of turnover VAT and consumption tax multiplied by coefficient of 0.3 percent, instead of the proportion of absolute amount of the two taxes to be turned over. Consistent with the development trends in other provinces, from 2000 to 2005, the refund increment of two taxes showed a falling tendency in proportion to the increment of two taxes to be turned over in Inner Mongolia, from 22 percent to 11.8 percent. See Zhu Xiaojun and Zhang Yongjun, "Establishing Fiscal Development Outlook of Leaving Wealth with the People," *Survey Research Report.* 10th issue, 2008.

27 Budget Department of Ministry of Finance, ed., ditto, p. 175.

28 According to CBRC statistics, by the end of 2009, local government loan balance was 7.38 trillion yuan, a year-to-year growth of 70.4 percent. See Lu Xiaoping and Zhang Dukang, *Local Government Is in Debt as Much as 7.38 Trillion; Experts from Chinese Academy of Social Sciences Claim It Is Still in Control*, People Net, May 21, 2010.

Bibliography

The original source of this chapter is: Feng, Xingyuan. *Features, Problems and Reform of County and Township Fiscal Administration System in China*, Lincoln Institute of Land Policy Working Paper, WP13FX1, 2012, available at: http://www.lincolninst.edu/pubs/2262_Features--Problems-and-Reform-of-County-and-Township-Fiscal-Administration-System-in-China.

Anhui Province Carries Out Systems of "County Supervising Township Finance" and "Province Directly Supervising County." *Zhong Guo Jing Ji Wang* (http://www.ce.cn/). June 23, 2006.

Budget Department of Ministry of Finance, ed. *Intergovernmental Fiscal Relations in China*. (Beijing: China Financial and Economic Publishing House), 2003.

Bureau of Finance of Anyue County. *Announcement of Anyue County People's Government on Adjusting Township Fiscal System.* Anyue County People's Government, No. 93, December 14, 2005.

Center for Public Policy Studies, Shanghai University of Finance and Economics. *China Finance and Economy Development Report*, 2007.

Chen, X. *The Public Finance System in China: Theory, Policy and Empirical Research.* (Beijing: China Development Press), 2005a.

Chen, X., ed. *Public Fiscal Systems in China: Theory, Policy and Empirical Study.* (Beijing: China Development Press), 2005b.

Chen, Y. and Gu, S. Four Disadvantages of "City Supervising County" and Five Problems of "Power Expansion and County Strengthening." *People Net Theory Channel*, March 4, 2009.

Feng, X. *Research Report on County and Township Fiscal Problems of Anyue County, Sichuan Province, Sub-report for Research on County and Township Fiscal Problems, Joint Project by NDRC and Australian Government*, October 28, 2006.

Gao, P. (Editor-in-chief). *China's Finance and Tax Reform during Twelfth Five-Year Plan Period.* (Beijing: China Financial and Economic Publishing House), 2010.

Guo, S., Li, C. and Chen, L. *Brief Analysis of Countermeasures Helping County Finance Get Through Difficult Situation.* Website of Research Institute for Fiscal Science of Ministry of Finance. December 21, 2005.

Han, J. and Xuan, W. Focusing on "Debt Risk" of Local Governments. *China Comment*, April 8, 2009.

He, K. and Li, S. *Rural Tax Reformation in China.* (Beijing: China Zhigong Press), 2000.

Hebei Province Tries Out Two Fiscal Systems of the County to the Township. *Economic Daily*, December 20, 2006.

Hu, Z. and Piyi, F. Yiwu's Power Expansion: Exploring New Road for 'Province Governing County'. *Economic Information Daily*, December 21, 2006.

Jia, K. and Bai, J. Overcoming Difficulties in Public Finance at County and Township Level and Innovation in Fiscal System. *Economic Research Journal*, (2), 2002, pp. 3–9.

Jiang, H. Strengthening County and Expanding Power: A Difficult Road of Sixteen Years. *China Business Journal*, February 16, 2009.

Krug, B., Zhu, Z. and Hendrischke, H. *China S Emerging Tax Regime: Devolution, Fiscal Federalism, or Tax Farming?* ERIM Report Series Reference No. ERS-2004-113-ORG, 2004.

Li, Z. General Transfer Payment Shifts from For "People" to For "Things." *China Taxation News*, July 7, 2008.

Lin, N. and Zuohua, H. Province Supervising County: A New Local Reform Tide. *China Comment*, January 28, 2006.

Local Affairs Department of Ministry of Finance, ed. *The Tax Sharing Fiscal Administration System in China.* (Beijing: China Financial and Economic Publishing House), 1998.

Lu X. and Zhang, D. Local Government Is in Debt as Much as 7.38 Trillion; Experts from Chinese Academy of Social Sciences Claim It Is Still in Control. *People Net*, May 21, 2010.

Ministry of Finance. *Report on Central and Local Budget Performance in 2007 and Central and Local Drafted Budget in 2008*, March 5, 2008.

"Province Directly Supervising County" Still in the Trial; Whether Prefectural Cities Relinquish Powers Is the Key. *China News Week*, August 7, 2008.

Song, L. and Shujie, L. *Deployment of Public Services Administrative and Financial Power in All Levels of Government.* (Beijing: China Planning Press), 2005.

Tao, R., Liu, M. and Zhang, Q. Analysis on Rural Taxation, Government Regulation and Fiscal Reform. *Economic Research Journal*, 38(4), 2003, pp. 3–12.

Wang, Q. Insisting on Scientific Financial Management and Developing County Economy. *Review of Economic Research*, (41), 2007, pp. 17–23.

Wang, Y. Reform Improves Fiscal Transfer Payment System. *China Investment*, December 27, 2008.

World Bank. *China National Development and Sub-national Finance: A Review of Provincial Expenditures*, Report No. 22951-CHA, April 9, 2002.

Wu, L. and Li, Z. A Preliminary Exploration on Township Finance and Reform – Investigation on Hong Town. *China Rural Survey*, (4), 2003, pp. 13–24.

Xie, X., ed. *China's Financial Reform for Thirty Years*. (Beijing: China Financial and Economic Publishing House), 2008.

Zhang, Y. and Zhu, X. Optimizing the Fiscal Expenditure Structure and Constructing a Harmonious Fiscal System. *North China Economy*, (4), 2007, pp. 19–21.

Zhang, Z. 25 Years for Implementing "City Supervising County" System across China: County Strengthening and Power Expansion in Deep Waters. *Decision Making*, January 29, 2008.

Zhejiang Provincial Department of Finance. Zhejiang Province's Overall Implementation of Ecological Finance Transfer Payment System. *Huangyan Financial Information Net*, June 3, 2008.

Zhejiang Rural Finance Research Association. *Rural Public Finance Issues*. (Hangzhou: Zhejiang University Press), 2006.

Zheng, Y. *De facto federalism in China: Reforms and dynamics of central-local relations*. Series on contemporary China. Vol. 7. (Hackensack, NJ: World Scientific), 2007.

Zhou, Y. County and Township Level Fiscal Expenditure System: Reform and Countermeasures. *Management World*, (5), 2000, pp. 122–132.

Index

For Product Safety Concerns and Information please contact our EU representative GPSR@taylorandfrancis.com Taylor & Francis Verlag GmbH, Kaufingerstraße 24, 80331 München, Germany

Batch number: 10725798

Printed by Printforce, the Netherlands